KARL SHAW has worked as a journalist, in advertising and in marketing. His books include *Royal Babylon: The Alarming History of European Royalty*, *5 People Who Died During Sex: And 100 Other Terribly Tasteless Lists*, *Curing Hiccups with Small Fires: A Miscellany of Great British Eccentrics* and *The Mammoth Book of Losers*.

Recent Mammoth titles

The Mammoth Book of Fun Brain Training
The Mammoth Book of Hard Bastards
The Mammoth Quiz Book
The Mammoth Book of Dracula
The Mammoth Book of New Tattoo Art
The Mammoth Book of Losers
The Mammoth Book of Codeword Puzzles
The Mammoth Book of Hot Romance
The Mammoth Book of Best New SF 26
The Mammoth Book of Really Silly Jokes
The Mammoth Book of Best New Horror 24
The Mammoth Book of Weird News
The Mammoth Book of Antarctic Journeys
The Mammoth Book of Muhammad Ali
The Mammoth Book of the Best of Best New Erotica
The Mammoth Book of Best British Crime 11
The Mammoth Book of Conspiracies
The Mammoth Book of Lost Symbols
The Mammoth Book of Sex Scandals
The Mammoth Book of Body Horror
The Mammoth Book of New CSI
The Mammoth Book of Best New Erotica 13
The Mammoth Book of Gangs
The Mammoth Book of SF Wars
The Mammoth Book of Shark Attacks
The Mammoth Book of Freddie Mercury and Queen
The Mammoth Book of the World Cup

The Mammoth Book of

Tasteless and Outrageous Lists

Karl Shaw

RUNNING PRESS
PHILADELPHIA · LONDON

ROBINSON

First published in Great Britain in 2014 by Robinson
Copyright © Karl Shaw, 2014

The moral right of the author has been asserted.

A CIP catalogue record for this book
is available from the British Library.

ISBN: 978-1-47211-744-1 (paperback)
ISBN: 978-1-47211-745-8 (ebook)

Typeset in Plantin by Hewer Text UK Ltd, Edinburgh
Printed and bound in Great Britain by
CPI Group (UK) Ltd, Croydon, CR0 4YY

Robinson
is an imprint of
Constable & Robinson Ltd
100 Victoria Embankment
London EC4Y 0DY

An Hachette UK Company
www.hachette.co.uk

www.constablerobinson.com

CONTENTS

CHAPTER ONE
JUST DESSERTS

CHAPTER TWO
THE GOOD, THE BAD AND THE ODD

CHAPTER THREE
AND SO TO BED

CHAPTER FOUR
RUDE HEALTH

CHAPTER FIVE
ART ATTACKS

CHAPTER SIX
ALL THINGS BRIGHT AND BEAUTIFUL

CHAPTER SEVEN
THE WONDER OF YOU

CHAPTER EIGHT
GOD'S MYSTERIOUS WAYS

CHAPTER NINE
MUSICAL MISCELLANY

CHAPTER TEN
R.I.P.

CHAPTER ELEVEN
TRIAL AND RETRIBUTION

CHAPTER TWELVE
LOOSE ENDS

FURTHER READING
487

CHAPTER ONE
Just Desserts

FROM FENDER TO FORK:
10 ROAD KILL RECIPES

1. Fox cub fricassee*

2. Hedgehog spaghetti carbonara

3. Groundhog hoagies†

4. Creamed coon casserole

5. Moose and squirrel meatballs

6. Skunk skillet stew

7. Bunny burgers

8. Burgoo‡

9. Raccoon Kebabs (also known as "Ringtail Surprise")

10. Pothole Possum Stew

---

* Arthur Boyt, a retired biologist from Cornwall, has been eating road kill for more than fifty years and is the author of several road kill recipe books. He calls himself a "freegan" and, although a dog lover, does not believe in waste and once ate a Labrador retriever, which he compared to lamb. His favourite snack is badger sandwich.
† America's Buck Peterson has written several recipe books for road kill including *Original Road Kill Cookbook*, *The International Road Kill Cookbook* and *The Totalled Road Kill Cookbook*. The more discerning may prefer Jeff Eberbaugh's *Gourmet Style Road Kill Cooking*.
‡ In Kentucky, a traditional road kill stew made from squirrel, rabbit or possum and vegetable.

FOOD FOR THOUGHT:
15 CULINARY CURIOSITIES

1. The first soup was made from hippopotamus around 6000 BC.

2. Hippocrates said that dogs were likely to give you indigestion, but he recommended boiled puppy as a tasty meal for invalids: the Greek physician Galen reckoned that the meat of a young castrated dog was best.

3. The hard skin of an elephant's trunk was a much sought-after delicacy in Roman times. Not because it was thought to taste good, but because it was considered the nearest you could get to chewing on hugely expensive but entirely inedible ivory.

4. The Arabs invented caramel around the year 1000. The women in the harem used it to wax their legs.

5. In ancient Greece, red mullet was a great delicacy and cooking it was a serious business. To prevent the stomachs of red mullet from bursting during the cooking process, the best chefs kissed them on the lips.

6. The Chinook Indian tribe ate a delicacy known as "Chinook Olives". The dish was made by soaking acorns in urine for five months.

7. Attila the Hun was the king of fast food. His warriors preserved their fresh meat by placing it under their

saddles. The bouncing action squeezed fluids from the meat and the horse's sweat salted it and removed moisture. When the Hun stopped to eat, he had a dried and salted ready meal.

8. Jews are forbidden to eat elephants.*

9. The largest joint found on any menu is roasted camel, offered by royalty in Morocco several hundred years ago and still served at some Bedouin weddings. The camel is cleaned and then stuffed with one whole lamb, twenty chickens and sixty eggs, among other ingredients, then spit-roasted for fifteen hours.

10. In ancient Rome, leeks became highly fashionable after the Emperor Nero started eating them to strengthen his voice for singing.

11. The only meat not banned by the Catholic Church for consumption during Lent is the capybara, the world's largest rat. It is a big favourite in South America.

12. The Elizabethan direction on how to test when an oven is hot enough to bake a cake is to make a kitchen maid hold her elbow there until it turns red.

13. An estimated 72 per cent of supermarket trolley handles are contaminated with more faecal matter than you will find in an average bathroom. If you eat takeaways on a regular basis, you will swallow about twelve pubic hairs a year.

---

* They are not kosher because they are not mentioned in Leviticus.

14. The first meal eaten in space was a tube of pureed apple sauce, enjoyed by John Glenn on Friendship 7 in 1962.

15. The most popular flavour of edible underwear is cherry. Chocolate is the least popular.

DATE RAPE:
10 MISUSES OF FRUIT

1. According to the Koran, Eve tempted Adam with a banana, not an apple.

2. King Henry VIII ate apples filled with goat's testicles to try to boost his sperm count. When this failed, he tried bull's testicles, although how he got them into an apple is unclear.

3. Elizabethan ladies kept slices of apple under their armpits to soak up their sweat, and then gave them to potential suitors as keepsakes.

4. The most nightmarish instrument of torture during the Holy Inquisition of the Middle Ages was a device called the Pear, also known as "the Pope's pear" or the "poire d'angoisse" (pear of anguish). It was a segmented device of bronze and iron in the shape of a pear designed to be inserted into various orifices of the human body. A screw-driven mechanism on the interior of the "pear" allowed it to be slowly expanded as the torturer turned the handle, thus stretching and tearing the tender flesh of the victim from the inside.

5. In 1900 Dr W. F. Morgan of the *New York Medical Times* warned his readers that eating watermelon caused "excitement of the penis", adding " . . . a fact that is fully appreciated by our coloured brethren".

6. In 1903 the sexologist Havelock Ellis interviewed an army officer in India who owned up to an active sex life, ranging from encounters with foreign prostitutes to affairs with his fellow military officers, but said he really preferred the "carnal use" of fruit, especially melons and papaya.

7. In 1941 three Ugandan men were convicted of manslaughter after they murdered an old man in their village they suspected was a wizard. They killed him by the traditional method for despatching a wizard, by forcing several unripe bananas into his anus.

8. Fruit can improve the quality of oral sex because Kiwi and pineapple make genital secretion taste sweeter. Dairy products, meat and alcohol are thought to make it taste worse.

9. In the Philip Roth novel *Portnoy's Complaint*, the main character, Alexander Portnoy, masturbates using a cored-out apple.

10. Every year there are approximately 300 banana-related accidents in the UK.

BAD TO THE BONE:
10 PEOPLE WHO HAD THEIR
NEIGHBOURS FOR DINNER

1. In 1098 starving Crusaders captured the Saracen fortress at Ma'arra in modern-day Syria. Finding little in the way of food, they improvised by slicing portions from the buttocks of their dead prisoners, then roasting and eating them.

2. In 1759, after encountering severe weather and lost in the mid-Atlantic for six months, the starving eight-man crew of the cargo ship *The Dolphin* ate everything that was edible on board, including the ship's dog and cat, their shoes and some leather shorts. Finally they ate the only passenger on board, a Spaniard called Anthony Galatio.

3. In 1809 Maoris in New Zealand killed and ate an entire ship's crew of between sixty-six and seventy people. It was revenge for the whipping of a young Maori chief by the crew of the sailing ship *Boyd*, which carried convicts and free settlers from England to Australia. The second mate was spared in the massacre and taken prisoner; he was killed and eaten when his usefulness in making fish-hooks was exhausted.

4. In 1822 Alexander Pearce, an Irishman transported to Australia for seven years for stealing several pairs of

shoes, escaped from his penal colony with seven other convicts. After four weeks on the run they were on the brink of starvation and after nine weeks Pearce was the last man standing. When he was recaptured, Pearce confessed to eating his fellow inmates, but his story was not believed; he was thought to be covering for companions still at large. He was sent back to prison, but a year later he escaped again with a young prisoner called Thomas Cox. When he was recaptured eleven days later, Pearce was carrying an old flour bag containing the half-eaten remains of his mate. The meat and fish he had taken when he escaped were still intact; when asked why, he explained that he just preferred the taste of human flesh.

5. The nineteenth-century Fijian tribal chief Ratu Udre Udre holds the Guinness World Record for "most prolific cannibal", having eaten between 872 and 999 people. He recorded his achievement with a huge pile of stones, adding to it with a new stone every time he ate. According to legend, his warriors would go to the battle and bring back body parts of their victims as titbits for their chief: his favourite snack was the head. He preserved what he couldn't finish in one sitting so he could eat it later.

6. You might guess from his nickname that John 'Liver-Eating' Johnson, a mountain man of the old American West, was not a man to be messed with. When Crow Indians attacked his home one day while he was out in the wilderness, killing and scalping his pregnant wife and burning his house to the ground, Johnson took revenge, embarking on a one-man war against the Crow nation, killing their warriors wherever he could find them, cutting out the livers of his slain enemies and eating them. During the course of his twenty-five-year blood feud, he claimed to have killed around 300 braves.

For all of his violent ways, thanks to his iron- and Vitamin-A enriched diet, Johnson died in his bed in 1900 at the grand old age of seventy-seven.

7. In 1997 Russia's most enterprising cannibal, Nikolai Dzhurmongaliev, butchered a hundred women and served them to his dinner guests in the republic of Kyargyzstan. When arrested, Nikolai explained that two women kept him in meat for a week.

8. In 2003 two crematorium workers in Cambodia were apprehended while eating the fingers and toes of a customer, washed down with a bottle of wine. Both men were set free by a local court on a technicality; Cambodia had no law against cannibalism.

9. In 2009 Russian police arrested three vagrants for killing a twenty-five-year-old man. They had sold his body parts to the local kebab house in the city of Perm, 720 miles east of Moscow.

10. In 2012 police in Miami, Florida, shot and killed a naked man whom they found eating the face of another man who was lying next to him on the roadside. Rudy Eugene was killed by a city police officer after refusing to step away from Ronald Poppo, who was left fighting for his life in hospital after suffering critical injuries. Witness Larry Vega said, "The guy just stood, his head up like that, with pieces of flesh in his mouth. And he growled."

15 FUSSY EATERS

1. The last Qing Dynasty Chinese Dowager Empress Cixi breakfasted every day on porridge laced with human breast milk, followed by a spoonful of powdered pearl.

2. The author Vladimir Nabokov ate butterflies. He said they tasted "like almonds and perhaps a green cheese combination".

3. The English journalist Henry Labouchere wrote despatches from the Siege of Paris in 1870. He dined on rats and frogs but turned his nose up at a slice of spaniel.

4. In his final years, the oil tycoon John D. Rockefeller lived on breast milk. He got it from several wet nurses he kept on his payroll.

5. Mark Antony employed a praegustator (food taster) because he feared Cleopatra might try to poison him. The idea caught on and praegustators assumed an important role in every imperial household. The names of many of them are recorded on their tombstones; the causes of their deaths, however, are not.

6. The nineteenth-century English noblewoman Helena, the Comtesse de Noailles lived on a diet of milk, champagne, fresh herring roe (to prevent bronchitis) and methane: she encouraged her cows to graze near open

windows because she thought the farts they produced were good for her health.

7. Henry Ford never ate granulated sugar because he thought it was dangerous; he imagined the sharp granules would cut up his stomach and he could bleed to death.

8. Convicted of murdering an insurance agent and executed by lethal injection in Texas in 1990, James Smith requested for his final meal a "lump of dirt". Smith was a Tarot card reader and the dirt was a vital ingredient in a voodoo ritual; his request was denied, so he settled for a yogurt instead.

9. To toughen up the boxer Joe Louis for a match, his trainers took him to Chicago's stockyards to drink blood fresh from the slaughterhouse.

10. In some ancient tribes in the Middle East, a new king would eat the penis of his predecessor to absorb his sacred authority.

11. The mathematician Kurt Gödel refused to eat anything that hadn't been prepared by his wife. When she was hospitalized in 1978, Gödel died of starvation.

12. In 1991 Californian housewife Omeima Nelson admitted killing and then eating portions of her abusive husband. She said that she had barbecued his ribs just like in a restaurant. "It's so sweet, it's so tender and delicious. I like mine tender."

13. The ocean liner RMS *Queen Mary* was converted into a troopship for the duration of World War II. The vessel was said to be haunted by the ship's cook. His cooking

was so terrible that a riot broke out among the troops being carried to the front: the violence got out of hand and the cook was stuffed in the oven and roasted alive.

14. Adolf Hitler employed fifteen female food tasters to sample his food. It was packed into boxes and delivered to the Führer at the Wolf's Lair, then the tasters were served a plate of food each and forced to eat it between eleven and twelve every morning.

15. Prince Charles likes his biscuits to be served at a special temperature; his staff keeps a warming pan to maintain them at the perfect level. When his mother has dinner guests, she has the potatoes and sprouts measured before they are served to make sure they are of similar dimensions and won't spoil the appearance of the dinner plate.

A WATCHED PET NEVER BOILS: 9 NATIONAL DELICACIES

1. Although chiefly famous for their chocolate and cheese, the Swiss also eat thousands of puppies and kittens every year. In one traditional Swiss recipe you cook a cat with sprigs of thyme; there's another for puppy pizza topping.

2. In America, the term 'dog' has been used as a synonym for sausage since the late nineteenth century. This was because some sausage makers were still putting dog meat in their bangers until at least the mid-1800s.

3. In the run-up to the 2008 Beijing Olympics, Chinese officials removed dog and cat meat from the menus of 112 official Olympic restaurants so as to not offend visitors. In Yulin, Guangxi, the locals still celebrate the "lychee dog meat festival" when they kill and eat more than 100,000 dogs. Until 2006, Shenzhen in China had a Cat Meatball Restaurant.

4. In Poland, dog fat is made into lard, which by tradition is believed to have medicinal properties. It is said to be very good for your lungs.

5. The expression *Dar gato por liebre* ("to pass off a cat as a hare") is the Spanish equivalent of "to pull the wool over someone's eyes". It derives from a Spanish butcher's scam whereby you rip off the skin, feet and head of a cat and pass it off as a hare.

6. In Hawaii, broiled puppy meat is prepared by flattening out the entire eviscerated animal and broiling it over hot coals. The traditional Hawaiian accompaniment for dog is sweet potatoes.

7. In Germany, dog meat has been eaten in every major crisis at least since the time of Frederick the Great; the Germans call it "blockade mutton".

8. In South Korea, butchers improve the flavour of dog meat by hanging or beating the mutt to death.

9. Thousands of edible guinea pigs are eaten every year in the United States. They arrive from Peru as whole, frozen, hairless rodents in plastic bags and in restaurants go for $17 a plate; the guinea pig is splayed down the middle like a lobster and served with a front leg and a back, an eye, an ear and a nostril. According to activists, eating guinea pig is good for the environment because they represent a low-impact meat alternative to carbon-costly beef.

15 FOOD FATALITIES

500 BC: the Greek thinker Pythagoras, who is a huge fan of the humble bean, dies when, on being pursued by his enemies, he refuses to flee across a field of pulses.

1624: Richard Sackville, third Earl of Dorset, dies in agony on Easter Sunday after dining on several potato pies to "enkindle his lust".

1784: the philosopher Denis Diderot chokes to death on an apricot. As well as writing the world's first great encyclopaedia, Diderot was an authority on how to make apricot jam.

1790: a man at Stillington in Lancashire is reported to have won a bet by drinking five quarts of ale from an earthenware mug then chewing and swallowing the mug. He dies two days later.

1824: *The Times* reports that a man from Jersey ate six raw eggs mixed with half a pint of gin for a bet. The wager was then repeated three times with higher stakes. With two pints of gin inside him, he got stuck into a pile of raw bacon and drank two large glasses of brandy. After this he "felt indisposed", went home and keeled over dead.

1987: in Seoul, South Korea, housewife Roh Ki Hwa hangs herself after forgetting to adjust her watch for daylight-saving time. She was said to be deeply embarrassed about preparing her husband's Sunday lunch one hour late.

1989: Londoner Leslie Merry dies of a ruptured spleen after a fatal encounter with a vegetable. While walking near his home in Leytonstone he is hit in the ribs by a turnip thrown from a speeding car.

1991: delivery driver Joseph Larose is killed while transporting ice cream to a supermarket in Tampa, Florida, when a 500lb rack of "Nutty Buddies" topples onto him, crushing his skull.

1998: Michael Gentner from Akron, Ohio, chokes to death while trying to swallow a live fish for a bet. Paramedics, who think they are responding to a routine food-choking incident, find him not breathing and the tail of the still-living fish sticking out of his mouth.

2002: chef Le Hung Cuong plucks a venomous sea snake from a tank in a restaurant in Haiphong, Vietnam, ready to turn it into the night's special – "porridge with snake's blood". The snake has other ideas and bites Cuong's left hand. He is dead on arrival at hospital.

2003: French chef Bernard Loiseau shoots himself in the mouth with his shotgun after a full day of work in his kitchen when newspaper reports hint that his restaurant might lose its Michelin three-star status.

2006: Janet Rudd dies of asphyxiation during a marshmallow-eating contest in London, Ontario. According to the rules of the contest, she was required to fill her mouth with marshmallows without swallowing or chewing, while saying the words "chubby bunny".

2009: Ukrainian chemistry student Vladimir Likhonos dies after dipping a piece of bubble gum into explosives he is using on another project. He mistakes the jar of explosive for the citric acid he often adds to increase the gum's sour taste. The gum explodes, blowing off his jaw and most of the lower half of his face.

2010: Usha, a female employee of Akansha food products in Lucknow, India, slips from her ladder and falls into a giant vat of tomato ketchup. Five co-workers jump in one after the other to save Usha; all six drown together.

2012: Edward Archbold from Florida dies shortly after winning a cockroach-eating contest. The cause of death was accidental choking due to "arthropod body parts".

HARD TO SWALLOW:
10 FREAKISH DIETS

1. In 1788 the Duke of Bedford bet Lord Barrymore 1,000 guineas that his Lordship couldn't eat a live cat. The wager attracted a lot of public attention and led to several letters in the press on the subject of cat eating; one reader claimed he had seen a Yorkshireman eat a live black tomcat to win a bet of two guineas. Barrymore was said to fancy his chances, having previously dined on kitten. However, in the event he got cold feet and wrote to the editor of *The World* claiming that they were mistaken in their report; he had only bet that he could find "a man who would eat a cat". There is no record as to whether he ever found a cat-eater to bail him out of the wager.

2. In 1805 Professor Martyn of Cambridge University reported that he knew a boy who could eat 370 lb (168 kg) of food in a week. Moreover, a pig fattened on the boy's vomit had been sold at the market for a good price; presumably the diet was not disclosed to the buyer.

3. The eighteenth century threw up a formidable clutch of polyphagi – extreme eaters. In January 1790 a reporter from *Sporting Magazine* saw a man eat a live cat in a public house in Windsor. The victim was a nine-pound cat; according to the report, the man "made a formidable attack on the head of his antagonist and, with repeated bites, soon deprived it of existence". He ate the

cat without stripping off the fur and skin, leaving only the bones.

4. Nicholas Wood, The Great Eater of Kent, who lived in the mid-seventeenth century, became a local folk hero on account of his enormous appetite. He could eat an entire sheep (except the skin, wool and horns) and once ate a washing-bowl full of porridge, nine loaves of bread and drank three jugs of beer in a single sitting. To prepare for these enormous meals, he rubbed his belly with grease to stop his skin from splitting. He once won a bet by eating seven dozen rabbits. At a market in Lenham, a trickster called John Dale bet that he could fill the Great Eater's stomach for just two shillings. He did this by soaking twelve one-penny loaves of bread in six pots of very strong ale. This time, Wood was defeated: he fell asleep and remained comatose for nine hours after finishing only half of the meal. The Great Eater was scheduled to make his debut before a London audience; according to his advance publicity, he would wolf down a wheelbarrow full of tripe followed by "as many puddings as would reach over the Thames". When the day arrived, however, Wood suffered from stage-fright, perhaps recalling some of the dangerous practical jokes he had encountered during his perilous career; shortly before leaving for London he had lost nearly all his teeth after being duped into eating a shoulder of mutton, bones and all, at a market in Ashford. He fled his lodgings in London and was never heard of again.

5. In the 1740s an Irish street performer called Thomas Echlin, according to the press, was "remarkable for his Vivacity and Drollery in the low Way". His act included eating several dogs and cats, then leaping head first into the freezing Thames. Echlin was also too fond of drinking vast amounts of gin and he died vomiting blood.

6. In the late-1770s a London street performer calling himself "The Stone Eater" chewed and swallowed large plates full of stones and gravel. His unusual talent emerged after he was shipwrecked off the Norwegian coast on an uninhabited rocky islet; after munching gravel for thirteen years, it was claimed, he was rescued by a passing ship, by which time his intestinal tract had become conditioned to minerals as the principal source of nourishment. The Stone Eater attracted the attention of the medical establishment including the Edinburgh surgeon Dr Munro who wrote a short article about him in his Medical Commentaries. A rival stone eater appeared in London called Siderophagus who also munched iron as well as pebbles. He was one half of a husband and wife act; under the stage-name Sarah Salamander, she downed pints of nitric acid and sulphuric acid.

7. Charles Domery was a Polish soldier who defected to the French army in return for food. He was said to have eaten 174 cats in a year and, although he hated vegetables, could get through 5 lb of grass a day if there was nothing else available. He once tried to eat the severed leg of a crew member hit by cannon fire, before it was snatched away from him. In 1799 Domery was captured by the Royal Navy off the coast of Ireland. He amazed his captors with his astonishing appetite; still hungry after double rations, he begged food from other prisoners and even ate dead cats and rats delivered to him by curious jailors. In spite of his excesses Domery was said to be around average build and, while he was never known to vomit, he never seemed to gain weight, although he sweated a great deal, particularly after a feast, and was constantly surrounded by a nauseating body odour. He showed no signs of mental illness and was said to be of average intelligence. In 1799 the

authorities performed an experiment to test the limits of his appetite. He breakfasted on 4 lb of raw cow's udder and 5 lb of raw beef, twelve large candles and a bottle of porter. For lunch, he devoured 5 lb of raw beef, 1 lb of candles and three large bottles of porter. He was returned to the prison, where it was recorded that he was in a good mood, albeit peckish, after his feast. The next morning he was up at 4 a.m. sharp demanding his breakfast. During the entire experiment he did not defecate, urinate or vomit, and his pulse and temperature remained steady.

8. In the early 1820s a French glutton, Jacques de Falaise, performed in taverns around Paris. During his act he swallowed eggs and walnuts whole, followed by live sparrows, crawfish, mice, adders and eels. On one occasion he almost died after swallowing fifty-five franc pieces for a bet. He hanged himself several years later; the autopsy showed that his stomach was badly scarred by the sharp and corrosive substances he had swallowed during his career.

9. The most extreme polyphagi was a Frenchman identified only as Tarrare. Born near Lyon around 1772, in his teens he was turned out of the house by parents who could no longer afford to feed him. For several years he wandered the French countryside, foraging for food in dustbins in gutters, at one point working as a warm-up act for an itinerant quack by swallowing small live animals. In 1788 he joined the French army where his depraved appetite came to the attention of military surgeons. They fed him a live cat, which he ate then drank its blood; he later threw up the fur and the skin. They followed up by serving him a menagerie of live animals, including puppies, snakes and lizards: Tarrare ate them all. The military were at a loss to know what to

do with him until someone came up with a bizarre plan. He was persuaded to swallow a small wooden box with a document inside; the intact box was recovered two days later from the hospital toilet. So began his brief career as a military courier-spy. His first mission was to swallow a message and take it to a French colonel held captive by the Prussians in a fortress near Neustadt. Tarrare, disguised as a German peasant, could speak no German and was quickly arrested. He was returned to the military hospital where he endured several bizarre attempts to curb his voracious appetite, including diets, laudanum, wine vinegar, tobacco pills and feeding him vast quantities of soft boiled eggs, but everything failed. At night, tormented by hunger, he stalked the back alleys of Paris looking for stray dogs to eat. Back at the hospital, he was apprehended in the morgue while attempting to eat a corpse. When a fourteen-month-old infant disappeared from a ward, the finger of suspicion was pointed at Tarrare and he was banished from the hospital, never to return. He was found in Versailles four years later, dying from tuberculosis. At the autopsy they discovered his gullet, liver and gallbladder were abnormally large and his enormous stomach was covered in ulcers and filled with pus.

10. In 1980 Werner Herzog said that if his fellow film director Errol Morris ever completed a documentary about pet cemeteries, *Gates of Heaven*, he'd eat his shoe. Morris made the film and Herzog kept his promise, dining on boiled loafer with garlic, herbs and stock.

PICK YOUR POISON:
10 GROSS FOOD ADDITIVES

1. The US government's Consumer Protection Agency sets a legal limit for the amount of rodent hair allowed in various foodstuffs; one rat hair for every 100 g of chocolate, twenty-two rat hairs for every 100 g of cinnamon and five rat hairs for every 18 oz jar of peanut butter.

2. Natural Red #4, also known as carmine, is a food colorant produced by boiling female cochineal insect shells in ammonia or a sodium carbonate solution. It takes about 70,000 of the bugs to produce 1 lb of dye and is a commonly used ingredient in yogurt, curries and alcoholic beverages.

3. Borax, or E285 as it's known in the food world, is used to control acidity and as a preservative. Although banned in North America, it is allowed in the EU and can be found in some caviars as well as various Asian noodle and rice dishes as it adds a firm, rubbery texture; it is also used in fire-retardants, in anti-fungal compounds and in enamel.

4. Yellow #5, also known as tartrazine, is a food dye made from coal tar and commonly found in pastries, soft drinks, snacks, spreads and processed foods including cereals and soups. In 2007 it was linked to childhood hyperactivity; since then any product in the EU that

contains tartrazine comes with a warning label, but in the US there is no such regulation.

5. Jelly and other gelatine-based foods contain collagen, a protein often collected from animal skins. The source varies depending on the type of food; the gelatine in desserts, for example, is made mainly from pigskin.

6. L-Cysteine is an amino acid made from human hair and used to prolong shelf life in products such as bread baps, pizza dough, biscuits, pastas and pastries. Most of the hair used to make L-Cysteine comes from China, where it's gathered from the floor of barbershops and hair salons.

7. Chewing gum contains lanolin, a secretion made from sheep's wool and also found in skincare products. It softens up your hands and your chewing gum.

8. Vanilla-, strawberry- and raspberry-flavoured ice creams often contain a bitter, smelly, orange-brown substance called castoreum. This food flavouring is extracted from the glands of the male or female beavers, which are located near the anus. You will find it described as 'natural flavouring'. In nature, it is combined with the beaver's urine and used to mark territory.

9. Your pint glass contains traces of fish bladder. Isinglass is a gelatine-like substance produced from the swim bladder of a fish and added to cask beers and Guinness, to help remove any residue yeast or solid particles in the beer.

10. The US Food and Drug Administration legally allows nineteen maggots and seventy-four mites in a 31/2 oz can of mushrooms.

10 STRANGE BREWS

1. The world's most expensive coffee is made from beans excreted by Thai elephants. The beans are eaten by the elephants and plucked a day later from their dung. A gut reaction inside the elephant creates the coffee's unique taste, described as "earthy in flavour and smooth on the palate".

2. St Bridget of Kildare was known for transforming her used bathwater into beer.

3. In 1663 Samuel Pepys reported that a drunken Sir Charles Sedley washed his penis in a glass of wine, then drank the wine, while toasting the king.

4. In remote China, people drink dog wine. It is a kind of fermented milk and is mixed with fresh dog meat before it starts to bubble.

5. India has a soft drink made from cow urine mixed with aloe vera and gooseberries.

6. Chicha, a traditional beer from Latin America, is made from corn and human saliva.

7. Baby mice wine is a traditional health tonic in China and Korea. Newborn mice, eyes still closed, are dropped alive into a jug of rice wine and left to ferment. After the wine is imbibed, the mice are eaten.

8. As recently as the 1970s, the Guiaca people of the upper Orinoco cremated their dead, then made the half-burned bones into a soup for drinking.

9. In Antigua, lizard soup is thought to be an effective cure for asthma, so long as the patient isn't told what's in it.

10. As a special treat, widows of the Buganda people of Uganda are allowed to drink beer in which the entrails of their recently deceased king have been washed.

CHAPTER TWO

The Good,
the Bad and the Odd

12 PERFECTIONISTS

1. The American cult leader Shadrack Ireland invented and preached the cult of Perfectionism, the idea that heaven was achievable on Earth and that, as a result, he would never die. When the inevitable happened in 1778 his followers left him sitting in his chair until the smell was so bad they had no choice but to bury him.

2. Jean Gericault's masterpiece *The Raft of the Medusa* was inspired by a nautical disaster that left several passengers from a wrecked ship adrift at sea. The artist prepared by locking himself in a morgue with several corpses, then took some severed body parts home with him to get "the colour of death" right.

3. The Holy Roman Emperor Charles V rehearsed his funeral several times before taking part in the real thing in 1558. He had his tomb erected in a chapel and made his servants march in procession while Charles followed behind dressed in a shroud. When the service began and the hymns struck up, the emperor jumped into his coffin, from where he would join in the prayers.

4. The French essayist Dominique Bouhours was a stickler for grammar. When he died in 1792 his last words were: "I am about to, or I am going to, die. Either expression is correct."

5. Philetas of Cos was a scholar and poet in ancient Greece. He was obsessed with the "liar paradox"; this is, if a man

says, "I am lying", is what he said true or false? Philetas had so many sleepless nights over this that it killed him.

6. The Ottoman Sultan Murad IV executed a musician for playing out of tune.

7. The poet Lord Byron's great-uncle William was known as the "Wicked Lord". He killed his cousin during an argument over the best way to hang game.

8. The German Emperor Frederick II cut off a notary's thumb who had spelled his name Fredericus instead of Fridericus.

9. Hans Christian Andersen commissioned a musician to compose his funeral march. Andersen told him, "Most of the people who will walk after me will be children, so make the beat keep time with little steps."

10. In February 1790 Thomas de Mahy, Marquis de Favras, became the first nobleman to lose his head to the French Revolution. When handed his death sentence, he noted, "I see that you have made three spelling mistakes."

11. Edward Russell White, forty-six-year-old bass-baritone, hanged himself in 1998. He was upset over a bad rehearsal for Cleveland Opera's production of *Lucia di Lammermoor*.

12. In his quest to rid the world of sexual ignorance, the American academic Alfred Kinsey (1894–1955) measured more than 5,000 penises. He experimented with masochism and was able to insert pencils into his penis and even a toothbrush, bristles first. He also circumcised himself with a penknife in the bath.

20 HARD MEN
(AND ONE HARD WOMAN)

440 BC: the Greek Herodotus reports that some Egyptian men prove their manliness by mating with female crocodiles.

320 BC: the philosopher Anaxarchus is pounded to death in a mortar with iron pestles by Nicocreon the tyrant. Anaxarchus is said to have made light of the punishment.

1194: after his horse falls on him during a jousting tournament, the dying Leopold V, Duke of Austria, helps amputate his own gangrenous foot by holding an axe head while a servant strikes it with a mallet.

1346: King John "The Blind" of Bohemia, despite having lost his eyesight a decade earlier, doesn't want to miss out on the action at the Battle of Crécy. He orders his men to strap him into his saddle and point him in the direction of the enemy. Unsurprisingly, he is very quickly killed along with the fifteen knights who escorted him. Before he sets off he is reported to have said, "Let it never be the case that a Bohemian king runs from a fight."*

---

* According to tradition, the King of England's son, the "Black Prince", was so impressed by this display of lunacy that he decided to adopt King John's personal crest of three white ostrich feathers and his motto "Ich Dien" (I serve) as his own. It is the Prince of Wales's motto to this day.

1424: with his dying breath, the Czech general Jan Zizka, one of only six commanders in history never to lose a battle,* asks for his skin to be made into a drum so that he can continue in military service.

1660: Thomas Harrison is the first of the Regicides to be executed for signing the death warrant of King Charles I. After being hanged for several minutes with his entrails exposed, he leans over and punches his executioner in the face.

1815: at the Battle of Waterloo, Henry Paget, 2nd Earl of Uxbridge, is riding close to the Duke of Wellington when the earl's leg is shattered by a cannon shot. Uxbridge observes, "By God, sir, I've lost my leg!"; Wellington replies, "By God, sir, so you have."

1844: after being mauled by a lion, Dr David Livingstone sets his broken bones himself, waits for his wounds to heal, then carries on exploring.

1849: despite being born without arms or legs, Arthur MacMorrough Kavanagh sets off on an epic trip across Scandinavia, Russia, Azerbaijan, Iran, Pakistan and India, having earlier taken in Egypt and Palestine. Later, Kavanagh is able to use the fingers of his vestigial upper stumps to shoot, paint and write and when strapped into a special saddle becomes a fearless horse rider.

1853: after being speared through the face by Somalian raiders, the explorer Richard Burton fights off his assailants and makes his escape with the weapon still stuck in his jaw.

---

* The others are Alexander the Great, Scipio Africanus, Genghis Khan, Alexander Suvorov and Khalid ibn al-Walid.

1856: while searching for the source of the Nile, explorer John Hanning Speke becomes temporarily deaf after a beetle crawls into his ear and he tries to dig it out with a knife. This causes an ear infection so severe that it eats a hole in the tissue. After this, his ear whistles whenever he blows his nose.

1897: while canoeing through African swamps, the lone female explorer Mary Kingsley uses her brolly to beat off crocodiles blocking her path. After falling headlong into a staked animal trap, she notes in her diary, "At these moments you realise the blessings of a good thick skirt".*

1909: while exploring Brazil's jungles, Percy Harrison Fawcett swims rivers infested with piranhas. He reports that the experience "made my toes tingle".

1912: despite his deteriorating condition, polar explorer Robert Falcon Scott continues to record his fate in grim detail right to the bitter end. He is puzzled when the blackish, "rotten-looking" nose of one of his colleagues seems likely to drop off. Scott notes, "to my surprise, he shows signs of losing heart over it".

1918: after being badly wounded eight times, losing a hand and winning the Victoria Cross, British army officer Adrian Carton de Wiart says, "Frankly, I enjoyed the war."

1922: after shaking hands with his firing squad, Irish republican Erskine Childers tells them, "Take a step forward, lads. It'll be easier that way."

1927: Arctic explorer Jack Hornby, known as the "hermit of

---

* While staying with suspected cannibals in Africa in 1895, Mary Kingsley found a bag in her hut containing a human hand, four eyes and two ears.

the north" for his efforts to live off the land with limited supplies, assures his two travelling companions that he can teach them "how to starve properly". He is as good as his word; all three die of starvation.

1937: during the Spanish Civil War, George Orwell is shot in the throat by a fascist sniper, an experience he finds "very interesting".

1991: while stepping out of a London club, "Mad" Frankie Fraser, one -time enforcer for south London crime-lords the Richardson brothers, is shot in the head at close range. Still upstanding and conscious, Frankie takes himself off to hospital, but refuses to inform on his assailant, because he's not a grass.

2007: Japanese motorcyclist Kazuo Nagata cruises 2 km down a road without noticing that he has lost his right leg after hitting a dividing barrier on a road. A friend returns to pick up his leg, which is transported by ambulance to a hospital.

2007: a Welsh rugby fan cuts off his testicles with wire cutters to mark his national team's victory over England, then puts his severed bits in a bag and takes them to his local social club to show his friends. Geoffrey Huish, thirty-one, tells *The Sun*, "It wasn't a bet, but I said I'd cut my balls off if we won. I can't have kids now but still want a family. Maybe I'll adopt."

10 HEROES OF ADVERTISING

1847: Thomas Holmes, the first American to develop and use embalming fluid, hones his technique on soldiers during the Civil War so their remains could be shipped home for burial. After the war, Holmes opens a pharmacy in Brooklyn, selling his home-made embalming fluid. He displays the pickled head of a young girl in his shop window as an example of his work.

1898: American Frank E. Young markets his "Rectal Dilator" in several respectable journals. Billed as a cure for piles, the device looks remarkably like a butt plug; he is able to convince the authorities that it is a medical device, despite a very explicit instruction manual included with each order, for the next forty years, until it falls foul of the 1938 Federal Food, Drugs and Cosmetics Act, which bans them for "false advertising".

1903: the inventor Thomas Edison launches a PR campaign to persuade the American public that his rival's Alternating Current electrical power supply is much more dangerous than his own Direct Current system. At Coney Island's Luna Park, Edison sets up the public execution of an elephant called Topsy by slamming 6,600 volts of AC through the animal's body. As Topsy dies, smoke billows from his feet. Edison personally supervises the filming of the event and releases it later that year as *Electrocuting an Elephant*. In the film he asks, "Is this what your wife should be cooking with?"

1909: the explorer Robert Peary fails to reach the North

Pole, but, down to his last two toes from previous attempts, finds time to endorse Shredded Wheat and his favourite brand of underpants before naming a remote cape on Ellesmere Island after another of his sponsors, Colgate.

1915: Harrods sells morphine and syringe kits, labelled "A useful present for friends at the front".

1933: during the Ukraine famine, cannibalism is widespread. Soviet officials respond with a poster campaign that advises: "Eating your own children is a barbarian act."

1965: after trying out various representations of masculinity, including athletes, gunsmiths and sea captains, Marlboro cigarettes go for the rugged cowboy image. Three men who appeared in the advertisements later died of lung cancer, earning the brand the nickname "Cowboy Killer".*

2001: as part of their government's advertising campaign to raise the birth rate, Singapore's leading newspaper publishes a guide explaining how to have sex in cars.

2011: the Benton Franklin Health District in Kennewick, Washington, scraps a colon cancer awareness campaign after complaints about billboards that pose the question "What's Up Your Butt?" The health authority accepts that this may have been in poor taste.

2012: a New York judge rules against a company making cat

---

* David McLean, the best known of the Marlboro Men, died of lung cancer in 1995. After his diagnosis, McLean became an avid anti-smoking crusader and once appeared at a Philip Morris shareholder meeting to denounce cigarette advertising. The company responded by buying up every copy of *Death in the Valley*, a documentary chronicling smoking-related cancer deaths. McLean's widow sued for damages.

litter, forbidding it to show a commercial that unfairly sought an advantage against a competitor. The judge said he found the claim, in the advert for Clorox Pet Products, to be "highly implausible" that eleven people on a panel would "stick their noses in jars of excrement and report forty-four independent times that they smelled nothing unpleasant".

10 REASONS WHY AMERICANS SHOULDN'T BE ALLOWED TO HAVE GUNS

1992: in Newtown, North Carolina, Ken Barger fatally shoots himself when, awakening to the sound of a ringing telephone beside his bed, he reaches for the phone but grabs instead a Smith & Wesson .38 Special and draws it to his ear.

1993: Illinois patrolman Todd Johnson is demonstrating a disarming technique, in which he invites a fellow officer to shoot him in the stomach. Unaware that the lesson is over and that Johnson has reloaded his weapon, the other officer points it and fires, killing Johnson instantly. Four days later, while trying to show another patrolman how their fellow officer accidentally killed himself, patrolman Richard Shurtz re-enacts the shooting. The twenty-year-old has, however, forgotten to unload his .357 Magnum and shoots himself in the stomach. He dies in a car crash while driving himself to the hospital.

1998: in Detroit, Michigan, a single shot from an AK-47 assault rifle kills two Detroiters in a combined suicide and accidental shooting. Elrod Hill deliberately shoots himself and the bullet passes through his head and mortally wounds his friend Brian Olesky, who was sitting on a couch next to him.

1998: in Jacksonville, Florida, minister Melvyn Nurse shoots himself in the head at the Livingway Christian Fellowship Church while delivering a sermon to young people about the dangers of carrying guns. A colleague notes: "He was trying to convey a point that guns kill. It's not up to us to question God's motives."

2000: in Kentucky, Larry Slusher dares his friend Silas Caldwell to shoot a beer can off his head, William Tell-style. Silas aims too low, fatally wounding his lifelong pal.

2000: in Bay City, Daniel Kobebel is shot in the leg by his dog while attempting to take a picture of the trigger-happy canine holding a rifle.

2002: in Pennsylvania, eighteen-year-old Christopher Daniel and a friend entertain themselves with some target practice, shooting down overhead high-voltage power lines. A line hits the ground and Daniel, attempting to prevent a serious fire, grabs it in his hand and is electrocuted.

2002: in New York, thirty-year-old Bronx man Michael Bent bleeds to death after accidentally shooting himself in the testicles while adjusting the illegal gun he had tucked in his waistband.

2003: Gregory Freeman shoots dead his friend Jeffrey Murr during a Ku Klux Klan initiation. Freeman and Murr are initiating Karl Mitchell III, who is strapped to a tree with a hood over his face. Murr shoots paint balls at Mitchell while Freeman fires a 9 mm pistol into the air to make Mitchell think he is being struck with real bullets. A paint ball accidentally hits Freeman, causing him to bend over and discharge the pistol, shooting Murr in the head.

2012: soldier Patrick Edward Myers pulls a gun on fellow soldier Isaac Lawrence Young and shoots him in the face, during a successful attempt to cure his hiccups.

10 ANGLOPHOBES

1. "I know why the sun never sets on the British Empire, God would never trust an Englishman in the dark."

    Duncan Spaeth, US academic and writer

2. "[England] is a pirate spreading misery and ruin over the face of the ocean."

    Thomas Jefferson, US founding father

3. "The English are, I think, the most obtuse and barbarous people in the world."

    Stendhal (Marie Henri Beyle), French writer

4. "The average cooking in the average hotel for the average Englishman explains to a large extent the English bleakness and taciturnity. Nobody can beam and warble while chewing pressed beef smeared with diabolical mustard. Nobody can exult aloud while ungluing from his teeth a quivering tapioca pudding."

    Karel Capek, Czech writer

5. "Thirty millions, mostly fools."

    Thomas Carlyle, Scottish historian and essayist, when asked what the population of England was

6. "All Englishmen talk as if they've got a bushel of plums stuck in their throats, and then after swallowing them get constipated from the pips."

    W. C. Fields, US actor

7. "The most repulsive people God has ever created. A grey, yawning monster of a people where breath smells of deathly boredom."
   "There is nothing on Earth more terrible than English music, except English painting."

   Heinrich Heine, German poet

8. "England is like a prostitute who, having sold her body all her life, decides to quit and close her business, and then tells everybody she wants to be chaste and protect her flesh as if it were jade."

   He Manzi, Chinese politician

9. "Paralytic sycophants, effete betrayers of humanity, carrion-eating servile imitators, arch-cowards and collaborators, gang of women-murderers, degenerate rabble, parasitic traditionalists, playboy soldiers, conceited dandies."

   East German Communist Party's approved terms of abuse when describing the English, 1953

10. "Cold-blooded queers with nasty complexions and terrible teeth who once conquered half the world but still haven't figured out central heating. They warm their beers and chill their baths and boil all their food."

    P. J. O'Rourke, US author

10 SPEED BUMPS ON THE ROAD TO SEXUAL EQUALITY

1654: the London physician John Bulwer notes that hairy women are "monsters"; he says that if you see one you should throw stones at her.

1664: Samuel Pepys tells his wife Elisabeth that he is sorry for giving her a black eye, just before going off to see his mistress.

1817: Napoleon Bonaparte writes: "Nature intended women to be our slaves. They are our property. They belong to us, just as a tree that bears fruit belongs to a gardener. What a mad idea to demand equality for women! Women are nothing but machines for producing children."

1870: Queen Victoria dismisses the women's suffrage movement as "the most hateful, heartless and disgusting of human beings".

1877: in his book *Diseases of Women*, American surgeon Lawson Tait warns young ladies about the dangers of taking music lessons. It will upset their ovaries and cause "a great deal of menstrual mischief".

1888: the philosopher Friedrich Nietzsche says: "When a woman becomes a scholar there is usually something wrong with her sexual organs."

1903: sexologist Havelock Ellis explains that walking upright is much more difficult for women, who "might be physiologically truer if they went around on all fours".

1905: former US President Grover Cleveland says: "Sensible and responsible women do not want to vote. The relative positions to be assumed by man and woman in the working out of our civilization were assigned long ago by a higher intelligence than ours."

1931: addressing a women's meeting in London, the pioneer vegetarian Dr Josiah Oldfield says that ugly women are "a crime against society" and suggests that they should be drowned.

1934: in an interview, the world's brainiest man Albert Einstein says: "In women, God may have created a sex without brains." When reminded about the Nobel Prize winner Marie Curie, Einstein replies, "Well, she may be the exception." He also has a non-PC way of explaining his most famous theory: "Supposing an ugly lady sits on your lap for a minute. It will seem like an hour. But if a beautiful girl sits on your lap for an hour, it will seem like a minute."

DWARFS OF SOME STATURE: A SHORTLIST OF 8

1. Jeffrey Hudson

   Arguably the most famous British dwarf in history, Hudson was born the son of a bull-baiting butcher "of lusty stature". Theories about how he came to be so small ranged from his mother's choking on a gherkin while pregnant to rumours about his parents keeping him in a box; in fact, he suffered from growth-hormone deficiency. In the 1620s, at just under 2 ft tall, Hudson became court dwarf to English royalty: King Charles I's favourite joke was to stick him in-between two halves of a loaf of bread and pretend to eat him. Hudson lost his job after shooting a fully grown man in the head.* He tolerated his role as royal pet with charm and good grace for many years, but the joke eventually wore thin and he let it be known that he would no longer suffer insults about his height. When offence was offered in 1644, he challenged his detractor to a duel. Hudson chose pistols on horseback – and planted a musket-ball through the man's forehead.

   ---

   * Dwarfs were so prized as servants and entertainers in royal households that the population of "natural" dwarfs was exhausted, so techniques were developed to manufacture them. In China, children were placed in large vases constructed to constrict the growing child. The children's bodies grew inside the vase, but with no room to grow up or down, they expanded outward to fill the space inside the vase. Eventually, the vase was cracked open and a "dwarf" was born.

2. Nicolas Ferry, aka Bébé

   Celebrated eighteenth-century court dwarf to King Stanislaw of Poland, one of his assignments was to peek under the skirts of the king's prospective mistresses and report back. Although he grew to be only 34 inches (86 cm) tall, Ferry was considered a novelty among dwarfs because his limbs and features were all in perfect proportion to his height, a condition known as "proportionate dwarfism". Ferry's health declined in his late teens and he showed signs of premature ageing and had difficulty walking. He became a chronic invalid and died in 1764 aged twenty-two. His skeleton was prepared and mounted for study, and is currently kept at the Musee de l'Homme in Paris.

3. Caroline Crachami

   Known as "the smallest person ever", the tragic "Sicilian Fairy" was first exhibited in London in 1824 by a Dr Gilligan, who claimed he was her father. Hundreds of people queued daily and paid one-shilling admission to view the nine-year-old, 19-inch marvel. For the most part, Miss Crachami's act involved wandering around the stage while listening to music. For a few shillings more, audience members were permitted to handle the tiny girl, dance with her, pat her head and feed her biscuits. King George IV was a big admirer, along with around 300 members of the English nobility. When she was presented at court, observers noted that she had a very bad cough; in the middle of her gruelling schedule, she collapsed and died onstage from tuberculosis in June 1824, age nine. A week later her real father, the Sicilian musician Louis Crachami, arrived in London and began legal attempts to retrieve his daughter's body for burial. Despite his best efforts, the corpse was acquired by the anatomist John Hunter, who dissected it and put her skeleton on display in the Hunterian Museum, where it remains to this day.

4. Richard Gibson

   Known professionally as "Dwarf Gibson" but to his friends as "little Dick", he served as court dwarf and court artist in England during the reigns of three monarchs, Charles I, Charles II and William and Mary. Married to Anne Shepherd, who was known as the "queen's dwarf", the couple were both said to be an identical 3 feet 10 inches tall and they had nine children. Appropriately, "little Dick" specialized in painted miniatures.

5. Charles Sherwood Stratton

   Under the stage name "General Tom Thumb", Stratton was the star attraction of the American circus pioneer (and distant relative) Phineas T. Barnum. Although a relatively large baby, he is said to have more or less stopped growing when he was six months old, whereupon his father happily agreed to consign his son as an attraction in Barnum's New York Museum. Dressed in military regalia "General Tom Thumb" took the US by storm and a European tour soon followed; Queen Victoria saw him three times. He became a wealthy man with a house in the fashionable part of New York, a steam yacht and designer wardrobe. When Barnum got into financial difficulty it was Stratton who bailed him out and eventually became his business partner. He died of a stroke aged forty-six.

6. George Washington "Commodore" Nutt

   Another of Barnum's little people, the showman described him as "a most remarkable dwarf, who was a sharp, intelligent little fellow, with a deal of drollery and wit ... and a splendid head". Nutt made his living dressed in miniature naval uniforms and riding in a tiny carriage in the shape of a walnut. He and General Tom Thumb were rivals for the affections of another Barnum attraction, Lavinia Warren. Thumb won and the gallant loser stood as Thumb's best man at the couple's wedding. At the time of his death he was 43 inches tall.

7. Aditya "Romeo" Dev
Listed in the *Guinness Book of Records* as the "world's smallest bodybuilder", the Indian dwarf can shoulder press 2 kg dumbbells, a notable feat given his 9 kg (20 lb) body weight and 84 cm (2 feet 9 inches) height.

8. Bridget "the Midget" Powers
The 3 foot 9 inch American hardcore porn star made her first film in 1999 and by her own count has appeared in at least sixty-five more. These include *Whack Attack 8: Straight Up Their Candy Asses!*, *Mechanical Elf*, *Little Fuckers*, *Pint Size Pussy*, *Only The A-Hole 7*, *Cellar Dweller 4*, *Sodomania* and *Slop Shots 4*. Describing the low point of her career, she told *Bizarre* magazine: "Once I did a film with a guy who had a penis of nearly a foot and a half and it scared me. That is like a six-foot-tall woman being impaled on a three-foot traffic cone." She is now retired from the industry.

15 PEOPLE WITH ANGER MANAGEMENT ISSUES

1. After the Battle of Edessa in 260, the Roman Emperor Valerian was taken captive by the Persian King Shakur and used as a living human footstool. When Shakur grew tired of the joke he had Valerian skinned and stuffed with straw and manure instead.

2. The word Zabernism means abuse of military power or authority, or unjustified aggression. It derives from an incident in 1912 in Zabern (the German name for Saverne in Alsace) when an overzealous German officer killed a cobbler for smiling at him.

3. The ninth-century Greek emperor Theophilus took revenge on two monks who had criticized him, by having eleven verses of obscene poetry tattooed on their foreheads.

4. The French nobleman Thomas de Marle, second Lord of Coucy, was considered violent by medieval standards. He was fond of hanging his enemies by their testicles, which would rip off under the strain, "spilling their vitals".

5. Vedius Pollio, a Roman official under Emperor Augustus, had a pool full of lampreys, which had been trained to eat human flesh. When his slave dropped a crystal cup, he had him thrown alive to his killer fish.

6. In 1079 Poland's Bishop Stanislaus criticized the sexual conduct of King Boleslaw the Generous, in particular for abducting a nobleman's wife. The king responded by sawing off the bishop's arms and legs.

7. The Sassanid king Chosroes II had a harem of 3,000 wives and 12,000 female slaves. He wanted Hadiqah, the daughter of the Christian Arab Na'aman, to become wife number 3,001, but Na'aman refused to allow his Christian daughter to enter the harem of a Zoroastrian. The king had him trampled to death by an elephant.

8. The North African ruler Ibrahim II ordered the execution of 300 palace servants after discovering at dinner that a napkin was missing.

9. During the War of the Roses, John Tiptoft, Earl of Worcester, was known as "the butcher of England". In 1470 he put down a rebellion in Southampton, then took some stakes sharpened at both ends and used them to attach the severed heads of rebels to their own rectums.

10. Elizabeth I's torturer-in-chief Richard Topcliffe was described by his Catholic enemies as "a veteran in evil" with a "cesspool" for a heart. He also liked to take his work home with him, building a torture chamber in the cellar of his house. One of his victims, Nicholas Owen, who was known for hiding Catholic priests, was found dead in his cell with his bowels hanging out. He suffered from a hernia, and Topcliffe had racked him so hard that he simply burst.

11. In 1602 the Scottish noble Patrick Stewart of Innervak caught his servant, Angus, sleeping with his daughter. Stewart cut off the servant's genitals and filled his scrotum with hot coals.

12. In 1867 while visiting a mountain village in western Fiji, the Irish Methodist missionary Revd Thomas Baker removed a comb from a chief's hair, unaware of a local tradition that touching the head of a chief is a grievous insult. Revd Baker was promptly killed and eaten, along with seven followers.*

13. During King Leopold's reign of terror in Belgian Congo, Leon Rom, his district commissioner of Matadi, decorated the flowerbeds around his house with human heads.

14. In 1906 the dying Spanish general Ramón Blanco y Erenas was asked by a priest, "Do you forgive your enemies?" The general replied: "No. I don't have any enemies. I've had them all shot."

15. In 2007 a twenty-four-year-old woman from Liverpool was jailed after she ripped off one of her former boyfriend's testicles with her bare hands. Amanda Monti pulled off Geoffrey Jones' left testicle and then tried to swallow it when her ex rejected her advances at a house party. After deciding not to devour the fresh man-sack, she spat it out. A friend handed it back to Jones saying: "That's yours."

---

* 136 years later the villagers offered an apology to Revd Baker's living descendants, who admitted he was slightly mad and confessed surprise that they hadn't eaten him earlier.

12 CHALLENGED MONARCHS

1. Louis "the Stammerer" King of Aquitaine (877–79)

2. Bermudo "the Gouty" King of Leon (984–99)

3. Magnus "the Blind" King of Norway (1130–39)

4. Sverker "the Clubfoot" King of Sweden (1130–56)

5. Inge "the Crouchback" King of Norway (1136–61)

6. Alfonso "the Fat" King of Portugal (1185–1223)

7. Eric "the Lisp and Lame" King of Sweden (1222–50)

8. Ivail "the Cabbage" Czar of Bulgaria (1278–79)

9. Wladislaw "the Short" or "the Elbow-high" King of Poland (1320–33)

10. Vasili "the Cross-eyed" Grand Prince of Moscow (1425–62)

11. Henry "the Impotent" King of Castile (1454–74)

12. Otto "the Crazy" King of Bavaria (1886–1913)

10 NAZI ODDITIES

1. The Nazi race theorist Professor Hermann Gauch was so racist that he was embarrassing even to the Nazi leadership. He once claimed that Italians were "half ape" and claimed that Aryans were better at singing because "the shape of the Nordic gum allows a superior movement of the tongue".

2. Hitler's successor, Admiral Donitz, was plagued with incontinence. When he surrendered to the British in 1945 he was wearing six pairs of underpants.

3. In 1941 Hitler banned several Gothic-style popular typefaces including Fraktur because they were "Judenlettern" – Jewish letters.

4. Hitler's right-hand man Hermann Goering seized Germany's biggest condom manufacturing business and gave it to his godmother, Baroness Elisabeth von Epenstein, in exchange for two large castles.

5. Concerned about sexually transmitted diseases picked up from foreign prostitutes of inferior races, Heinrich Himmler provided his Nazi troops with blow-up sex dolls. The dolls were smaller than life-size and could fit easily into a soldier's backpack. Allegedly, Himmler asked Hungarian actress Kathy von Nagy to model for them, but she turned him down.

6. It was illegal in Nazi Germany for apes to give the Heil Hitler salute.

7. Hitler once ordered a team of phrenologists to take measurements of his skull. They concluded that his skull was "just like Napoleon's" and they had seen "nothing like it since Frederick the Great". It contradicted a medical report written when he was on trial for attempting to seize power in 1923, which said that Hitler's features demonstrated "bad race, mongrel, low receding forehead, ugly nose, broad cheekbones, small eyes and dark hair".

8. Hitler weighed around 155 lb. It's just an estimate because he refused to undress even for medical examinations.

9. The SS liked to torture concentration camp inmates by tickling them with goose feathers.

10. Martin Bormann owned a special edition of *Mein Kampf* bound in human skin.

IDLE WORSHIP:
10 FAMOUS SLACKERS

1. René Descartes, who said "Cogito, ergo sum" – "I think, therefore I am" – did most of his thinking in bed, which is where he stayed most days until noon. He had a theory that if he didn't exert himself he could live for at least 100 years and perhaps even up to 500 years; he died of pneumonia aged fifty-four.

2. The writer Samuel Johnson rarely rose before noon, and then spent the rest of his day either in the theatre or hanging out in the coffee shops of London with his friends. He always tried to get his work out of the way as quickly as possible and rarely read over what he had just written. As he hardly ever worked, he was often too poor to buy the basics of his trade, ink and paper.

3. In 1827 "the father of computing" Charles Babbage was appointed Lucusian professor of mathematics at Cambridge, a prestigious post once held by Isaac Newton. It came with a generous income and the sole requirement of the job was to deliver one course of lectures a year. Babbage held the post for eleven years but couldn't be bothered to deliver a single lecture.

4. On the evening he was assassinated in Ford's Theatre, Abraham Lincoln's bodyguard was John Frederick Parker, a Washington police officer. He turned up three hours late for his shift, and then sloped off to have a

drink with his mates at the pub next door to the theatre. That's how John Wilkes Booth was able to simply walk in, put a pistol to Lincoln's head and pull the trigger.

5. The thirtieth US President Calvin Coolidge rarely worked more than four hours a day and took a two-hour catnap every afternoon. The first thing he did after he was sworn in as President of the United States was to go back to bed.

6. Albert Einstein liked to sleep ten hours a night, unless he was working on an idea, then it was eleven. He claimed that his dreams helped him to invent.

7. James Joyce did his writing in bed. He said that if he could write two good sentences he considered that he had done a decent day's work.

8. The poet W. H. Auden always clocked off promptly at 5 p.m. and refused to work into the evening; he said: "Only the Hitlers of the world work at night; no honest artist does." Auden kept up his energy levels with amphetamines; he called them a "labour-saving device in the mental kitchen".

9. Adolf Hitler didn't work at night, or much at all. Apart from his carefully crafted speeches, he rarely put much effort into anything. He was never seen until 2 p.m., after which he would eat lunch and then go for a walk. After dinner, he would watch a movie and then go to bed. Some of his ministers found it difficult to get meetings with him for months at a time. As the war became more desperate, he started working longer hours, but by then it was too late.

10. For the last forty-five years of his life, from 12 June 1965, the day that "Hapworth 16, 1924" appeared in the *New Yorker*, until 10 January 2010, the day he died, *The Catcher in the Rye* author J. D. Salinger didn't publish a single story or novel.

10 CELEBRITY ENDORSEMENTS

1. The first ever celebrity endorsement featured Queen Victoria in a Cadbury's Cocoa advertisement. She was shown sipping the milk chocolate drink with the legend "Drink Cadbury's Chocolate". When it first appeared in 1854, sales of Cadbury's Cocoa skyrocketed.

2. In the 1870s Pope Leo XIII allowed his name and face to be used in advertising for Vin Mariani, a wine laced with cocaine. According to the copy, his Holiness carried a hip flask of the stuff under his robes at all times. With the Pope's blessing, the surprisingly addictive beverage sold better than anyone could have guessed and Leo XIII went on to become the oldest pope in history. It also inspired one John S. Pemberton to come up with a similar product called Coca-Cola.

3. In 1885 when the designers of the iconic Victorian coffee brand Camp needed a poster boy to promote their new product, they turned to the man of the hour, Major-General Hector Macdonald, the legendary "Fighting Mac", one of Britain's greatest Victorian military heroes. In 1902, while in command of British troops in Ceylon, Macdonald, scourge of Afghans, Boers and Whirling Dervishes, was accused of gross indecency with four schoolboys in a railway carriage. On his way back to Ceylon to face trial, Macdonald stopped off in Paris at the Hotel Regina, sat on his bed, put a pistol to his head and blew his brains out. Macdonald's image, however, is still used on the Camp bottle today.

4. Theodore "Teddy" Roosevelt, twenty-sixth President of the United States, gave his official endorsement while still President to a twelve-bore double-barrelled shotgun made by the Fox Gun Company. He described it as "the most beautiful gun I have ever seen", and plugged it in an article for *Scribner's Magazine*: "I had a Fox No. 12 shotgun; no better gun was ever made."

5. In 1927 Al Jolson became famous as one of the first actors and singers to star in a talking motion picture. Two years later he put his name to Lucky Strike cigarettes, the "healthy alternative to fattening sweets". Jolson is quoted as saying: "Folks, let me tell you, the good old flavour of Luckies is as sweet and soothing as the best 'Mammy' song ever written ... There's one great thing about the toasted flavour ... it surely satisfies the craving for sweets. That's how I always keep in good shape and always feel peppy." Jolson died of a massive heart attack aged sixty-four.

6. In 1905 the Hollywood star Fatty Arbuckle was hired to promote Murad cigarettes, but privately had doubts. Arbuckle told his sponsors: "You can make me praise them in print but don't make me smoke 'em. I gotta career to think of and it's a live show. What if I cough? They'll stop the money for sure. And those things make me cough."

7. The Hollywood child actress Shirley Temple lent her name to a non-alcoholic beverage. When her life was insured with Lloyds of London, Temple's contract stipulated that no benefits would be paid if she met with death or injury while intoxicated. She was only seven years old at the time.

8. In 1958 the actor Tyrone Power was shooting the costumed epic *Solomon and Sheba*. While filming a complicated duelling scene with George Sanders requiring several retakes, Power complained of arm and chest pain and was rushed to the nearest hospital, where he died within the hour of a heart attack. He had just finished making an educational movie short sponsored by the American Heart Association, in which he warned his audience about the perils of overwork, because "time is the most precious thing we have".

9. In 1987 the US meat industry was concerned about the growing menace of vegetarianism. The Beef Industry Council decided to hit back with an advertising campaign starring Cybill Shepherd, best known for her starring role in the hit TV drama *Moonlighting*. She signed up to an alleged one-million-dollar deal as spokeswoman for American beef with the slogan "Real food for real people". The campaign was only weeks old when she told a magazine: "I've cut down on fatty foods and am trying to stay away from red meat." Ms Shepherd was swiftly dropped from the campaign.

10. Next, the Beef Industry Council turned to the actor James Garner, star of *The Rockford Files*. Surely Jim Rockford was not a secret vegetarian? Of course he wasn't. Garner loved a steak as much as the next man, but he was a less than ideal representative for their artery-clogging product, as it turned out. Shortly after he was shown carving his way through mountains of roasts and grills he was rushed to a cardiac unit for emergency quadruple by-pass surgery.

12 LOST EXPLORERS

1311: Abubakari II, ruler of the Mali Empire in Africa, heads off across the Atlantic to explore "the limits of the ocean"; he is never seen again.

1499: King Henry VII of England sends the Italian John Cabot to Newfoundland and eastern Canada "to discover and investigate whatsoever islands, countries, regions or provinces of heathens and infidels, in whatsoever part of the world placed, which before this time were unknown to all Christians". Cabot and his ships, crew and passengers are all assumed lost at sea.

1788: French explorer Jean-François de Galaup and his crew vanish without trace while attempting to sail around the world. It was good news for one of the men who applied for the voyage, sixteen-year-old Corsican Napoleon Bonaparte – he was on the shortlist but didn't make it onto the ship.

1791: Irishman Daniel Houghton is picked to lead a British expedition to explore the hinterland of Africa's west coast and find the fabled "lost" city of Timbuktu. After being robbed by a local trader who offers to take him directly to Timbuktu for a fee, Houghton dies alone of starvation, his unburied corpse assumed to have been eaten by scavengers.

1803: George Bass, a thirty-two-year-old British surgeon and explorer of Australia, sets sail from Sydney for South

America on the *Venus* and is never heard from again. One story has it that he was captured by the Spanish in Chile and sent to work in the silver mines.

1845: Arctic explorer John Franklin and more than a hundred seamen set off to find the Northwest Passage – the fabled shortcut to China via the Arctic Circle. The remains of some crew members are found later showing signs of cannibalism, but most are never discovered and the reason for their disappearance remains a mystery.

1848: Ludwig Leichardt, thirty-four-year-old German explorer, sets off on a 4,500-km east-to-west crossing on horseback of the unknown Australian interior. He and his team of four Europeans, two Aboriginal guides, seven horses, twenty mules and fifty bullocks vanish somewhere in the Great Sandy Desert.

1897: the heroic Swede Saloman August Andrée and his companions Knut Fraenkel and Nils Strindberg set off to reach the North Pole in a leaky hydrogen balloon, despite having little experience in large balloons and none at all in Arctic conditions. All three men survive a crash landing, but die a couple of weeks after landfall; this is attributed to severe food poisoning after dining on undercooked polar bear.

1900: the German naturalist Carl von Hagen goes to Papua New Guinea to collect butterflies. One of the specimens he encounters, the bright-green Paradise Birdwing, said to be the most beautiful butterfly in the world, "survives" to this day at the Harvard Museum of Comparative Zoology. Von Hagen is less lucky: shortly after netting *Onithoptera paradisea* he is captured and eaten by cannibals.

1924: Andrew Irvine, a twenty-two-year-old English mountaineer, takes part in the British Mount Everest Expedition with climbing partner George Mallory. Both disappear somewhere high on the mountain's northeast ridge. Mallory's body turns up in 1999, but the search for Irvine continues.

1925: British archaeologist and explorer Colonel Percy Harrison Fawcett, his eldest son Jack and his friend Raleigh Rimmell are last seen walking into the jungle of Mato Grosso in Brazil to search for a lost city called "Z". Despite several unconfirmed sightings and many conflicting reports and theories explaining their disappearance, and the loss of at least a hundred people in more than a dozen futile follow-up expeditions, their fate remains a mystery.

1928: Roald Amundsen, Norwegian Arctic explorer and the first expedition leader to reach the North Pole in 1926, disappears while flying on a search-and-rescue mission in the Arctic. His plane probably crashed in fog: his body has never been found.

KING SIZE:
10 OBESE MONARCHS

1. Eglon of Moab
   The sorry tale of the fat Biblical king is told in Judges 3:12–30. Eglon was sitting on the toilet when he was stabbed in the stomach by an Israelite called Ehud. When Ehud tried to withdraw his weapon it got lost in the folds of fat in the king's paunch. The king's courtiers, assuming that their master was still relieving himself, left him to his business. When they finally broke the lock and entered, they found Eglon lying on the floor dead.

2. Dionysius of Heracleia (r337–305 BC)
   The gluttonous ancient Greek king was so bloated that he could barely move or breathe and stuffed himself to the point where he often fell asleep on the throne during audiences; his courtiers stuck needles in him to keep him awake. He grew so big that he couldn't feed himself and food had to be introduced into his stomach by artificial means. The king aspired to end his days "on my back, lying on my many rolls of fat, scarcely uttering a word, taking laboured breaths, and eating my fill". Ultimately he was choked by his own fat at the ripe old age of fifty-five.

3. Sancho "the Fat" of León (r956–966)
   Two years after Sancho took the throne, a group of nobles led by Fernán González of Castile overthrew him on account of his extreme obesity. While in exile, the

Jewish court doctor Hasdai ibn Shaprut put Sancho on a diet and he managed to lose some of his girth and take back the throne. Within a couple of years he had put it all back on again.

4. Charles III "the Fat" (r881–888)

The Carolingian dynasty wasn't short of unflattering nicknames (see also Charles the Bald, Charles the Simple, Pepin the Hunchback, Louis the Stammerer and Odo the Insane). This porky monarch was too lazy to fight the Vikings and took to bribing them to stay away. Charles was eventually overthrown by his slim nephew, Arnuff.

5. William the Conqueror (r1066–1087)

A strapping, healthy six-footer when he invaded England, in his later years William "the Bastard" became William "the Fat Bastard"; King Philip of France said the corpulent conqueror looked like a pregnant woman about to give birth. In 1087 William went off to the Norman equivalent of a weight-loss clinic in Rouen, France where he planned to shed a few pounds with a strict diet of herbs and medications; he never made it. At his funeral he was found to be too big for his coffin and it took some poking and prodding to try to force his body into it; his guts burst, filling the church with an "intolerable stench", sending the mourners racing for the doors.

6. Edward IV (r1461–1470, 1471–1483)

When he was young, Edward IV was tall, handsome and very athletic, but he was a man of large appetites – for women, food and drink; he enjoyed epic banquets and forced himself to throw up between courses so that he could pack more in. By the time he was forty he had ballooned (although he never quite reached the proportions of his grandson Henry VIII). In March 1483 he died suddenly and unexpectedly from a heart attack while he was on a fishing trip (although one contemporary historian recorded that the king died from eating too much fruit and veg).

7. Henry VIII (r1509–1547)
   Henry was still a lithe lothario in his thirties but the latter years of his life saw an alarming physical deterioration, especially after a leg injury sustained in a jousting accident stopped him from exercising. By the end of his reign the tubby Tudor had a 52-inch waist and 53-inch chest – morbidly obese by modern standards. When he died aged fifty-six, caught between fluid retention caused by circulatory problems and chronic constipation, Henry was so heavy that his coffin broke the supports that were provided for it in at least one of the churches in which it was displayed.

8. Queen Anne (r1702–1714)
   Although her reign was a byword for elegance, "Brandy Nan" was profoundly fat and unhealthy. When she came to the throne at the age of thirty-seven she had already given birth to six children, had eight stillbirths and four miscarriages, none of which did much for her figure. It was a struggle to find ceremonial robes to fit her for her inaugural speech to Parliament. The visiting French ambassador was astonished by the amount of food she could eat and was afraid that "she might burst". Anne was also so crippled by gout that she had some of the old machinery that was used to move Henry VIII around refitted for her own use. When she died, Anne's coffin was almost as wide as it was long.

9. Edward VII (r1901–1910)
   All of the Hanoverian monarchs were on the hefty side,

especially Edward's mother Queen Victoria. Edward was immensely fat and nicknamed "Tum Tum" and "Dirty Bertie": the latter nothing to do with revolting table manners (although he had those in large portions as well). When he wasn't chasing women in Paris, or killing animals, he was eating; when he got too fat to walk he had animals driven directly at him, straight down the barrel of his gun. A lifetime of binge eating and binge drinking finally caught up with Edward when he died of heart failure, aged sixty-eight, having reigned for only nine years.

10. King Farouk of Egypt (r1936–1965)
Weighing nearly 136 kg (300 lb), he was described by a courtier as "a stomach with a head": he was said to get through 600 oysters a week. In 1952 the CIA initiated a secret plan to overthrow Farouk; it was known internally as "Project Fat Fucker".* He collapsed and died at his dinner table in the Isle de France restaurant in Rome in 1965 following a characteristically gigantic dinner.

---

* Farouk fled Egypt, abandoning his huge stash of pornography.

10 WARDROBE MALFUNCTIONS

1667: the forty-three-year-old Duchess of Newcastle surprises a London theatre audience by attending topless, her "scarlet-trimmed nipples . . . all laid out to view".

1813: Napoleon's army retreat from Moscow. Out of an initial half a million soldiers, only 10,000 Frenchmen make it out of Russia alive. Many freeze to death partly because of the tin buttons used in their army uniforms; they turn to dust when the temperature drops to -30°C.

1862: Emma Livry, a prima ballerina at the Paris Opera catches her tutu, plumped up by layers of petticoats, in one of the gas-lamps that lights the theatre. In flames, she runs across the stage three times before she is caught and the fire extinguished with the help of firemen and other dancers, but later dies from her burns.★

1920: the French President Paul Deschanel receives the British Ambassador to France, stark naked apart from the ceremonial decorations of his office.†

1923: working on location in San Antonio, Texas, on the film *The Warrens of Virginia*, twenty-four-year-old silent film actress Martha Mansfield is anything but silent when a

---

★ Both of Oscar Wilde's half-sisters met a similar fate: one tried to save the other but was burned to death herself.
† Deschanel stepped down from the presidency soon afterwards, citing mental health issues.

match, tossed by a cast member, ignites her Civil War costume of hooped skirts and flimsy ruffles, causing her clothing to burst into flames. She dies in hospital the following day.

1927: the dancer Isadora Duncan gives a cheery wave as she sets off as a passenger in a brand-new convertible sports car that she is learning to drive. As she leans back in her seat to enjoy the sea breeze, her long red chiffon scarf winds around a rear wheel axle, tightening around Duncan's neck and dragging her from the car and onto the cobblestone street. She dies instantly.

1944: the actress Tallulah Bankhead is notorious for not wearing underwear. When the film crew on the set of *Lifeboat* complain about one of her many exposures, Alfred Hitchcock replies: "I don't know whether that's a concern for wardrobe or hairdressing."

1966: the singer P. J. Proby has his scheduled appearance on TV cancelled after he split his pants during a live London show, amid concerns that he has used his "pants-splitting routine" to gain attention once too often.

1973: Ugandan dictator Idi Amin gives a poolside TV interview, during which one of his testicles is constantly exposed.

1999: two women shelter under a tree during a thunderstorm in Hyde Park when a lightning strike is drawn to the metal in their underwired bras, killing them both instantly.

10 BUSINESS EXPERTS

1. "Drill for oil? You mean drill into the ground to try and find oil? You're crazy."

   > Associates of Edwin L. Drake when he proposed his project to find oil in 1859

2. "The phonograph has no commercial value at all."

   > Thomas Edison, American inventor, 1880

3. "Stocks have reached what looks like a permanently high plateau."

   > Irving Fisher, economics professor at Yale University in 1929, days before the Wall Street Crash

4. "Who the hell wants to hear actors talk?"

   > H. M. Warner, Warner Brothers, 1927

5. "In all likelihood world inflation is over."

   > Per Jacobsson, International Monetary Fund CEO, 1959

6. "Remote shopping, while entirely feasible, will flop because women like to get out of the house, like to handle merchandise, like to be able to change their minds."

   > TIME magazine writing off e-commerce in 1966

7. "And for the tourist who really wants to get away from it all, safaris in Vietnam."

   > Newsweek magazine, predicting popular holidays for the late 1960s

8. "With over fifty foreign cars already on sale here, the Japanese auto industry isn't likely to carve out a big slice of the US market."

Business Week, 2 August 1968

9. "My biggest fear is that we will be too successful."

Walt Disney chairman Robert Fitzpatrick on the opening of Disneyland Paris in 1992.
More than twenty years later it has losses of €1.9 billion and according to financial experts may never turn a profit

10. "[Apple's iPhone] is the most expensive phone in the world and it doesn't appeal to business customers because it doesn't have a keyboard which makes it not a very good e-mail machine . . ."

Steve Ballmer, Microsoft CEO, 2007

14 PEOPLE WHO SUED

1. In 1878 James Whistler sued the art critic John Ruskin over a poor review of one of his paintings. Whistler won and was insultingly awarded damages of a farthing (a quarter of a penny). Meanwhile, the legal costs bankrupted the American artist.

2. In 1967 the British Prime Minister Harold Wilson sued the pop band The Move, who had just promoted their new single 'Flowers in the Rain' by publishing a postcard featuring a cartoon of Harold naked and in bed with his personal secretary Marcia. The PM won and the band forfeited all the royalties for the single – about £200,000. The story of Wilson's alleged affair with Marcia Williams was retold in a 2006 BBC Four drama, *The Lavender List*, and proved equally provocative. Williams, by then known as Lady Falkender, successfully sued the BBC for £75,000 plus costs in respect of the unfounded suggestion.

3. In 1985 New Yorker Jay Shaheri filed a $20 million suit against the estate of a banker's widow who landed on him in a suicide leap from her nineteenth-floor apartment. He said Mildred Walker jumped "without regard for human safety".

4. In 1992 Robert Flynn, a retired civil servant from Farnham in Surrey, sued a utility company for the loss of his dead parrot. He had put her in the freezer but during a power cut she decomposed. He won the case and was awarded £200.

5. In 1996 Paul Shimkonis sued a Florida topless club claiming whiplash injuries sustained when a dancer thrust her breasts in his face. He said the impact of the sixty-inch bust was "like two cement blocks hit me".

6. In 1997 James Van Gorder filed a lawsuit against a chiropractic centre in Detroit, Michigan for negligence during treatment for back pain. According to Van Gorder, the chiropractor made him take off his clothes and lie face down on the two-part examining table; his genitals fell between the crack and got trapped when the chiropractor adjusted the table. Van Gorder claimed for extreme pain, suffering, disfigurement and "loss of sexual desire".

7. In 1999 Donald Drusky from Pennsylvania sued God for not granting him the skills to play the guitar. Drusky named Presidents Reagan and Bush, as God's earthly representatives, as co-defendants. A federal judge in Syracuse, New York, threw out the case.

8. In March 2003 Norwegian death metal fan Per Kristian Hagen filed a lawsuit against Blasphemer and his Mayhem bandmates for involuntary assault and battery when a dead sheep that Mayhem front man "Maniac" was carving up as part of the entertainment flew off the stage, striking Hagen and fracturing his skull. Hagen noted: "My relationship to sheep is a bit ambivalent now."

9. In 2004 Liza Minnelli's bodyguard accused the singer of forcing him to have sex with her. M'hammed Soumayah sued Minnelli for $100 million damages, claiming she made "many repeated attempts" to compel him into sex and he "eventually succumbed".

10. In 2005 Christopher Roller from Minnesota sued the celebrity magicians David Blaine and David Copperfield for stealing his "godly powers without permission to perform magic on stage". Roller demanded 10 per cent of their total income for life; he lost.

11. In 2005 Anna Ayala sued a Wendy's restaurant in San Jose, California, for emotional distress after allegedly finding a finger in a bowl of chilli. When the authorities could find no evidence of missing digits anywhere along Wendy's supply chain, the finger of suspicion pointed to Ayala, who was arrested and found guilty of attempting to extort money. The finger was eventually traced to a co-worker of Ayala's husband, who lost it in a work accident and gave it to the couple to settle a $100 bet.

12. In 2006 Allen Heckard, from Portland, Oregon, sued basketball legend Michael Jordan and Jordan's promoter, former Chicago Bull and Nike co-founder Phil Knight, for a combined $832 million. Claiming personal injury and emotional pain and suffering, Heckard said he had been mistaken for Jordan almost every day for fifteen years and was sick of it. This was despite being 6 inches (15.24 cm) shorter and eight years older than his more famous counterpart.

13. In 2009 a New York doctor, Richard Batista, sued his ex-wife for the return of a kidney that he had donated to her eight years prior while they were still married. Batista's lawyers said that, if the return of the organ proved impractical, their client would settle for $1.5 million compensation.

14. When their hero died in 2009, thirty-four French Michael Jackson fans sued his doctor, Conrad Murray, for "emotional distress". Five of them won their case and received a payout of one euro (88p) each.

VICTORIAN VALUES: 10 THINGS YOU MAY NOT HAVE KNOWN ABOUT PRINCE ALBERT'S WIFE

1. Queen Victoria survived six attempts to kill or harm her, a record she shares with Tsar Alexander II of Russia, who was finally blown to pieces at the seventh attempt in 1881.

2. She spoke no English at all until she was three years old, and thereafter in private spoke more German than English.

3. At 150 cm tall, 28 cm shorter than her husband, Queen Victoria was England's shortest monarch.

4. She was once prescribed cannabis by her personal physician, Dr J. R. Reynolds, to "assist sleep during menstrual cramps".

5. She described her own children as "ugly", "nasty" and "frog-like". When her daughter Vicky told her that she was pregnant by her husband Prince Frederick, Victoria replied that she was "dreadfully upset" by the "horrid news".

6. Her doctors never saw her undressed. They only discovered that she had a hernia and prolapsed uterus after she died.

7. She wore crotchless knickers because she thought they were more hygienic. Consequently, her underwear change was infrequent.

8. She hated the sight of pregnant women and described them as "quite disgusting".

9. She refused to breastfeed, which she thought "animalistic" and only suited to women of low social class.

10. She was a hypochondriac and would call for her doctor up to half a dozen times a day with various imaginary complaints, usually about her digestive system. He was surprised while on his honeymoon to receive a message from the Queen, which informed him "the bowels are acting fully".

7 MILITARY ECCENTRICS

1. Admiral Charles Beresford, commander-in-chief of the Royal Navy, had his entire back tattooed with a hunting scene showing the fox disappearing up his anus.

2. While fighting rebels in County Kerry in 1567, English soldier Humphrey Gilbert lined the path to his tent with severed Irish heads.

3. During the Indian Mutiny of 1857, in a furious bayonet charge a British soldier in the Scottish Highlanders known as "Quaker" Wallace drove his blade into twenty men while reciting verses from Psalm 116.

4. In 1904, during the decisive battle in the Russo-Japanese War, the Japanese commander-in-chief, Admiral Togo, invited his second-in-command to feel his "loose-hanging testicles" – a sign of his calmness in battle. Reassured, the officer returned to his post.

5. World War II British guerrilla leader Orde Wingate always scrubbed his body with a toothbrush. He was also said to be an authority on Donald Duck.

6. The Chinese general Lin Biao was Chairman Mao's designated successor until his plane mysteriously crashed in Mongolia. Lin had an extreme fear of water, which led to his refusal to ever bathe; the sound of running water made him suffer violent diarrhoea.

7. In 1973 Ehud Barak, Israel's defence minister, led a commando attack on Palestine Liberation Organization targets in Beirut, wearing a blonde wig and padded bra.

HISTORY'S 10 MOST MURDEROUS REGIMES*

USSR, 62 million deaths, 1917–87

People's Republic of China, 35 million, 1949–87

Germany, 21 million, 1933–45

Nationalist China, 10 million, 1928–49

Japan, 6 million, 1936–45

Pre-revolutionary Chinese communists ("Mao Soviets"), 3.5 million, 1923–49

Cambodia, 2 million, 1975–79

Turkey (Armenian genocide), 1.9 million, 1909–18

Vietnam, 1.7 million, 1945–87

Poland, 1.6 million, 1945–48

---

*   R. J. Rummel – *Encyclopaedia of Genocide*

CHAPTER THREE

And so to Bed

SHE AIN'T HEAVY:
10 HISTORIC SEX TOYS

54 BC: Egypt's Queen Cleopatra is rumoured to have invented the vibrator: a gourd, hollowed out and filled with angry bees.

1610: French and Spanish sailors on long sea voyages fashion their own life-sized 'sex dolls' out of cloth or old clothes held together with dried semen. Several men share a single doll, known as a Dame de Voyage.

1649: the French philosopher René Descartes takes a sex doll with him on his sea journey to Sweden. Made of metal and leather, he calls it Francine and often refers to it as his daughter. The crew is so freaked by this that they throw it overboard.

1757: Harris's List of Covent Garden Ladies, an annual guide to London's prostitutes, notes that dildos are made of "wax, horn, leather, and diverse other substances . . . and are to be had at many of our great toy shops and nick nackatories".

1869: American doctor George Taylor invents a steam-powered vibrator called "The Manipulator". About the size of a dining-room table, it has a hole in the middle with a vibrating sphere and users have to shovel coal into it.

1883: Dr Joseph Granville's electromechanical vibrator has

a wet cell battery weighing about 40 lb; it reduces the time it takes to achieve "paroxysm" in female patients from an hour down to around five minutes.

1890: Dr Macaura patents the Pulsocon Hand Crank Vibrator. It looks very much like a heavy old-fashioned egg whisk.

1894: advertisements for Vigor's vibrating saddle, as ordered by HRH the Princess of Wales, promise to "invigorate the system by bringing all the vital organs into inspirating [*sic*] action" and claims it has given the Countess of Aberdeen "complete satisfaction".

1901: electric vibrators available via mail order are advertised as a cure for various illnesses ranging from headaches and asthma to tuberculosis.

1908: Paris catalogues offer mass-manufactured vulcanized rubber dolls that can "imitate ejaculation". They also offer a custom version resembling "any actual person, living or dead".

CREATURE COMFORTS:
15 ZOOPHILES

1565: Louis de Gonzaga, Duke of Nevers, goes to war with 3,000 soldiers and 2,000 she-goats, some of the goats dressed in velvet; the goats are recruited to serve his men "for the most brutal purposes imaginable".

1566: an unnamed Montpellier farmer is apprehended while committing an "act that cannot be mentioned" with a mule. Both farmer and mule are sentenced to be burned alive, but the mule refuses to go without a fight until the executioner cuts off all four of her feet.

1641: in New Haven, Connecticut, a piglet with human features is delivered by a sow owned by Mrs Wakeman. It looks suspiciously like George Spencer, a local man with one glass eye; despite a lack of witnesses, or evidence, Spencer is hanged for the crime of bestiality.

1642: in Massachusetts, a mare, a cow and other "lesser cattle" are executed along with Thomas Graunger, the teenage boy who sexually assaulted them.

1646: John Brown of Fife denies sexually molesting a cow. The charge sticks when witnesses say they found the violated animal surrounded by imprints in the snow made by Brown's wooden leg.

1662: William Potter of New Haven, Connecticut, is hanged

along with his eight accomplices – a cow, two heifers, three sheep and two sows. It is reported that he has been buggering farmyard animals for "no less than fifty years".

1677: Mary Hickes appears at the Old Bailey, London, charged with bestiality. The key prosecution witness is the dog in question, who seals her (and his) fate by wagging his tail when he sees her in court. Hickes and the dog are hanged at Tyburn.

1789: on the island of Dominica, a soldier named Sparrow, "the tallest, straightest and cleanest Grenadier in the whole Regiment", is tarred, feathered and discharged for sodomizing a turkey.

1811: Thomas James, a labourer from Staffordshire, is hanged for having non-consensual sex with a donkey.

1849: French troops, surprised by the frequency their quartermaster is serving duck, pay a surprise visit to the kitchen to see what's going on. Their suspicions are confirmed when they catch him buggering a duck that is being prepared for the dinner table. The quartermaster is cashiered from the regiment.

1952: a Nigerian is convicted of indecency with a pigeon in Trafalgar Square. He is fined £50, and another £10 for taking it home and eating it.

1998: Sidney Carlton, a painter and decorator from Bradford, admits having sexual intercourse with a Staffordshire bull terrier called Badger. In defence, Carlton claims that Badger made the first move. He tells the court, "I can't help it if the dog took a liking to me."

1999: James Donald Ray is found guilty in San Diego of

molesting three sheep. Ray was caught having sex with a ewe outside a local school. Two other sheep, part of the school's agricultural programme, died after sexual assaults a few weeks earlier, prompting a stakeout.

2005: Kenneth Pinyan from Seattle, Washington, dies of acute peritonitis after receiving anal intercourse from a stallion. The case leads to the criminalization of bestiality in Washington State.

2011: Carol Hickey, a forty-three-year-old mother of four from Patrickswell, Ireland, dies after having sex with an Alsatian dog. Test results identify the cause of death as anaphylaxis, a severe allergic reaction to the dog's semen.

10 FERTILITY TREATMENTS

1. The ancient Egyptians tested a woman's fertility by making her sit in a bucket of dates mixed with beer; if she vomits, she will conceive.

2. The ancient Greek Hipponax advised that in married couples struggling to conceive the wife should whip the husband's testicles with the branch of a fig tree.

3. To avoid problematic births, the eleventh-century physician Trotula of Palermo advised drinking a potion made from ivory shavings or "the white matter from the excrement of a hawk".

4. In 1260 the German friar Albertus Magnus wrote: "Whoever shall eat of two goat's testicles and has intercourse thereafter shall conceive a male child."

5. A medieval cure for impotence included mixing the steeped brains of thirty male sparrows, the grease surrounding the kidneys of a freshly killed goat and as much honey as required: the man was to eat it before intercourse.

6. When King Henry VIII's old codpiece was displayed in the Tower of London, barren women would prick pins into the lining in the hope it would bring them babies.

7. In 1490 an Italian cleric warned women not to make

love in the same room as a portrait of John the Baptist, or they will give birth to a hairy baby.

8. In his 1598 medical guide *The General Practice of Physicke*, the German physician Christopher Wirtzung suggests that to conceive a male child, a gentleman should sprinkle his member with a powder made from the following: the testicle of a two-year-old hog, the penis of a shaven shag, two pairs of fox testicles, fifty sparrow brains, the penis of a bull, cloves, saffron, nutmeg and rosemary.

9. The sixteenth-century Transylvanian medic Paulus Kyr advised people not to eat cannabis seeds, because they are "bad for the head, create foul humours and dry up the genital seed".

10. In 1694 the Edinburgh doctor and fertility expert James McMath noted that the best time for conception was when menstrual fluid has a "bright florid colour" and smells like marigolds.

HEAVY PETTING:
10 CHUBBY CHASERS

1. Ibrahim I
   The mad Ottoman sultan caught sight of a cow's genitalia one day and was so aroused that he had a gold cast made of the animal's nether regions. He sent his aides to scour the land to find him a human match to the bovine privates. They returned with a 300-lb Armenian girl called Sechir Para (Sugar Cube) who became his favourite concubine. According to legend, on her say-so he had the rest of his 280-strong harem drowned in the Bosphorus.

2. Rembrandt
   The old Dutch master was evidently attracted to the larger lady or, as the art critic Kenneth Clark put it, women who were "monstrously fat". These included Rembrandt's wife Saskia and various mistresses who were used as cheap models for his work, especially his son's nursemaid, Geertje Dirck, who posed as the ample figure in many of his erotic etchings.

3. Peter Paul Rubens
   Rubens was very fond of plus-size women and featured them wherever possible in his paintings. It was fashionable for women at the time to carry some weight but he took it to a whole new level, making it the standard in all his work, giving rise to the term Rubenesque.

4. Samuel Pepys

   In June 1663 the diarist described having sex with his mistress Betty Lane, for which he rewarded her with a lobster: According to Pepys, ". . . she hath a very white thigh and leg, but monstrous fat." Pepys also had at least two sexual encounters with her hefty younger sister Doll in public houses.

5. Prince Frederick of Denmark

   In 1741 the English writer and parliamentarian Horace Walpole wrote to Lord Lincoln about Princess Louisa, sixteen-year-old daughter of the recently widowed King George II. Walpole noted: "Princess Louisa is grown so fat and, like the queen, has such a monstrous pair of flummey bubbies that I really think it indecent for her to live with her father." Two years later Princess Louisa and her huge breasts were married to Prince Frederick, resulting in six pregnancies, the last of which was fatal for her.

6. Wilkie Collins

   The Victorian author was drawn to women with huge backsides. He never married but kept two mistresses within a stone's throw of each other in Marylebone where he lived for most of his life. One was his house-keeper Caroline Graves, the other Martha Rudd, a "buxom wench" he first met serving in a pub and the mother of his three children.

7. J. M. W. Turner

   Although widely acknowledged as the master of storms, smoke and sunsets, the English artist also had a "chubby" period. When he died in 1857 his huge collection of twenty thousand paintings, drawings and sketches was bequeathed to the nation and among them were hundreds of erotic drawings of obese nude ladies.

8. Le Corbusier
The Swiss-French architectural master and self-confessed hogger★ said he liked his women "Rubenesque". He got the inspiration for designing his chaise longue from "the fat thighs of women" and spent his spare time painting brothel scenes featuring fuller-figured ladies. He once tried to chat up a female journalist with the line, "You are fat and I like my women fat."

9. Brian May
Queen guitarist and writer of "Fat Bottomed Girls", a song about a young boy who is raped by his overweight nanny and as a result grows up seeking ladies of larger girth in brothels.

10. Bill Clinton
Although he had a lithe wife, the forty-second US President kept an orally animated chunky secretary on the side. Or as Chris Griffin put it in an episode of *Family Guy*, "Dude, Bill Clinton got a beej† from a fat chick in the oval office."

★ A person who enjoys sex with a plumper: i.e. a fat yet very alluring female woman. Curvy. Plumper than the average lady. but nonetheless very attractive – *The Urban Dictionary*. See also "veeter".
† Short-form pronunciation of blowjob, for those people who are too lazy to pronounce its abbreviated form "BJ" – *The Urban Dictionary*.

12 WEDDING TRADITIONS

1. Originally, bridesmaids wore gowns similar to that worn by the bride to confuse evil spirits.

2. Bedouin girls often begin to sew their wedding dresses when they turn nine years old. It gives them time to finish their gown before they marry at the age of fourteen.

3. The original job of groomsmen was to help the groom kidnap the bride. At the altar, the groom always stands on the bride's right side so that his sword hand is free to fend off jealous rivals.

4. In some cultures, on the morning after the wedding the groom is expected to show off the virginal blood on the bed sheets.

5. The tradition of not letting the bridegroom see his bride before the wedding came from the time when many more marriages were arranged and the groom might never have seen the bride. There was a good chance that if he saw her, he would bolt.

6. The Talmud has strict laws about marital sex including a timetable for how often husbands should "rejoice" their wives. For men of independent means it is every day; for labourers, twice a week; for ass-drivers, once a week; for camel-drivers, once a month; and for sailors, once every six months.

7. Some tribes in central Asia believed that the bride's hymen should be broken not by her husband, but by her maternal grandfather. If he was unwilling (or dead) a cousin from her mother's side was expected to do the honours.

8. In the Middle Ages, the most popular month for marriage was June. Most people had their annual bath in May so they were still fairly clean when June came around: just in case, brides carried bouquets of flowers to cover up any bad smells.

9. In ancient Chaldea (present-day southern Iraq) a man could get a divorce by writing a letter to his wife's father or by saying, "Thou are not my wife." However, if the wife ever said, "Thou are not my husband," they could drown her.

10. It is legal to marry a dead person in France, as long as you can prove the wedding was already planned.

11. The phrase "always the bridesmaid, never the bride" originated with an advert for Listerine mouthwash in *Ladies Home Journal* in 1924. It featured a girl who couldn't get a man because of her bad breath.

12. At Iranian weddings it is traditional for the bride and groom to lick honey off each other's fingers to ensure their life together starts sweetly. At a wedding in Qazvin in 2001, a twenty-eight-year-old bridegroom choked to death on one of his new wife's false fingernails.

12 PEOPLE WHO MARRIED THEIR NIECES

1. Roman Emperor Claudius and his niece, Agrippina the Younger.

2. King Amedeo I of Spain and Maria Letizia Bonaparte.

3. Prince Augustus Ferdinand of Prussia and Margravine Elisabeth Louise of Brandenburg-Schwedt.

4. Ferdinand II, Archduke of Austria and Anne Juliana Gonzaga.

5. King Ferdinand VII of Spain and his nieces
   (1) Maria Isabel of Portugal and
   (2) Maria Christina of the Two Sicilies.

6. King Pedro III of Portugal and Maria I.

7. King Philip II of Spain and Anna of Austria.

8. King Philip IV of Spain and Mariana of Austria.

9. King Kamehameha the Great of Hawaii and Queen Keopuolani.

10. Porfirio Díaz, president of Mexico and Delfina Ortega Díaz.

11. James Mayer de Rothschild (of the Rothschild banking family) and Betty Salomon von Rothschild.

12. Voltaire and Marie Louise Mignot.

MASTURBATION:
10 STEPS TO RECOVERY

1842: a Boston medical journal publishes a short essay by Dr Aldred Hitchcock titled "Insanity and Death from Masturbation". The author describes at length the case of a twenty-three-year-old man suffering from fatigue, anaemia, sleeplessness, poor posture, dry skin, body odour and bad breath, the result of wanking continuously for six years. Despite Dr Hitchcock's best efforts the patient refused to give it up – resulting in his death five months later. At the autopsy it is noted that the deceased's testicles are dried and shrivelled while the abdomen, intestines and lower spine are infected and choked with pus.

1861: Dr Jackson lists the telltale signs of a masturbator: he or she will gorge on spicy food, eat pencils and lick lime off the wall.

1870: Philadelphian Dr Peter Remondino recommends circumcision as a cure for masturbation. More controversially, the doctor also calls for the "wholesale circumcision of the Negro race", a measure he claims will prevent black men lusting over white woman, thus reducing America's "great number of lynchings".

1871: *The Lancet* medical journal advises putting "blistering liquid" onto the male organ to "render erection painful".

1872: Dr Joseph Howe, professor of surgery at New York

University, claims to have successfully cured patients of their "foul habit" with a course of electric shocks to the genitals. The Howe technique involves inserting one electrode into the urethra and the other behind the scrotum.

1889: the American paediatrician Mary Wood-Allen publishes her book *What A Young Woman Ought To Know* highlighting dangerous activities "known to incite self-abuse". These include reading novels and standing on one foot.

1892: the American gynaecologist Robert Morris recommends clitoridectomy – surgical removal of the clitoris – as a treatment for masturbation, hysteria and female depression.

1893: Frank Orth patents his anti-masturbation device. Comprising a pair of rubber underpants, an electric pump and a water cistern, in the event of arousal, the device pumps cold water around the genitals to lower their temperature.

1898: Boston physician Dr Ira Warren describes the symptoms of prolonged masturbation, including ". . . headache, wakefulness, restless nights, indolence, indisposition to study, melancholy, despondency, forgetfulness, weakness in the back and private organs, a lack of confidence in one's own abilities, cowardice, inability to look another full in the face". To cure habitual masturbation, ". . . avoid solitude and sleep with some friend. He should sleep on a mattress and never on feathers; always on the side, never on the back."

1904: American gynaecologist Dr Bernard Talmey advises young girls to avoid spicy foods, coffee, tea or cocoa, bicycle riding, novels and daydreaming.

10 MILESTONES IN PORN

1150 BC: the Turin Erotic Papyrus, dubbed the "world's first porno mag", contains twelve erotic vignettes depicting various sex positions.

c. 1077: the Bayeux Tapestry shows a scene of sexual assault – a naked woman being menaced by a man with a large erection.

1516: the Renaissance master Raphael decorates the Vatican bathroom in the Papal Apartments with erotic frescos. The *Stufetta del Bibbiena* shows paintings of naked nymphs being spied upon by lusting satyrs with no anatomical detail spared.

1666: Samuel Pepys knocks one out while reading the smutty *L'Ecole des Filles*, a French work considered to be the beginning of pornography in France, then burns the book so that his wife won't see it.

1675: London bookseller and founder of Guy's Hospital Thomas Guy sets himself up as a publisher of Bibles for Oxford University. Guy's Bible is a huge hit, although this may have something to do with the 107 engravings of bare-breasted biblical women.

1748: John Cleland publishes his novel *Memoirs of a Woman of Pleasure*, later re-titled as *The Life and Adventures of Miss Fanny Hill*. Although the text is far from explicit (Cleland employs fifty different euphemisms for the word penis) the author is arrested for "corrupting the King's subjects" and the Bishop of London claims the book has caused two small earthquakes.*

1833: British explorer and cunning linguist Richard Francis Burton shocks his countrymen with a translation of the *Kama Sutra*, half sex-manual, and half relationship-handbook. Burton also complains about an associate who "could not be persuaded to try fucking a Muscovy duck while its head was cut off".

1860: excavations of Pompeii reveal large amounts of Roman erotica. Victorians, shocked by the frank depictions of sexuality, decide to hide them away from everyone but upper-class scholars. The moveable objects are locked away in the Secret Museum in Naples and the rest are covered and cordoned off so as not to corrupt the sensibilities of women, children and the working classes.

1978: Pope John Paul I, known as the Smiling Pope, dies of a heart attack. It is rumoured that he expired while reviewing the Vatican's huge stash of pornography.

1999: The British Museum pays £1.8 million for a Roman goblet depicting two men sodomizing boys while another secretly watches.

---

* It became one of the most banned books in history and was still banned in the United States until the 1960s.

SIZE MATTERS:
12 REMARKABLE ORGANS

1. The Hindu god Buddha was said to have a huge retractable member resembling that of a horse.

2. In Greek mythology, Priapus had an impressive penis and a permanent erection. In addition to his job as God of fertility, he doubled as protector of fruit plants, gardens and male genitalia.

3. Iraqi poetry from the third millennium BC identifies the creative force of the world as Enki or, more precisely, Enki's knob. It was so mighty that it dug the world's first irrigation ditches, created rivers and invented human sexual reproduction. After he fathered the first human baby, Enki said: "Now let my penis be praised."

4. According to the ancient Egyptians, the mighty dong of their god Atum created all life, divine and mortal, through the act of sacred masturbation.

5. The French Saint Foutin (rough equivalent in modern English, Saint Fuck) was amazingly well hung. Statues of the saint emphasize his prominent member, upon whose helmet wine was poured to ensure fertility. Quite often on these representations Foutin's manhood was fashioned from wood, from which splinters could be taken: no matter how many were retrieved, the size of his erection never diminished. Some say this was a miracle;

others suspect that a wooden broomstick-like object was hammered through a hole in order to lengthen the saintly member each time it grew shorter. His worship continues in Oiloules in south-eastern France.

6. The Dutch explorer Pieter de Marees wrote about his trip to the Gold Coast in 1602. He noted that the men of Guinea all have "a great privy member" but are afflicted with worms "in their cods".

7. Grigori Rasputin was a Russian mystic seen by many as a malign influence over the Russian Czar Nicholas II and his wife Alexandra. There were several testimonies to his allegedly huge penis. Once, while blind drunk in a posh Petrograd restaurant, Rasputin danced the *kazachok* with his flies open and his member exposed. His potency as a lover was enhanced by a well-positioned wart; one woman said that the first time she made love to him her orgasm was so violent that she fainted. When Rasputin was murdered by a group of noblemen in 1916, according to some accounts his penis was hacked off. Since then several people have claimed to be in possession of his severed manhood, although none has been proved definitively.

8. The Italian priest and author Ludovico Sinistrari (1622–1701) was an expert on sexual relations with demons. He claims he encountered a prostitute in Venice who sported a clitoris the size of a "goose's neck".

9. The French judge Pierre de l'Ancre wrote three books on witchcraft in the early 1600s and in one left a vivid description of the Devil's penis: according to the author, "a half-yard long", dark in colour, bent acutely and "very rough in texture".

10. In 1704 the London surgeon John Marten wrote a book about the causes of venereal disease, noting that the "bigness of a man's yard" was seldom cause for complaint by women, but he reported one exceptional case of marital sexual incompatibility caused by an excessively large one. He wrote: "I knew a very lusty man that married a very small woman, and by means of his yard being of almost the longest size, his wife could not suffer him . . . without a great deal of pain . . ." The unfortunate wife had endured four years of painful intercourse, despite the efforts of physicians who prescribed "styptic and astringent fomentations" to reduce the size of the offending organ, without success. Marten concluded, ". . . 'twas the length of it that did the mischief . . . to remedy it I advised him . . . to make a hole through a piece of cork, lined with cotton on both sides, of about an inch-and-a-half in thickness, and put his yard through the hole, fastening the cork with strings round his waist". According to the doctor, this device did the trick.*

11. The biggest vagina in recorded history most likely belonged to Anna Swann (1846–88). The "Nova Scotia Giant" was seven feet five tall and weighed 350 lb. She gave birth to a 23 lb baby with a 19 inch head.†

12. John Curtis Holmes, better known as Johnny Wadd, was one of the most prolific male porn stars of all time,

---

* In 2002 Dr Marten was fingered as the author of a famous, anonymously published pamphlet called *Onania*, which circulated around the 2,000-odd coffee houses of London, about the perils of masturbation. *Onania* went into twenty-eight editions and was widely translated in Europe.
† Runner-up: in 2011 a twenty-seven-year-old woman was charged with possession of heroin after fifty-four bags of the drug were found inside her.

appearing in about 2,500 adult movies in the 1970s and 1980s. He was best known for his exceptionally large organ, said to be the longest in the industry. Holmes claimed his penis length was 15 inches but his manager disagreed: "I saw John measure himself several times, it was only 131/2 inches." It is doubtful whether Holmes ever achieved a full erection. According to a 1970s porn industry in-joke, he was incapable of achieving a hard-on because the blood flow from his head into his penis would cause him to pass out. His co-stars likened it to "doing it with a big, soft kind of loofah".

10 CONTRACEPTIVES

1. To terminate a pregnancy, the second-century Greek physician Soranus advised jumping up and down vigorously, then a "hard spanking" followed by a "bumpy wagon ride".

2. The Byzantine physician Aetius of Amida said that the key to avoiding pregnancy was to place a cat's testicles in a hollow leather belt and wear it around your hips during sex.

3. The medieval physician Trotula of Salerno advised women to avoid pregnancy by wearing the womb of a childless goat. Failing that, a weasel's testicles wrapped in goose skin did the trick.

4. An eleventh-century Persian scholar advised that dogs have two testicles, one hard and dry, the other soft and moist; eat the hard one to prevent conception.

5. The eleventh-century Muslim scholar Constantine the African said that women who do not wish to conceive should carry a piece of elephant dung with them at all times.*

6. In the sixteenth century, Canadians avoided pregnancy by drinking strong alcohol fortified with ground-up beaver testicles.

---

* To be fair, this one probably works – Ed.

7. Seventeenth-century London prostitutes prevented pregnancy by inserting into their vaginas large nutmegs pickled in vinegar.

8. In 1886 Dr Edward Foote unveiled his "Electro-Magnetic Preventative Machine", a device that delivered small electric shocks to the uterus during sex. He promised a painless process in which "the womb is too greatly excited to retain the seed of the male".

9. In 1890s New York, women aborted pregnancies by sitting over a pot of hot stewed onions.

10. A can of Coca-Cola was the 1960s equivalent of the morning-after pill. According to American urban myth, if a woman had a douche with it after sex, the combined effects of carbonation and sugar would act as a spermicide. In southern states women preferred Dr Pepper.

LOVE HURTS:
10 DEATHS BY SEX

1986: in São Paulo, Brazil, a husband takes revenge by super-gluing his wife's hands to her lover's penis. The unidentified lovers undergo delicate surgery to separate them, but the man dies several days later from the toxic chemicals absorbed through the porous membranes of his member.

1986: Frederik, a sixteen-year-old elephant in Jutland, Denmark, dies after being pushed into a pond by three aggressive she-elephants. His keeper says that whenever Frederik tried to have sex with one of the four females he shared his enclosure with, the others got jealous and beat him up.

1987: a twenty-two-year-old Peruvian woman dies from an infection caused by a rusty padlock on the chastity belt her husband made her wear while he was away on business trips. Rosa Vela died from blood poisoning when the rusty lock on the tight leather belt dug into her flesh.

1988: a Cairo man jumps to his death from a fourth-floor balcony on his wedding night when he realizes that his mother-in-law has tricked him into marrying her ugly daughter, instead of the younger and prettier sister. Mohammed Abdel Rahman had arranged the proxy marriage while he was out of the country on a business trip and didn't learn about the deception until he turned up to consummate it.

1998: a court in Darwin, Australia, sends Christopher Payne, thirty-four, to prison for causing the drowning of a twenty-five-year-old woman at a local beach. She went underwater to perform fellatio on Payne but he held her under too long. According to the judge, Payne was motivated by "a selfish desire to prolong his pleasure".

1999: Raul Zarate Diaz, a Mexican jail warden, falls to his death while spying on couples during their conjugal visits. He crashes through a skylight carrying binoculars and a porno magazine, narrowly missing a Nicaraguan prisoner and his wife while they are having sex.

2003: Jean-Louis Toubon, a forty-four-year-old from Marseilles, chokes to death on his girlfriend's edible panties.

2009: Sergey Tuganov, a twenty-eight-year-old Russian, bets two women that he can have sex with them both, continuously, for twelve hours. Several minutes after winning the $4,300 bet, he suffers a heart attack and dies, apparently having ingested an entire bottle of Viagra.

2012: Uroko Onoja, a Nigerian businessman, dies after being forced by five of his six wives to have sex with them. Onoja had been found in bed with his youngest wife by the remaining five, who were jealous of him paying her more attention. Allegedly threatening him with knives and sticks, they demand sex as well; he stops breathing after his fourth fuck.

2013: a woman is mauled to death by a lion while having sex with her boyfriend in the African bush. Sharai Mawera is enjoying a passionate moment with her lover in Kariba, northern Zimbabwe when the big cat strikes. Her partner runs off naked in a bid to raise the alarm. It is thought to be the same lion that has recently eaten a local man who had been walking home from a nightclub.

MUMMY'S BOYS:
10 OEDIPAL COMPLEXES

1. Charles Baudelaire
   The kinky French poet wrote a collection of sexually explicit poems *Les Fleurs de Mal,* considered some of the naughtiest lines in the history of erotic literature, leading to a famous obscenity trial when they were published in 1857. His muse was a local prostitute, but the true love of his life was his mother, with whom he was said to be "suffocatingly intimate". He described his relationship with her as "romantic . . . as if I were courting her" – Baudelaire died of syphilis of the brain, in her arms, in a Paris clinic, unable to remember his own name, aged forty-six.

2. Gustave Flaubert
   The French novelist never married and was completely devoted to his mother, with whom he lived until she died when he was fifty. He spent his last years in reclusive poverty and died of a cerebral haemorrhage, so obese that his coffin was too big to fit into the grave and had to be left stuck at an angle.

3. Thomas Carlyle
   His domestic arrangement with the writer Jane Welsh was one of the unhappiest literary marriages ever. The problems began on their wedding night when the shaggy-bearded Sage of Chelsea refused to sleep in the marital bed. A few days into the honeymoon he wrote a

letter to his mum, to whom he was said to be "abnormally attached", explaining that he hadn't slept with his wife because he was suffering from insomnia and their bed was too narrow. For the next forty years of their marriage the Carlyles rarely shared a bedroom.

4. J. M. Barrie
   The creator of Peter Pan, the little boy who refused to grow up, was the ninth of ten children and had a complicated relationship with his mother Margaret. When his thirteen-year-old brother David died in a skating accident, Barrie, aged six, tried to gain his stricken mother's affection by dressing up in his dead brother's clothes. *Peter Pan* has been interpreted as Barrie's own Oedipal tale, a consolation for the lack of affection he received from his mum as a small child.

5. Marcel Proust
   Proust's chauffeur, manservant and sleeping partner Alfred Agostinelli accommodated the author's various bizarre and unpleasant habits, not least of which was his erotic attachment to butchers: he had Agostinelli procure a young butcher's apprentice for sex and, during sexual activity, the lad was required to answer questions about butchery. Agostinelli also brought Proust caged live rats; he became sexually aroused by watching them being stabbed with hatpins. Proust wrote his greatest work after the devastating news of his mother's death when he was thirty-five. He withdrew completely from public life and became a reclusive hypochondriac.

6. Kaiser Wilhelm II
   "Kaiser Bill", the son of Queen Victoria's eldest daughter Vicky, suffered a permanently paralysed arm as a result of a breech birth and spent his childhood enduring futile treatments ranging from having a freshly

slaughtered hare wrapped around his arm to electro-therapy treatment and metal restraints. When he was a young man he became fixated on his mother and wrote her a series of letters detailing several erotic dreams he had about her: his mother simply corrected his grammar and sent them back.

7. D. H. Lawrence

He had a complicated relationship with his mother, therapy arriving in the form of his first successful novel *Sons and Lovers*, written when he was twenty-eight soon after his mother's death; he confessed, "I loved her like a lover." In 1912 Lawrence eloped with Frieda Weekley but complained that his new wife, like women in general, seemed to have "sex on the brain" and he would never make love unless the lights were turned off.

8. Sigmund Freud

Although he spent a lifetime writing about other people's sexual hang-ups, the father of psychoanalysis was always very careful to keep his own private fantasies under wraps – about his mother, for example. When he was two-and-a-half, seeing his mum naked on a train aroused him; from this, Freud had a lifelong terror of travelling on trains. She adored him and called him her "darling Sigi".

9. Percy Grainger

Although drawn to blonde, blue-eyed Nordic types of either sex, Australia's most popular composer had an intense relationship with his mother Rose, "the only truly passionate love affair of my life". "Bubbles", as mum always knew him, slept in his mother's bed – until she committed suicide by throwing herself from a fourth-floor window, driven insane by tertiary syphilis, when he was twenty-two.

10. Adolf Hitler

   Dr Bloch, the Jewish physician who looked after Hitler's mother, said that, in all of his fifty years as a doctor, he had never seen a young man as devastated as Adolf was at the death of his mother. He carried her picture with him everywhere, right up to his final days in the bunker. Some in Hitler's inner circle doubted if he had ever experienced normal sexual relations with any woman; a top British spy concurred, describing Hitler's relationships with women as "of a platonic nature".

WOMEN WITH BALLS:
10 MALE IMPERSONATORS

1. Francisco de Loyola, conquistador
   Born Catalina de Erauso in the early 1600s, she was
   raised in a Spanish convent from the age of four. After
   taking a beating when she was fifteen, she ran away from
   the nunnery to look for adventure in the New World
   and, calling herself Francisco de Loyola, she fought as a
   soldier in the Spanish army. The Basque (as in region,
   not item of underwear) transvestite played her part too
   well, gambling, duelling and drinking her way into a lot
   of bother – and along the way even broke a few female
   hearts. After getting into a fight and killing a man and
   finding herself seriously wounded, she confessed all to a
   sympathetic bishop and was allowed to return to Spain
   where she became a celebrity. She even got the Pope to
   let her continue to dress as a man, although the Church
   expressly forbade this.

2. Anne Bonny, pirate
   Born in County Cork, Ireland, she was the illegitimate
   daughter of lawyer William Cormac and his housemaid.
   They immigrated to America after Anne's birth in the
   late 1600s and settled on a plantation near Charleston,
   South Carolina. She demonstrated an unruly temper at
   an early age by killing a servant girl with a knife.
       In 1718 she met and fell in love with the swaggering
   pirate Captain Jack Rackham. Disguising herself as a
   male, she began sailing with him on his sloop *Vanity*,

preying on Spanish treasure ships off Cuba and Hispaniola. It is said that she became pregnant by Jack and retired from piracy only long enough to have her baby and leave it with friends in Cuba before rejoining him and her adventurous life on the high seas. None of her shipmates ever suspected her of being a woman had not another woman pirate, Mary Read, attempted to seduce her. It was also a surprise for Bonny, who had taken Mary to be a boy. When another potential suitor made advances she beat him up so badly that he never spoke of it again.

3. James Gray, soldier
   Born Hannah Snell in Worcester, England, she married James Summs in 1744 and two years later gave birth to a daughter. Within a year her daughter had died and her husband had deserted her. Borrowing a suit and an assumed name from her brother-in-law James Gray, she went in search of her errant husband only to find that he had been executed for murder. Still posing as a man, she went to Portsmouth and tricked her way into the Royal Marines. Sent to battle twice, she was wounded twelve times, including once in the groin, but incredibly her secret went undetected during treatment. When her unit returned to England she "came out" to her astonished shipmates and petitioned for a military pension, which, surprisingly, was granted. She later opened a pub called The Female Warrior, remarried and had two children.

4. James Barry, doctor
   Margaret Ann Bulkley was the daughter of a Cork grocer who wanted her to go to medical school – an option not available to women at the time. In 1809, posing as James Barry, she became the first ever female Briton to become a qualified doctor. Four years later she became a medic in the British Army, rising through the ranks to Principal

Medical Officer, on the way performing the first successful Caesarean section by a British surgeon. Having
fooled the medical establishment for half a century (and
having earned notoriety for an intimate relationship with
the Governor, Lord Charles Somerset, which resulted in
a libel action after the pair were accused of homosexual-
ity) her secret was discovered when she died from
dysentery in 1865. British army officials were appalled
and locked away Dr Barry's service records for almost a
hundred years hoping the story would go away.

5. William Cathay, Buffalo soldier
Cathay Williams, a freed slave, enlisted in the US army
in 1866 after telling a recruiting officer that she was a
22-year-old cook called William Cathay. She served for
two years fighting Apaches in New Mexico and was
hospitalized at least five times. Eventually the combined
effects of smallpox, heatstroke and years of marching
left her hospitalized again and, during the last illness, an
army surgeon discovered her secret and she was dishon-
ourably discharged. In 1891, suffering from diabetes
and having had all her toes amputated, she was denied
an army pension.

6. Murray Hall, US politician
In the late 1800s Hall was a fixture in New York politics,
a "man about town" who played poker with his politician cronies, smoked huge cigars and drank whisky. In
fact, "he" was Mary Anderson, a Scottish orphan who
had fled to America wearing her dead brother's clothes.
There were slight clues, like feet so small that he had to
custom-order shoes and a coat worn two sizes too big to
add bulk to his frame, not to mention his odd fondness
for romantic novels, but he succeeded in his deception
for twenty-five years. Hall eventually developed breast
cancer, but refused to seek treatment to keep his gender

under wraps. When she died in 1901 news of her secret life was confusing to even those who had known her well (at the time she was living with her second wife and their adopted daughter). A colleague offering a tribute to the press lamented: "She's dead, the poor fellow."

7. Charley Parkhurst, stagecoach driver
   A legend of the Old American West, Charley was a fearless, one-eyed Wells Fargo stagecoach driver. What no one suspected was that old "Cock-eyed Charley" was in fact Charlotte. Despite several close calls on account of her "graciously endowed" rack (as described by the attending physician at her death), she managed to maintain the subterfuge by never staying in one place too long. Along the way she lost an eye to a horse kick and became the first woman ever to vote in a US presidential election – fifty-two years before women were granted the vote. Her cover was finally blown when she died from tongue cancer in 1879; further examination revealed that old "Cock-eyed Charley" had once given birth to a child.

8. Frank Thompson, soldier spy
   Cross-dressing nineteen-year-old Canadian Sarah Edmonds was the adventurous sort, so when the American Civil War broke out she reinvented herself as Frank Thompson and enlisted as a male field nurse to battle the Confederacy. The disguise was a complete success and she took part in the Battle of Blackburn's Ford, the First Battle of Bull Run, the Peninsular Campaign and Fredericksburg. On at least two occasions she undertook intelligence missions behind Confederate lines "disguised" as a woman. Frank was forced to desert after she contracted malaria, but couldn't check into a military hospital for fear of revealing her true identity. She later ditched her disguise,

worked as a nurse at a hospital for wounded soldiers and had three children.

9. Denis Smith, war journalist
   No relation to the bone-crunching Stoke City centre-half of yore, Denis was an ambitious teenage girl named Dorothy Lawrence from Warwickshire who wanted to work as a war correspondent in World War I. Fabricating papers to become Private Smith she landed a job as a Royal Engineer, but after enduring ten days of the full horror of the Western Front in 1915 she decided to fess up. Arrested and taken into custody as a suspected German spy, the brass eventually released her and sent her back to London, making her swear not to reveal how she had fooled the authorities, just in case it would inspire thousands of other women to also try to infiltrate the military. Dorothy's experience was not revealed until many years later when a historian found her story in an archive.

10. Billy Tipton, jazz musician
    Tipton played in jazz clubs around Oklahoma where he built a name as an accomplished musician and writer. He was also married five times: so imagine the coroner's surprise in 1989 when the corpse he was doing a routine job with turned out to be a woman. Dorothy Tipton began dressing as a man and calling herself Billy in 1933 when she was nineteen. Amazingly, four of Tipton's five wives had no idea they'd married a woman (one figured it out later), a fact she had hidden from them by claiming a medical condition that required the wearing of a truss; even three adopted children didn't have a clue. More problematic was her refusal to go anywhere near a doctor, until the seventy-four-year-old Tipton was admitted to hospital dying of an untreated ulcer.

QUEER AS FOLK:
20 FETISHES

1. Apotemnophilia: sexual arousal by having one of your limbs amputated, or being made to look like an amputee.

2. Chasmophilia: sexual arousal by rock fissures.

3. Climacophilia: sexual arousal by falling down stairs.

4. Coprophilia: sexual arousal by faecal matter.

5. Dacryphilia: sexual arousal by watching someone cry.

6. Emetophilia: sexual attraction to vomit; also known as a Roman shower, after the commonly supposed practice of throwing up during Roman feasts.

7. Erotophonophilia: sexual arousal by killing someone.*

8. Formicophilia: sexual attraction to ants.†

9. Galactophilia: sexual attraction to human milk or lactating women.

---

* Some of history's most notorious erotophonophiles include Jeffrey Dahmer, John Wayne Gacy and Ted Bundy.
† If you must know, formicophiles like putting small insects on their willies.

10. Harpaxophilia: sexual arousal from being a robbery victim.

11. Klismaphilia: sexual pleasure from enemas – flushing out your colon leading to a large bowel movement.

12. Menophilia: sexual arousal by menstruation.

13. Mysophilia: sexual attraction to decaying human flesh or rotting animal carcasses.

14. Objectophilia: sexual attraction to an inanimate object.★

15. Paraphilic infantilism: turned on by dressing up as and being treated like a baby.

16. Plushophilia: attraction to stuffed animals.

17. Symphorophilia: sexual arousal by watching, or being involved in, accidents.

18. Urolagnia: sexual attraction to urine.

19. Ursusagalmatophilia: sexual attraction to teddy bears.

20. Vorarephilia: sexual arousal at being eaten by, or eating, another person.

★ A wall, for example. Eija-Riitta Berliner-Mauer, fifty-four, whose surname means Berlin Wall in German, married the concrete structure in 1979. Mrs Berliner-Mauer fell in love with the wall when she first saw it on television when she was seven. She is now a widow.

CHAPTER FOUR

Rude Health

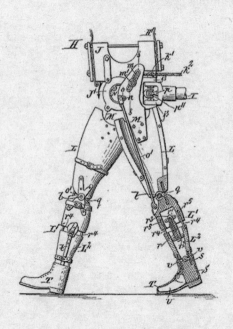

15 CURES
FOR ERECTILE DYSFUNCTION

AD 30: to guarantee an erection, Roman men are advised to wear an amulet made from the right molar of a small crocodile.

1250: the German friar Albertus Magnus writes: "If a wolf's penis is roasted in an oven, cut into small pieces, and a small portion of this is chewed, the consumer will experience an immediate yen for sexual intercourse." He adds helpfully: "Sparrow meat being hot and dry enkindles sexual desire and also induces constipation."

1400: Nicholas Flamel, celebrated scholar at the University of Paris, says that impotence can be cured by eating rotting wood that has been soaked for three days in the urine of a sixteen-year-old virgin.

1520: men incapable of impregnating their wives should return to the church where they were married and urinate through the keyhole: either that or piss through your wedding ring.

1531: impotent Frenchmen are advised to place wax effigies of their "useless members" upon a shrine to Saint Foutin, who was respected for his impressively large penis.

1563: rub your member with bile obtained from a raven.

1599: in his best-selling cookbook *Dyets Dry Dinner*, Henry Buttes says that chestnuts are best for erectile problems, as "this nut in his husk much resembleth testes, the instruments of lust".

1800: Samuel Solomon, an unsuccessful boot-polish salesman from Newcastle upon Tyne, introduces his best-selling Cordial Balm of Gilead for "impotency or seminal weakness". He advises patients to drink the cordial while bathing their testicles in cold water or a mix of vinegar and alcohol.

1853: Dr Hollick's second book of anatomy says that, to avoid premature ejaculation, "toughen" the head of the penis by soaking it regularly in alum, limewater or "mild caustics".

1886: J. S. Pemberton, inventor of Coca-Cola, asserts that his new beverage "is a most wonderful invigorator of the sexual organs and will cure seminal weakness, impotence etc".

1914: Dr G. Frank Lydston performs the first human testicle transplant when he transplants the gonad of a suicide victim into his own scrotum. Lydston expresses his disappointment that "vulgar prejudices" had prevented the exploitation of more sex glands from dead people.

1920: the penile splint, devised by Dr Thad W. Williams enables "the introduction of the non-erected penis into the vagina under all circumstances".

1922: L. L. Stanley, resident physician of the California state prison in San Quentin, transplants testicles from executed convicts, and then moves on to injecting into his subjects via a dental syringe a solution of goat, ram, boar and deer testicles.

2002: a Nigerian man is arrested after he kills a woman and eats her stewed intestines in a bid to cure an abnormally persistent erection. Fifty-year-old Folorunso Olukotun led police officers to his victim's disembowelled body in the bush near his home village having admitted attacking her with a machete, taking her intestines home and cooking them in a stew and eating them with pounded yam. Police said that someone had suggested to Olukotun that cannibalism was a cure for his problem as a joke, but had no news as to whether the erection had subsided.

2009: a study at King's College London concludes that pickled cabbage is at least as effective as Viagra at improving sexual function.*

---

* In 1998 Viagra became the first oral medication to be approved by the United States Food and Drug Administration to treat erectile dysfunction and immediately became the fastest-selling pharmaceutical in history. Pfizer's stock went up 150 per cent in 1998; sales of Viagra topped one billion dollars the following year.

10 STUART MEDICINES

1. The skin of dead puppies: apply as an ointment for your skin.

2. Oil of swallows: apply on your "shrunken sinews" (withered limbs).

3. Juice of snail: stick a pin in the snail and drip the juice into your eyes to cure eye infections.

4. Hen's dung: also used to cure eye problems.

5. Toenails and pubic hair: to treat a hernia, bore a deep hole into a willow tree and plug it with the patient's.

6. Candles used at a funeral: a cure for burns.

7. Hair and nail clippings from a small child: place under a patient's bed to cure convulsions.

8. The hand of a corpse: a cure for just about everything. Sick people would be brought to a house where a dead person was laid out so that the hand could be laid on them. The corner of the sheet used to wrap a corpse was also used to cure a headache or a swollen limb.

9. A hot boiled egg: to relieve constipation, "apply to the fundament or arse hole".

10. Goose turds: for jaundice or skin ailments, take two turds, dissolve in white wine, strain and drink two hours before meals.

10 MOST COMMON CAUSES OF DEATH IN STUART LONDON*

1. Spotted Fever and Purples

2. Griping in the Guts

3. Surfit

4. Stopping of the Stomach

5. Rising of the Lights

6. Itch

7. Fainting in a Bath

8. Frighted

9. Stitch

10. Stone and Strangery

---

* As listed in the London Bills of Mortality, 1658.

FIT TO RULE:
10 BRITISH ROYAL ILLNESSES

1. Alfred "the Great": haemorrhoids. He prayed to God for a cure for his very painful piles. Alfred was also quite obsessed with sex and prayed to God to give him something that would take his mind off it. God delivered: on Alfred's wedding night he developed a severe dose of stomach cramps, probably Crohn's disease, which plagued him to his death aged forty-five.

2. Richard III: scoliosis, a curvature of the spine. He was also infested with parasitic worms that grew up to a foot in length.

3. Henry IV: leprosy. His face was covered with huge red pustules; the Church said this was divine retribution for his execution of the Archbishop of York. Others believed that his second wife Joanna of Navarre was a witch and had cast a spell on him. Some say it was just a really bad case of acne.

4. Henry VI: bipolar disorder. Suffering from recurrent bouts of melancholia, depression and catatonia, he was thought to have inherited madness through his mother Catherine, daughter of Charles VI "the Mad" of France. His illness paved the way for the War of the Roses.

5. Henry VIII: experts have long speculated as to why his wives suffered so many miscarriages. Some say it was

because the king had syphilis, or had a rare blood type called Kell positive; if a male with this type impregnates a Kell negative woman, she is at increased risk of miscarrying, especially in the third trimester when several of Henry's wives apparently suffered miscarriages. Since we can't test Henry's blood, we'll never know for sure. Experts also think that his transformation from generous young prince to cruel, paranoid tyrant was down to a violent head trauma he suffered in a jousting accident.

6. Mary I: stomach cancer. Although some attributed her death to the outbreak of flu that was sweeping the country, the cancerous tumour was probably misinterpreted by Mary as pregnancy.

7. Charles II: renal failure and possibly syphilis. It has also been suggested that he had mercury poisoning as a result of inhalation that occurred while conducting experiments with the Royal Society.

8. Mary II: smallpox killed her in 1694. She was in good company: smallpox claimed five reigning European monarchs in the eighteenth century: King Louis I of Spain in 1724, Tsar Peter II of Russia in 1730, Louise Hippolyte, Sovereign Princess of Monaco in 1731, King Louis XV of France in 1774 and Maximilian III Joseph, Elector of Bavaria in 1777. King Charles II, his daughter Henrietta, King William III and Queen Anne all caught smallpox and survived.

9. Queen Anne suffered from severe gout from the age of thirty-three and Lupus, which is also strongly associated with increased and increasing difficulty in carrying healthy children to term in pregnancy. She was also massively obese from the age of about thirty, which is

not helpful for pregnancies either; she had at least eighteen but produced only three healthy children. To improve her health, in 1619, on the advice of her doctor, the queen took up sawing and chopping wood. She was dead within two months.

10. Edward VII, George V, Edward VIII and George VI: three generations killed by smoking-related illnesses. The first three kings succumbed to heart and circulatory disorders; George VI died from lung cancer.

12 FAMOUS PHOBICS

1. John Bunyan: simantrophobia or fear of church bells and church steeples. The author of *Pilgrim's Progress* was terrified that if he went near a church steeple it would topple onto his head.

2. Thomas Edison: nyctophobia or fear of the dark. It was the driving force behind his invention of the light bulb.

3. Samuel Johnson: agoraphobia or fear of crowded or public places. The great lexicographer asked to be excused from jury duty because the very thought of being in a packed courtroom made him feel faint.

4. Johannes Brahms: aquaphobia or a fear of large bodies of water. He developed a terror of travelling by boat after a bad sea-going experience in a skiff. Brahms declined an honorary doctorate from Cambridge University in 1877 because the offer was conditional on his crossing the Channel to accept it in person.

5. Franklin Delano Roosevelt: triskaidekaphobia. The US President who said, "The only thing you have to fear is fear itself" was afraid of the number thirteen. He avoided hosting dinner parties with thirteen people and he refused to travel on the thirteenth day of the month.

6. Alfred Hitchcock: astynomiaphobia or fear of police. As a child he was sent to the local police station with a letter from his father. The desk sergeant read the letter then

locked up the boy for ten minutes, explaining, "This is what happens to people who do bad things." Hitchcock had a morbid fear of police from that day on.

7. Ritchie Valens: aviophobia or fear of flying. The one and only time the pioneer rock 'n' roller flew, the plane crashed and killed him and everyone else on board including fellow musicians Buddy Holly and J. P. "the Big Bopper" Richardson.

8. Clark Gable: cetaphobia or fear of bath water. He never took a bath because he was disgusted by the thought of sitting in dirty water.

9. Richard Nixon: nosocomephobia or fear of hospitals. "Tricky Dicky" feared that if he ever went in one he would never come out alive. Turns out he was right.

10. Evel Knievel: aviophobia or fear of flying. The famous stuntman could jump over Snake River Canyon and the fountains of Caesars Palace but he couldn't face a short-haul flight from Idaho to Las Vegas.

11. Oprah Winfrey: chiclephobic or fear of chewing gum. It began when she was a child and she found a stash of her grandmother's old chewed gum in a cupboard.

12. Angela Merkel: cynophobia or fear of dogs. The German Chancellor was bitten by a dog as a child. Vladimir Putin, with this information in hand, once offered a dog as a gift to the chancellor and would let his black Labrador sit in on their meetings.

10 HEALTH FREAKS

219 BC: Chinese Emperor Qin Shi Huang sends his alchemist Xu Fu off with 500 young men and 500 young women to the eastern seas to find the elixir of life and is disappointed when none of them returns. Legend has it that they found Japan instead.

37 BC: Democritus, "the laughing philosopher", dies of natural causes having reached the great age of 107 by applying hot loaves to his nostrils.

c. 330: the Han dynasty chancellor Chang Ts'ang lives to be 180 years old by regularly sucking on women's breasts.

343: the prominent Chinese alchemist Ge Hong says that you are what you eat, and so, by eating gold, man can attain perfection.*

1510: the Spanish explorer Juan Ponce de León leads an expedition around the Caribbean islands and into Florida to find the Fountain of Youth: many die.

1567: Chinese Emperor Jiajing overdoses and dies of mercury poisoning, believing mercury to be the Elixir of Life.

1928: the Soviet physician Alexander Bogdanov tests his

---

* He also prescribes a method for walking on water and for raising the dead.

theory that blood transfusions from much younger donors will grant him eternal youth – or at least stop him going completely bald. Bogdanov has eleven blood transfusions, claiming improvement in his eyesight, suspension of balding and other positive symptoms. The twelfth transfusion costs him his life when he takes the blood of a student suffering from malaria and tuberculosis; the student makes a complete recovery.

1930: Russian surgeon Serge Voronoff grafts monkey testicle tissue on to the testicles of men. By the early 1930s, more than 500 men had been treated in France by his rejuvenation technique, including the elderly Prime Minister of Turkey.

1932: Eben Byers, American golfer and industrialist, dies from multiple cancers caused by drinking nearly 1,400 bottles of a radioactive health potion called Radithor and is buried in a lead-lined coffin.

1974: Basil Brown, a forty-eight-year-old health food enthusiast from Croydon, drinks himself to death with a gallon of carrot juice a day. He is bright yellow when he expires from liver failure.

10 TUDOR REMEDIES

1. Asthma: swallow young frogs or live spiders coated in butter.

2. Gout: boil a red-haired dog in oil then add worms and the marrow from a pig bones; apply the mixture.

3. Headache: rub the forehead with a rope used to hang a criminal.

4. Rheumatism: wear the skin of a donkey.

5. Jaundice: drink a pint of ale containing nine drowned head-lice every morning for a week.

6. Boils: apply a poultice to the boil. When you remove the poultice, place it in a coffin containing a corpse. The boils will leave you and pass on to the dead person.

7. Whooping cough: take a ferret, feed it with milk then give the leftover milk to the sick child.

8. Warts: lay half a mouse on the wart for half an hour and then bury it in the ground. When the mouse rots, the wart will vanish.

9. Baldness: rub dog or horse urine into your scalp.

10. Deafness: take the gallstone of a hare and the grease of a fox, warm the mixture and place in your ear.

5 MEDICAL EMERGENCIES IN THE MIDDLE AGES THAT DIDN'T END WELL

892: the Viking Sigurd "the Mighty" invades Scotland and cuts off the head of a local warlord Mael Brigte, nicknamed "the Tusk" because of his big front teeth, then straps the severed head to his horse's saddle and rides off with it. On the journey home one of the teeth scratches Sigurd's leg, which becomes badly infected and he dies.

1143: King Fulk of Jerusalem is startled by a rabbit, which dashes out in front of his horse at a bad moment. The horse stumbles and throws him, crushing his head until his brains pour out of his ears and his nose.

1159: Adrian IV, the only Englishman ever to become Pope, suffers from a strange form of tonsillitis known as quinsy, which makes it difficult for him to swallow. One day he takes a sip of wine and chokes to death on a fly, which was floating in his goblet.

1387: King Charles II of Navarre wraps himself from head to toe in bandages soaked in brandy to try to cure an illness, but is burned alive when a servant accidentally sets the bandages on fire.

1410: King Martin of Aragon has a fit of hysterical laughter at a banquet, and then falls dead. He probably died from indigestion after eating too many eels, but we don't know what it was that he found so funny.

6 MONORCHIDS

1. The Roman dictator Sulla. He ruled with vicious severity in the early years of the first century BC and was said
   to have been an excellent singer but had only one testicle, a deficiency that did not bar him from military
   service.

2. King Carlos II of Spain. When he died in 1700, five days
   before his thirty-ninth birthday, the physician who
   carried out his autopsy found that the king had "a single
   testicle, black as coal".

3. Adolf Hitler. The Führer's allegedly half-empty scrotal
   sack is the stuff of legend. According to one version, the
   testicle was lost when young Adolf took part in an ill-
   advised barnyard prank in which he attempted to urinate
   down the mouth of an alpine goat. More likely, he
   received a wound in the groin in 1916 at the Somme.
   Hitler's World War I company commander has said that
   a VD exam found that Hitler had only one ball.*

4. General Francisco Franco. Much like the Nazi leader,

---

* According to the music-hall song, the other was in the Albert Hall.
In the original version, however, it was "Goring has only got one ball"
and went on to state that Hitler had two small ones and Himmler was
"similar". The final line of this original and some later forms ends with
the word play that Goebbels had "no balls". Either way, the Allies had
a clear testicular advantage. According to WWII records detailing the
health of conscripted men, the British Army had nine soldiers with
three testicles apiece.

Franco's loss stemmed from an injury he suffered in battle when he was wounded in the lower abdomen at El Biutz, near Ceuta, in June 1916.

5. Chairman Mao Zedong. As well as an undescended right testicle, the Chinese leader suffered from various venereal diseases including gonorrhoea and genital herpes.

6. J. D. Salinger. According to his biographer, the reclusive author of *The Catcher in the Rye* was so self-conscious about his undescended testicle that it drove him to seclusion.

10 OCCUPATIONAL HEALTH HAZARDS

1. Prostitute's Pupil
   Also known as "Argyll Robertson pupils" after the
   Scottish ophthalmologist who associated it with late-
   stage syphilis in 1869. The sufferer's pupils act like a
   prostitute, i.e. they "accommodate but do not react".

2. Gamekeeper's Thumb
   A chronic dislocation of the joint where the thumb meets
   the wrist. For Scottish fowl-hunters it was the result of
   carrying game draped over their shoulder suspended
   from a leather thong attached to their thumb. English
   gamekeepers sustained the injury by killing rabbits with
   a forceful blow from their thumb to the back of the
   animals' necks.

3. Miner's Nystagmus
   It affects the nerves of the eyes, causing a spasmodic
   movement of the eyeball, either rotary or from side to
   side. It is caused by poor lighting but exposure to
   noxious gases and neurosis could also be contributory
   factors.

4. Chimney Sweep's Cancer
   Also known as chimney sweep's scrotum or soot warts,
   it generally affected chimney sweeps in their late teens
   and early twenties, although the youngest recorded
   victim was eight. It was the result of being in contact

with soot from early childhood and was characterized by large painful growths in the scrotum.

5. Cheese Washer's Lung

   An allergic inflammation of the lung leading to shortness of breath, wheezing and overall poor respiratory health caused by inhalation of *Pencillum casei* or *P.roqueforti*, commonly found on the rinds of cheeses. Similar to: *Bird-Breeder's Lung* (exposure to feathers and bird droppings); *Farmer's Lung* (exposure to mouldy hay); *Mushroom Worker's Lung or "dung lung"* (exposure to mushroom compost); *Mollusc Shell Lung also known as pearl worker's lung* (exposure to mollusc shell dust).

6. Rag Picker's Disease

   Wool and animal skins harbour anthrax spores, which become airborne when the hide or hair is handled and can be inhaled into the lungs, causing an infection. If not treated quickly, anthrax has a near 100 per cent mortality. Simply handling the spores can cause a skin infection, which shows up as a boil-like lesion that eventually forms a large black ulcer.

7. Cobbler's Femur

   All that hammering of shoes makes the body lay down extra bone in response to micro-fractures. Similar characteristic conditions can be seen in blacksmiths; the condition was also evident in archers found in the wreck of the *Mary Rose*.

8. Fiddler's Neck

   A thickening of skin and redness just below the jaw line on the left side of the neck of violin and viola players. Scaling, pimples and occasional cysts may also occur, with clogged pores and inflamed hair follicles. It's caused by pressure on a player's neck due to a poor grip on the instrument, a badly fitting chin rest or the wrong size or weight of instrument.

9. Guitar Nipple

An inflammation referred to as "guitar nipple" was mentioned in the *British Medical Journal* in 1974. It is caused by chafing from the guitar sound box. Another occupational hazard for guitarists is dermatitis caused by guitar strings.

10. PlayStation *Palmar hidradenitis*

A skin disorder marked by painful lumps on the palms caused by keeping too tight a grip on the console while playing video games and furiously pushing the buttons.

10 ANCIENT REMEDIES CONTAINING HUMAN BODY PARTS

1. To staunch internal bleeding, drink a tincture made from crushed Egyptian mummy.

2. To relieve the pain from rheumatism or arthritis, apply an ointment made from human fat, or soak bandages in human fat to make your wound heal more quickly.

3. Human fat as an aid to remove wrinkles. Queen Elizabeth I used "man's fat" to fill in the pockmarks she was left with when she recovered from smallpox.

4. To relieve a nosebleed, push powdered moss from a dead man's skull up your nose.

5. To cure epilepsy, eat some treacle mixed with the powdered skull of a young woman.

6. For relief from a headache, drink powdered human skull. To banish apoplexy, eat chocolate mixed with human skull.

7. As a general pick-me-up, drink the warm blood of a recently executed person. For those who prefer their blood cooked, a 1679 recipe from a Franciscan friar describes how to make it into marmalade.

8. Cure leprosy by bathing in the blood of a dog. If you haven't got a dead dog, a two-year-old child will do.

9. Bezoar stones – repulsive bundles of hair, vegetable fibres or food that form in the stomachs of humans (or animals) were a cure-all for a wide range of illnesses. Queen Elizabeth I had a bezoar stone in her crown jewels.

10. The ancient Chinese made human toffee apples by steeping whole corpses in honey.* Old men nearing the end of their lives would donate their bodies to science by offering themselves to a process of mummification in honey to create a healing confection. This process would start before death; the donor would stop eating any food other than honey – even bathe in honey. When this diet finally proved fatal, the cadaver was placed in a stone coffin filled with honey. After a century or so, the contents turned into a thick, toffee-based gloop, which was then ladled into jars and sold as a health tonic. It was allegedly still available in Paris up to the 1900s.

---

* The recipe was included in *Chinese Materia Medica* put together by Li Shih-chen, a naturalist, in 1597, but he said that he was unsure of its authenticity.

10 HOME PREGNANCY KITS

1800 BC: Egyptian ladies, leave an onion in your vagina overnight; if you wake up and can taste onion, you are not pregnant.

1350 BC: urinate on wheat and barley seeds. If the wheat sprouts, a female child is on its way; if the barley sprouts, it's a boy. No sprouts, no pregnancy.

1200 BC: grasp your woman's fingers in your hand and squeeze her arm: if the veins in her arms beat against your hand, you're going to be a daddy.

1100 BC: ladies, examine your nipples for unusual pigmentation, then drink breast milk from a woman who has borne a son. If you throw up, pregnancy is confirmed.

360 BC: Hippocrates says that a woman who has missed her period should drink a solution of honey in water at bedtime. A bloated stomach the next morning will indicate the presence of a child.

340 BC: apply perfumed linen to the lady's genitals. Her mouth and nose will take on the odour of the perfume if she is pregnant.

1300: place a needle in a woman's urine. If the woman is pregnant it will rust red or black.

1478: give a woman a sweet drink before going to bed and,

if she complains of pain in the navel in the morning, pregnancy is confirmed. It is important not to tell the woman the purpose of the drink because "women are cunning".

1920: inject a woman's urine into a young female mouse or rabbit. If the animal dies, the woman is pregnant.

1952: a refinement arrives with the frog test; inject a female African Clawed Frog with the urine of the patient. If the frog produces eggs within the next twenty-four hours, the test is positive: very usefully, the frog stays alive and can be used again.

10 INFANT MEDICATIONS YOU WON'T FIND IN SUPERDRUG

1. Mrs Winslow's Soothing Syrup (1849); contained morphine*

2. Dr Drake's German Croup Remedy (1875); contained opium

3. Children's Comfort (1880); contained morphine

4. Dr Pierce's Extract of Smart Weed (1889); contained opium

5. Hooper's Anodyne, the Infant's Friend (1890); contained morphine

6. Dr Seth Arnold's Cough Killer (1892); contained morphine

7. Dr Moffett's Teething Powders (1895); contained opium

8. Dr James Soothing Syrup Cordial (1900); contained heroin

---

* Promoted as "likely to sooth any human or animal", it effectively silenced restless infants and small children. It was still available in the UK until 1930.

9. One Day Cough Cure (1903); contained marijuana and morphine

10. Gowan's Pneumonia Cure (1905); contained opium

10 REASONS WHY THERE HAS NEVER BEEN A BETTER TIME IN HISTORY TO HAVE A DOSE OF THE CLAP*

300 BC: the ancient Egyptians treat unwanted vaginal discharges with garlic, acanthus resin, cow horn and the grist of vegetable seeds combined with oil; apply to a sponge and insert into the orifice.

1400: syphilis† patients have their open blisters cauterized or sealed with a red-hot poker.

1495: the French king Charles VIII orders foreigners with syphilis to leave Paris within twenty-four hours on pain of death.

1496: Giorgio Sommariva of Verona is the first European to use mercury to treat syphilis. Symptoms of mercury poisoning include chest pains, heart and lung problems, coughing, tremors, violent muscle spasms, psychotic reactions,

---

* "The clap", possibly from the Middle English *clapper* meaning a rabbit burrow, which was slang for a place of prostitution.
† Syphilis is named after a mythological Greek shepherd named Syphilus who was cursed with a horrible disease as a punishment for insulting the god Apollo. Doctors in the late 1400s and early 1500s were so afraid of syphilis they would not write down its name. Instead they used the Greek letter Sigma as its symbol.

delirium, hallucinations, suicidal tendencies, restless spleen syndrome, testicular twisting and anal implosion.

1507: For an ulcerated penis, wash thoroughly then "apply to it a cock or pigeon flayed alive ... or a live frog cut in two".

1520: patients diagnosed with gonorrhoea* have mercury injected directly into the urethra.

1700: Stuart STD sufferers are given mercury creams, or are forced to inhale mercury fumes or given oral doses of mercury.

1840: gonorrhoea patients are given daily irrigations of the urethra with potassium permanganate.

1908: Paul Ehrlich tests hundreds of different arsenic compounds on syphilitic laboratory rats. At the 606th attempt he finds a compound that effectively destroys the syphilis without destroying the rat. He calls it Salvarsan – "arsenic saves".

1917: Austrian physician Julius Wagner-Jauregg discovers that you can cure syphilis by giving the patient malaria. From now until the 1940s, all syphilis sufferers are treated this way.

---

* Gonorrhoea got its name in AD 131 from Galen, one of the greatest Greek physicians. Its name literally means "flow of seed" because Galen mistakenly thought the penile discharge was "seed" flowing out against its will.

10 MEDICAL EXPERTS

1. "The flesh and the whole disposition of the body are softened and the pores open, and as a result, pestiferous vapour can rapidly enter the body and cause sudden death, as has frequently been observed."

   Ambroise Pare, the French royal surgeon who lived in the reigns of Henry II, Francis II, Charles IX and Henry III, warning about the diabolical effects of bathing, 1568

2. "Erection is chiefly caused by scuraum, eringoes, cresses, crymon, parsnips, artichokes, turnips, asparagus, candied ginger, acorns bruised to powder and drank in muscadel, scallion, sea shell fish, etc."

   Aristotle's *The Masterpiece*, 1684★

3. "One half of the children born die before their eighth year. This is nature's law; why try to contradict it?"

   Jean-Jacques Rousseau, 1762

4. "The abolishment of pain in surgery is a chimera. It is absurd to go on seeking it. 'Knife' and 'pain' are two words in surgery that must forever be associated in the consciousness of the patient."

   Dr Alfred Velpeau, 1839

★ A sex manual that was popular in England from the seventeenth to the nineteenth centuries. First published in 1684, it was written by an unknown author who falsely claimed to be the philosopher Aristotle.

5. "The abdomen, the chest and the brain will forever be shut from the intrusion of the wise and humane surgeon."

> Sir John Eric Erichsen, Surgeon Extraordinary
> to Queen Victoria, 1873

6. "Heroin possesses many advantages over morphine. It's not hypnotic, and there's no danger of acquiring a habit."

> *Boston Medical and Surgical Journal*, 1900

7. "Experimental evidence is strongly in favour of my argument that the chemical purity of the air is of no importance."

> L. Erskine Hill, quoted in the *New York Times*, 1912

8. "If your eyes are set wide apart, you should be a vegetarian, because you inherit the digestive characteristics of bovine or equine ancestry."

> Dr Linard Williams, Medical Officer
> to the Insurance Institute of London, 1932

9. "If excessive smoking actually plays a role in the production of lung cancer, it seems to be a minor one."

> Dr W. C. Heuper, National Cancer Institute, 1954

10. "That virus is a pussycat."

> Dr Peter Duesberg, molecular-biology professor
> at U. C. Berkeley, on HIV, 1988

10 HISTORIC UNSOLVED MEDICAL MYSTERIES

1. Akhenaton

   The strangest and most controversial of all the Egyptian pharaohs ruled for seventeen years until *c.* 1335 BC. Pharaohs were generally represented in their iconography as very athletic types, but Akhenaton was depicted with a long, thin, very feminine face, huge thighs and pendulous breasts. It has been speculated that he suffered from a genetic abnormality, possibly Marfan's Syndrome. It's also just possible that there was nothing medically wrong with him at all and that "he" was in fact a "she".

2. The plague of Athens

   Between 430 and 426 BC Athens suffered outbreaks of a killer plague that wiped out almost a third of the population. The Greek historian Thucydides had the illness and survived, but, despite his description of the rash that accompanied it, two millennia later we still don't know exactly what caused it. One plausible explanation is typhus, a bacterial disease spread by fleas and rodents. Or it may have been a disease that no longer exists, in which case the exact nature of the Athenian plague may never be known.

3. Alexander the Great

   The Macedonian king enjoyed robust good health until he died suddenly aged thirty-two. Some accounts say he was poisoned, or he drank himself to death. Plutarch hinted at a more lingering death, during which Alexander had difficulty walking, then lost his speech and became so weak that as his troops filed past him he could only follow them with his eyes. One theory is that he suffered from ascending paralysis, a symptom of typhoid fever. This could also explain why embalmers arrived a week after Alexander's death and found him so uncannily life-like that they were afraid to go near him; it is possible that the paralysis made it seem like he was dead, since he wasn't moving and only breathing very shallowly.

4. Sweating sickness
   Also known as "English sweating sickness" or "The English sweat". The first outbreak was in 1485 and it spread rapidly, striking down apparently healthy people; the onset of symptoms was dramatic and sudden, with death occurring within three hours. In 1502 it killed young Arthur, Prince of Wales, paving the way for his younger brother to become King Henry VIII of England.* Although at first confined to England, it spread to Europe and there were more outbreaks in 1506, 1517 and 1551. Then just as quickly as it arrived, the disease disappeared.

5. The dancing plague
   In mid-July 1518 around 400 people in Strasbourg, France, began dancing for days on end without rest, causing dozens of participants to die of stroke and

---

* In June 1528 when Henry VIII was courting Anne Boleyn, one of her ladies was taken ill with sweating sickness. Henry, who was para-noid about illness "took off on a flight from safe house to safe house". Anne became ill with "the sweat" but was one of the lucky ones. She survived sweating sickness, but others, including her brother-in-law, Sir William Carey and Thomas Cromwell's wife and daughters, lost their lives to the sickness.

exhaustion. At the time it was thought to be "natural disease" caused by "hot blood". One suggestion is that the dancers were in some kind of trance state. Strasbourg's poor were suffering from severe famine and disease at the time and they believed in a saint called St Vitus who had the power to take over their minds and inflict a terrible, compulsive dance.

6. Christopher Columbus
   During his first journey to the Americas, Columbus fell ill with an unspecified virus with symptoms including burning pain while passing water, swelling in the knees and swelling and infection in the eyes; his eyes were so painfully inflamed that they actually bled. After that he had months of debilitation before becoming completely bedridden. His contemporaries thought it was gout or rheumatoid arthritis, but it is possible he acquired this crippling condition from the tropical birds he carried back from the New World as gifts to Spanish monarchs Ferdinand and Isabella. Literally, he was sick as a parrot.

7. Wolfgang Amadeus Mozart
   On 20 November 1791, while struggling to complete his *Requiem Mass in D Minor,* Mozart unexpectedly took ill, developing a high fever, headache, sweats and severe swelling and pain in his hands and legs. Within a couple of weeks his entire body was swollen; with the swelling came nausea and vomiting, diarrhoea, a persistent rash and a terrible body odour. Fifteen days after the onset of this illness, he had a fit, lapsed into a coma and died aged thirty-five. According to the official record he was taken by "severe military fever", a description that does not tally with any diagnosis in modern medicine. Researchers since have posited at least 118 causes of death, including trichinosis, influenza, mercury poisoning (for treatment of syphilis, or foul play by the composer Antonio Salieri),

parasitic infestation or acute rheumatic fever. It is impossible to prove the cause of death because no autopsy was performed and the remains can't be studied because he was buried in an unmarked grave.

8. The madness of King George III

People suspected something was very wrong in the late 1780s when George took to wearing a pillowcase on his head and began foaming at the mouth. His courtiers tried to keep it a secret from the outside world by pretending that the king had flu; the cat was finally out of the bag when he opened his address to the House of Commons with "My Lords and Peacocks".* Eventually, George was too far gone to be trusted to perform even the basic royal tasks such as waving from the balcony at Buckingham Palace or meeting visitors and saying, "Hello, have you come far?" In 1810, shortly after celebrations to mark the seventy-two-year-old king's golden jubilee, he was laced into a straightjacket and packed off to Windsor Castle, where he spent the last few years of his life blind, deaf and senile. There have been many theories down the years as to what may have brought on the king's "madness" including failure to take a mistress, having a very ugly wife, lead poisoning (the one favoured by Prince Charles) and arsenic poisoning. In the 1960s scientists thought they knew the cause of these ravings – porphyria, an inherited genetic defect. This theory formed the basis of a long-running play by Alan Bennett, *The Madness of George III*, and later a film starring Nigel Hawthorne in the title role. New research, however, suggests that it is more likely that George III did suffer from some type of mental illness after all.

---

* It was a tricky time for everyone, not least the Poet Laureate, who was expected to write a cheerful ode every year about the king on his birthday.

9. Charles Darwin

The great naturalist took to his bed for months at a time with a baffling list of ailments, including abdominal pain, bouts of vomiting after every meal, sleeplessness, headaches and giddiness. The country's most prominent physicians diagnosed lactose intolerance, lead poisoning, hypochondria and gout. More recent research has offered up various suggestions including cyclic vomiting syndrome, Chagas' disease – a parasitic illness contracted during his five-year voyage on the HMS *Beagle* – and *Helicobacter pylori*, the bacteria now known to cause peptic ulcers. He died of heart disease, aged seventy-three.

10. Florence Nightingale

During the Crimean War she volunteered to go to Turkey where she was put in charge of running a hospital for sick and injured British soldiers. She was very dedicated to her job and worked long hours, carrying a lamp as she walked the halls of the battlefield hospital at night and became immortalized as "The Lady with the Lamp".* After her return home at the end of the Crimean War, she showed rather less stoicism. She went to bed, where she more or less remained for the last fifty-three years of her life. Some suggest she was simply a hypochondriac, others that she suffered disabling depression caused by post-traumatic stress disorder from the horrors she observed in the war. She died of natural causes, aged ninety.

---

* She also kept a small pet owl in her pocket, which she took with her everywhere, but "Lady With the Pet Owl In Her Pocket" didn't catch on.

5 MODERN MEDICAL MYSTERIES

1. Water allergy
   Given that your body is around 60 per cent water, it might seem improbable but for some people a few minutes in the bath or shower causes their skin to erupt in itchy red welts and blisters; even tears and sweat can cause a reaction. *Aquagenic urticaria* was first described in 1964 and affects only one in 230 million people worldwide. Medical opinion is still divided; one theory has it that the condition is caused by the release of histamine in sufferers' skin cells.

2. Chimeric people
   In mythology, a chimera was a fantastical beast that had other animals' parts – for example, a wolf with a snake for a tail. Chimeric people are a mix of two individuals, a composite of two non-identical twins that had fused in the mother's womb. In practice, a woman could go for a DNA test along with her children, only to find that in theory she is not their biological mother despite the fact that she gave birth to them. No one knows for certain how many commonplace human chimeras exist but with the rise of fertility treatments and genetic testing it is possible that many more will be discovered.

3. Foreign accent syndrome
   If you wake up talking with a strong Croatian accent, despite the fact that you've never heard a Croatian

accent before, you're probably suffering from foreign accent syndrome. One of the most famous cases occurred in Norway in 1941 when a young woman suffered a head injury from shrapnel during an air raid and was left with a strong German accent and was shunned by her fellow Norwegians. One possible explanation is that the sufferer's accent might be due to the listener struggling to interpret the change in the head-trauma sufferer's speech patterns.

4. Putrid finger
   In 1996 the medical journal *The Lancet* carried a distressing case study of a twenty-nine-year-old man who had pricked his finger on a chicken bone five years earlier, leaving him with an infection that made him stink ... "a putrid smell emanating from the affected arm, which could be detected across a large room, and when confined to a smaller examination room became almost intolerable".* The cause of the smell could not be identified and it did not respond to antibiotics. The doctors ordered a skin biopsy, hoping to discover some noxious foreign body but found nothing of interest. Meanwhile, the finger continued to stink. The case ended happily but mysteriously; the patient's infection cleared up spontaneously.

5. Shrinking genitalia
   A condition called "Koro" or "penis panic" is a type of mass hysteria, more common in Africa and the Far East, in which people believe that his or her genitals – for example, nipples or penises – are retracting. One sufferer was forty-one before he sought treatment for Koro, and had spent fifteen years tying a string around his penis

---

* The article was called, accurately, "A Man Who Pricked His Finger and Smelled Putrid for Five Years".

and attaching the string to a hook above his bed at night in order to keep it from shrinking. In 1967 there was a Koro epidemic in Singapore after newspapers reported cases of Koro as a result of eating pork from a pig inoculated against swine fever. Pork sales collapsed and hundreds of Koro cases followed. Scientists haven't yet figured out whether Koro is caused by a cultural tendency towards a specific type of anxiety, or whether it started as a rumour or legend that's being taken literally.

12 ACCIDENTS IN THE WORKPLACE

1620: George Abbott, archbishop of Canterbury, shoots gamekeeper Peter Hawkins dead while aiming at a deer.*

1753: Russian scientist Georg Wilhelm Richmann is trying out his new apparatus for studying lightning for the first time. While leaning forward to look into his electroscope, a bolt of lightning strikes the apparatus, enters the top of his head and exits from his foot, blasting a hole in his shoe and throwing him into a seated position on a nearby chest. He is the first scientist to die while studying electricity.

1869: although twenty-seven men will die during the construction of the Brooklyn Bridge, the structure's famed designer, John Augustus Roebling, avoids that fate: he dies from injuries sustained before construction has even begun. On a visit to the site, a docking boat crushes Roebling's right foot and his toes have to be amputated. Suffering from tetanus and lockjaw, he lapses into a coma and dies.

1889: George Stephens, elephant keeper with Barnum and Bailey's circus at Olympia in London, dies after being sat on by an elephant.

---

* A zealous persecutor of heretics, Abbott sent 140 people to prison for failing to remove their hats in his presence. Hawkins is still the only person known to have been shot dead by an archbishop.

1911: Tennessee whiskey distiller Jasper Newton 'Jack' Daniel kicks his safe in frustration because he can't remember the combination. He breaks his big toe and dies from a gangrene infection.

1949: on board the RMS *Queen Mary*, Second Officer William Stark steals a swig from the captain's secret stash of gin. Too late, Stark realizes that the captain is using the old gin bottles to store the lethal cleaning solvent tetrachloride.

1959: ignoring the advice of safety experts, the Soviet military commander Mitrofan Ivanovich Nedelin sets up his chair next to the launch pad to get a better view of the testing of the USSR's new missile, the R-16. He and an estimated 250 people are incinerated when the fully fuelled rocket explodes, engulfing them in a giant fireball 120 m in diameter.

1983: a naked, screaming stripper is found trapped under a man's crushed body on a piano pinned against a nightclub ceiling. San Francisco topless-club owner James "Jimmy the Beard" Ferrozzo was under a baby grand piano used by Carol Doda, who makes her entrance by reclining across the instrument while it is lowered by cable to the stage. She says she was too drunk to remember how he got there.

2003: Devan Young, twenty-nine, is found dead in the bowling alley where he worked in Wichita, Kansas. He had been crushed to death by the machine that resets the pins.

2005: Kyle Lake, a pastor of University Baptist Church in Waco, Texas, is standing in water up to his shoulders in a baptismal pool when he adjusts his microphone. He is electrocuted in front of 800 worshippers.

2010: a female suicide bomber from Chechnya who intends

killing hundreds of people during New Year's Eve celebrations in Red Square, Moscow, dies prematurely when her suicide belt explodes in a safe house hours before the planned attack. It was triggered by a message from her mobile phone operator wishing her a happy new year.

2012: gravedigger Zailan Hamid is killed when the grave he is digging collapses and buries him in Mentakab, Malaysia.

10 FAMOUS PEOPLE WITH 10 GOOD EYES BETWEEN THEM

1. King Philip of Macedon (359–336 BC)
   The father of Alexander "the Great" was struck in the right eye by an arrow or a spear at the siege of Methone. He got angry if anyone ever referred to eyes at all.

2. Hannibal (247–183/182 BC)
   Carthaginian leader. Lost an eye when it became infected while crossing a swamp with his army.

3. Grigory Potemkin (1739–71)
   Russian military leader, statesman and lover of Catherine "the Great". A huge man known as "Cyclops", he lost an eye during an argument over a game of billiards.

4. Leonhard Euler (1707–83)
   Pioneering Swiss mathematician and physicist, he lost the sight in his left eye after staring at the sun for too long.

5. Horatio Nelson (1758–1805)
   Lost the sight of his right eye at the siege of Calvi in 1794, but he never wore an eye patch: he didn't really need to because his blind eye was externally undamaged and there was no disfigurement to be covered up.

6. Louis Braille (1809–52)
   The inventor and designer of Braille became blind in

one eye after accidentally stabbing himself in the face with his father's awl.

7. Edgar Degas (1834–1917)
   The French impressionist attributed his sight problems to cold weather he encountered doing guard duty in the army. He couldn't stand bright light, especially sunlight, and was forced to work indoors until eventually he had to give up painting completely.

8. Theodore Roosevelt (1858–1919)
   The twenty-sixth US President was blinded in his left eye in a White House boxing match. He boxed with sparring partners several times a week until a blow detached his left retina.

9. James Thurber (1894–1961)
   American comedian and cartoonist. While playing with his brother William, James was shot in the eye with an arrow.

10. Gordon Brown (b. 1951)
    The former British Prime Minister lost the use of his left eye when he received a kick in the head during an end-of-term school rugby union match.

CHAPTER FIVE

Art Attacks

15 CREATIVE ECCENTRICITIES

1. The French poet Baudelaire claimed he had eaten the brains of a child and had a pair of trousers made from his father's skin.

2. Frederic Chopin wore a beard on only one side of his face. It was the side facing the audience while he was playing the piano.

3. Lewis Carroll wrote 98,721 letters to his friends, usually in black ink, but he preferred violet ink when he was writing to young girls.

4. Victor Hugo always ate two raw eggs in the morning to get him in the mood for writing, then forced himself to meet his daily writing goals by locking away all of his clothes to resist the temptation of going out.

5. Truman Capote chain-smoked and kept his cigarette butts in his pockets. He never dialled a number or stayed in a hotel room if the number was "unlucky".

6. Charles Dickens couldn't write unless his study was precisely arranged with a small vase of fresh flowers, a large paper knife, a gilt leaf with a rabbit perched on it and two bronze statuettes of fat toads wielding swords in a duel.

7. Edith Sitwell liked to lie in an open coffin before a day's work.

8. Salvador Dalí said he fantasized about Adolf Hitler. He said, "I often dreamed of Hitler as a woman. His flesh, which I had imagined whiter than white, ravished me." The other Surrealists didn't kick him out of the movement, however, until Dalí declared his support for General Franco in 1939.

9. The Norwegian dramatist Henrik Ibsen always kept a live scorpion in a jar on his desk while he was writing.

10. Marcel Proust slept all day and wrote at night, while lying on his bed, with his head resting on two pillows. When he awoke in the late afternoon, the first thing he did was smoke a little opium to relieve his asthma.

11. Agatha Christie got inspiration for her murder plots by munching on apples in the bathtub.

12. The writer Thomas Wolfe liked to gear himself up to put something exciting down on paper by masturbating.

13. The American novelist Patricia Highsmith, who claimed she had ideas "as frequently as rats have orgasms", bred snails. She said she was more comfortable with their company than with people.

14. The Belgian writer Georges Simenon, creator of the fictional detective Maigret, claimed he slept with more than 10,000 women; it explained the "Do not disturb" sign that was always on his office door.

15. Salvador Dalí claimed he christened all his paintings by ejaculating onto the canvas after they were finished.

10 SCATHING FILM REVIEWS

1. "No."

   US film critic Leonard Maltin's
one-word review of *Isn't It Romantic?* (1948)

2. "And to Hell it can go."

   Ed Naha – *From Hell it Came* (1957)

3. "I hated this movie. Hated hated hated hated hated this movie. Hated it. Hated every simpering stupid vacant audience-insulting moment of it. Hated the sensibility that thought anyone would like it. Hated the implied insult to the audience by its belief that anyone would be entertained by it."

   Roger Ebert, who hated *North* (1994)

4. "This movie doesn't scrape the bottom of the barrel. This movie isn't the bottom of the barrel. This movie isn't below the bottom of the barrel. This movie doesn't deserve to be mentioned in the same sentence with barrels."

   Roger Ebert – *Freddy Got Fingered* (2001)

5. "I'm sure movies like this give people pimples."

   Pauline Kael, *New Yorker* – *Sweet November* (2001)

6. "The general opinion of *Revenge of the Sith* seems to be that it marks a distinct improvement on the last two episodes, *The Phantom Menace* and *Attack of the Clones*.

True, but only in the same way that dying from natural causes is preferable to crucifixion."

Anthony Lane, *New Yorker* – *Star Wars: Revenge of the Sith* (2005)

7. "Hulk smash all hope of interesting time in cinema. Hulk take all effort of cinema, effort getting babysitter, effort finding parking, and Hulk put great green fist right through it. Hulk crush all hopes of entertainment."

Peter Bradshaw, *The Guardian* – *The Incredible Hulk* (2008)

8. "It is 146 minutes long, which means that I entered the theatre in the bloom of youth and emerged with a family of field mice living in my long, white moustache. This is an entirely inappropriate length for what is essentially a home video of gay men playing with giant Barbie dolls."

Lindi West – *Sex and the City 2* (2010)

9. "The green space outside the Odeon Leicester Square may well be covered in cellophane-covered bouquets in the days to come, in memory of this new woe.

"I hesitate to use the term 'car crash cinema'. But the awful truth is that, 16 years after that terrible day in 1997, she has died another awful death."

Peter Bradshaw, *Guardian* – *Diana* (2013)

10. "It is a film so awe-inspiringly wooden that it is basically a fire risk."

Peter Bradshaw, *Guardian* – *Grace of Monaco* (2014)

WOE IS ME:
10 LITERARY AFFLICTIONS

1. Shakespeare may have had syphilis. It would certainly explain his apparent obsession with "the pox", not to mention his familiarity with the symptoms. The standard treatment was mercury vapour treatments, which left the victim with several physical problems, especially tremors: it would also explain why his handwriting was so terrible.

2. The poet John Milton started to lose the sight in his left when he was thirty-six and was blind in both eyes within eight years. He tried various medications, including "Goddard's drops", used for "faintings, apoplexies, lethargies and other sudden and alarming onsets". It didn't cure his blindness, but it did give him acute lead poisoning.

3. The Irish satirist Jonathan Swift suffered from vertigo, hearing loss and tinnitus, which he likened to "the noise of seven windmills". In his later years he probably developed Pick's Disease, a type of dementia characterized by painful inflammation of the eyes and inability to control emotions: his friends thought he had simply gone mad. He also liked to binge on apples, chomping his way through a hundred golden pippins at a time. It gave him terrible stomach ache. His doctors prescribed antimony – mercuric sulphide – which gave him mercury poisoning, and which in turn may have given him brain damage.

4. Fyodor Dostoyevsky was literature's most famous epileptic. From 1860 he recorded the dates of his seizures in a notebook; from that time, up to his death twenty years later, he listed 102 fits, preceded by "heaviness and even pain in the head, disorders of the nerves, nervous laugh and mystical depression". He used his experiences to create characters with epilepsy in four of his twelve novels.★

5. *Moby Dick*'s author Herman Melville was bipolar, an alcoholic and probably suffering from post-traumatic stress disorder. He also endured agonizing arthritis to write *Billy Budd*. The vast amount of opium he took didn't help.

6. Karl Marx suffered from constipation, liver trouble, rheumatism, shingles, ulcers, insomnia, bronchitis, laryngitis, pleurisy and painful boils around his genitals. He complained to his friend Engels: "I shan't bore you by explaining the carbuncles on my posterior and near the penis, the final traces of which are now fading but which made it extremely painful for me to adopt a sitting and hence a writing posture. I am not taking arsenic because it dulls my mind too much and I need to keep my wits about me." Marx was so troubled by the boils on his backside that he had to write most of *Das Kapital*, his masterpiece, standing up.

7. Charles Dickens suffered from insomnia. He spent sleepless nights treading the streets of London, often

---

★ Dostoyevsky's father died in 1839 in mysterious circumstances. According to one account, he was murdered by his own serfs, who restrained him during one of his drunken rages and poured vodka down his throat until he drowned. Another account says that he died of natural causes and that a neighbour invented the story of his murder so that he could buy the Dostoyevsky estate at a knock-down price.

encountering the inspirations for his novels. He thought he could sleep better in a north-pointing bed, so he carried a compass with him everywhere so he could realign his bed northwards if he was away from home.

8. Wilkie Collins suffered from neuralgia, rheumatism, "spasm suffocation" and "gout in the eyes", which a journalist friend said made his eyes look like "literally enormous bags of blood!" When Collins was writing Armadale, he was plagued by a large, sore boil on his groin and swollen testicles. His female companion administered an unusual treatment: he noted in his diary, "Caroline to mesmerise my feet".

9. George Orwell suffered from multiple bouts of bronchitis, whooping cough, dengue fever and tuberculosis, but at least he got something out of his misery. Orwell admitted that *1984* had "much to do with my illness". He underwent "collapse therapy", a treatment designed to close the dangerous cavities that form in the chests of tuberculosis patients. This treatment inspired him to write about the tortures of Winston Smith in the Ministry of Love.

10. The Irish poet W. B. Yeats suffered from prosopagnosia – an inability to recognize faces – which he tried to cure by dosing himself with arsenic. His illness probably came in handy on his deathbed when he was visited by his wife and two mistresses at the same time.

10 MUSES

1. For some artists there is nothing like a dalliance to get the creative juices flowing. For the French poet Baudelaire it was a Jewish prostitute, Sarah la Louchette, the "Squint-eyed Sarah" mentioned in some of his works. She gave him the inspiration for some of the naughtiest poems and the syphilis of the brain that eventually killed him.

2. Salvador Dalí painted a picture of his wife Gala with a lamb chop on each of her shoulders. He explained later: "I liked my wife, and I liked chops, and I saw no reason why I should not paint them together."

3. J. M. Barrie's inspiration for Peter Pan was Peter Llewellyn-Davies, the middle child of a family of five boys whom he met and befriended in Kensington Gardens, London. Unlike Pan, Davies grew up – only to throw himself under a train.

4. When the Italian composer Carlo Gesualdo found his wife in bed with her lover, he hacked and shot them to death then left their mutilated bodies outside the house for all to see. It inspired him to write some remarkably tortured pieces about the faithlessness of women.

5. Peggy Guggenheim was the muse of many artists, despite her oddly shaped nose, the result of botched rhinoplasty (after her plastic surgery Jackson Pollock suggested putting a towel over her head while one had

sex with her). At her gallery she showed paintings by Marcel Duchamp, Jean Cocteau, Jean Arp, Wassily Kandinksy, Yves Tanguy and Wolfgang Paalen, and is said to have slept with most of them; she also had affairs with Samuel Beckett and married Max Ernst. When asked by an interviewer how many husbands she'd had, Guggenheim replied: "Do you mean mine, or other people's?"

6. James Joyce was inspired by the sound and smell of his wife Nora's farts. He wrote: "I think I would know Nora's fart anywhere. I think I could pick hers out in a roomful of farting women. It is a rather girlish noise not like the wet windy fart which I imagine fat wives have."

7. Lewis Carroll, whose real name was Charles Dodgson, had many "child friends" and was an avid photographer who enjoyed taking pictures of young girls, often nude. He wrote *Alice in Wonderland* and *Through the Looking Glass* after telling stories to nine-year-old Alice Liddell while on picnics with her and her family on the river in Oxford, where he was a mathematics don. Dodgson was a close friend of Alice's family until there was a sudden cooling of relations in 1863 when she was eleven. After his death, pages from his diaries were censored or destroyed by his family and not one of his ten brothers and sisters ever spoke about him in public.

8. The painter Francis Bacon met George Dyer, a homeless, unemployed alcoholic in 1964 while Dyer was breaking into Bacon's house. Over the years Bacon painted Dyer many times in some of his best works. When Bacon severed all ties with him, the day before the artist's Paris retrospective in 1971, Dyer committed suicide.

9. The Austrian artist Oskar Kokoschka was regarded as one of the greatest Expressionists of the twentieth century.* Kokoschka's muse was Alma Mahler, widow of the great composer. When she ended their affair, Kokoschka reacted badly. He obsessed over her for the rest of his life and even had a life-size doll made of her, anatomically correct in every detail, which he then treated like a living companion. He bought it new clothes and underwear and took it with him on public engagements and rented a box for her at the opera to show her off. Kokoschka said that the doll was a big improvement on the original, because, unlike the real Alma, it never answered back. He was distraught when some of his friends got drunk at a party and kicked the doll to pieces.

10. In 1993 Suede's singer/songwriter Brett Anderson told *Melody Maker*, "I honestly think lack of sex is vital to my writing process. I don't know if the same goes for Aerosmith."

---

* Although not by the soon-to-be assassinated Archduke Franz Ferdinand, who visited an exhibition of Kokoschka work and observed, "This fellow's bones ought to be broken in his body."

THERE WILL BE BLOOD: 12 MOVIE MISHAPS

1928: three people die and one man loses a leg when several hundred extras are caught in the Great Flood scene during the making of *Noah's Ark*.

1936: in *The Charge of the Light Brigade*, during the charge sequence, a stuntman is killed when he falls off his horse and lands on a broken sword. Thirty-six horses receive broken legs and have to be shot, resulting in a ban on the use of trip wires.

1939: while making *The Wizard of Oz*, the Wicked Witch of the West, Margaret Hamilton, is badly burned when her character is required to vanish in a burst of flame and smoke and a delayed trapdoor leaves her exposed to the pyrotechnic device. Her stunt double is also injured in a scene involving a smoking broomstick. Meanwhile, the original Tin Man, Buddy Ebsen, suffers an allergic reaction to his aluminium make-up resulting in a collapsed lung and permanent respiratory problems.

1941: in *They Died With Their Boots On*, three extras are killed during a cavalry charge. Jack Budlong, is riding alongside Errol Flynn when he is pitched forward from his saddle. Sensing danger, he tosses his sword ahead of him, but it lands handle down and he is impaled upon it.

1941: the Nazi propaganda machine releases the anti-British film *My Life for Ireland*. During the epic final battle scene, several people are killed when an extra steps on a live landmine. The footage is included in the final release.

1969: during the filming of *Shark!* a stuntman is chewed to death on camera when a shark, which is supposed to have been sedated, suddenly springs to life and attacks.

1972: sound technician James Chapman is mauled to death by a lion during production on *The Last Lion*.

1972: while filming *Aguirre, the Wrath of God*, Klaus Kinski is so enraged by a noisy card game being played in a nearby tent that he takes a pistol and fires three shots into the tent, blowing off the tip of a crewman's finger. Later, when Kinski threatens to walk off the set, the director Werner Herzog shows him a rifle and tells him that, if he tries to leave, Herzog will shoot him, and then turn the gun on himself; Kinski stays put.

1983: during the making of *The Twilight Zone*, actor Vic Morrow and child actors Myca Dinh Le, aged seven, and Renee Shin-Yi Chen, six, are decapitated when a helicopter spins out of control and crashes during an explosion scene.

1994: on the set of *The Crow*, actor Brandon Lee, son of Bruce, is killed by a prop .44 Magnum when a live round, unwittingly lodged in the barrel, hits Lee in the stomach. It is one of several accidents. On the first day of shooting, a carpenter is seriously burned when he comes into contact with high-voltage power lines; a worker is injured when a screwdriver is accidentally driven through his own hand and a stuntman falls through the roof of the set.

1994: during the filming of *Troy*, George Camiller breaks his leg while filming an action sequence. He is operated on the following day, but suffers complications and dies two weeks later.

2011: during production of *Harry Potter and the Deathly Hallows*, Daniel Radcliffe's stunt double David Holmes suffers a serious spinal injury while practising a flying sequence in a harness. An explosion, which is part of the stunt, causes him to fall to the ground, leaving him paralysed from the waist down.

HOMER'S CURSE: 50 CELEBRITIES WHO DIED AFTER GUESTING ON *THE SIMPSONS*

Doris Grau – died on 30 December 1995

Audrey Meadows – 3 February 1996

George Fenneman – 29 May 1997

Linda McCartney – 17 April 1998

Phil Hartman – 28 May 1998

Jim Varney – 10 February 2000

Tito Puente – 20 April 2000

Steve Allen – 30 October 2000

Joseph "Joe C" Calleja – 16 November 2000

Werner Klemperer – 6 December 2000

Joey Ramone – 15 April 2001

Jack Lemmon – 27 June 2001

George Harrison – 29 November 2001

Ron Taylor – 16 January 2002

Lawrence Tierney – 26 February 2002

Stephen Jay Gould – 20 May 2002

Dee Dee Ramone – 5 June 2002

John Entwistle – 27 June 2002

Rod Steiger – 9 July 2002

Chick Hearn – 5 August 2002

Johnny Unitas – 11 September 2002

Barry White – 4 July 2003

Bob Hope – 27 July 2003

Johnny Cash – 12 September 2003

Paul Winfield – 7 March 2004

Isabel Sanford – 9 July 2004

Johnny Ramone – 15 September 2004

Rodney Dangerfield – 5 October 2004

Henry Corden – 19 May 2005

Ann Bancroft – 6 June 2005

Bob Denver – 2 September 2005

Johnny Carson – 23 October 2005

James Brown – 26 December 2006

Dennis Weaver – 24 February 2006

Tom Poston – 30 April 2007

Robert Goulet – 30 October 2007

Kevin Dubrow – 19 November 2007

George Carlin – 22 June 2008

Paul Newman – 26 September 2008

Eartha Kitt – 25 December 2008

Patrick McGoohan – 13 January 2009

John Updike – 27 January 2009

Ed McMahon – 23 June 2009

Michael Jackson – 25 June 2009

Gary Coleman – 20 May 2010

Jack LaLanne – 23 January 2011

Elizabeth Taylor – 23 March 2011

Harry Morgan – 7 December 2011

Dick Clark – 18 April 2012

Ernest Borgnine – 8 July 2012

TOIL AND TROUBLE: 10 MOST CURSED PERFORMANCES OF *MACBETH*

1606: Shakespeare is forced to play Lady Macbeth when Hal Berridge, the boy designated to play the lady, falls mysteriously ill and dies. According to legend, the bard played the role so badly that he told his fellow actors never again to mention "that play", thus starting the tradition of not referring to it by name. When King James sees the play he is so spooked by the "realistic" witches that he bans it for five years.

1672: during a performance in Amsterdam, the actor playing Macbeth substitutes a stage prop dagger for the real thing and kills Duncan in full view of the audience.

1849: two rival actors, Briton William Charles Macready and American Edwin Forrest, stage competing productions in New York. An audience of Forrest fans throw fruit and chairs at Macready during his performance at the Astor Place Opera House, disrupting the show. A riot ensues, and National Guardsmen fire on the crowd, injuring rioters and innocent bystanders. By the time the disturbance is finally brought under control, twenty people are dead and thirty-one injured.

1896: London newspaper *The Sketch* reports that Mr Gordon Craig, playing the part of Macduff, got carried away and attacked his fellow actor "with such an excess of zeal that the unfortunate Macbeth suffered somewhat severely about the head". Macbeth, however, gave as good as he got and the stage fight cost Macduff both of his thumbs.

1937: as Laurence Olivier takes on the role of Macbeth, a 25 lb stage weight crashes within inches of him; later, his sword breaks onstage and flies into the audience, hitting a man who suffers a heart attack as a result. During the same run, Old Vic founder Lilian Baylis dies on the night of the final dress rehearsal.

1942: during a production headed by John Gielgud, three actors, Duncan and two witches, die, and the costume and set designer commits suicide.

1947: actor Harold Norman is stabbed during the final sword fight in act five and dies from his wounds. His ghost is said to haunt the Coliseum Theatre, Oldham, where the fatal scene was played.

1953: during an open-air production, Charlton Heston rushes off stage, pointing at his thighs, screaming: "Get them off me!" Someone had laundered his tights and dipped them in kerosene and the heat caused serious burns to Heston's legs and groin. Later, the wind blows flames and smoke into the audience, causing a stampede.

1990: at the Old Vic, Peter O'Toole unexpectedly exits the stage and walks straight into a wall.

2013: in Manchester, an actor receives treatment from paramedics after being accidentally struck by Kenneth Branagh's sword.

12 ARTISTS WHO HATED THEIR OWN WORK

1. A. A. Milne
   The author hated *Winnie-the-Pooh* because it pigeon-holed him as a writer of children's books and he had always wanted to write adult fiction. Milne considered killing Pooh off at the end of his second book. Pooh's illustrator E. H. Shepard was similarly indisposed towards the little bear because he overshadowed his more serious work as a political cartoonist. Milne's son Christopher Robin cursed Pooh because he was constantly bullied over his association with it, although, ironically, he also owned a bookshop, where it was impossible to avoid someone popping that question.

2. Arthur Conan Doyle
   He resented his most famous creation Sherlock Holmes because it overshadowed all of his other writings. After killing him off in *The Final Problem*, Conan Doyle wrote to a friend confessing that writing about Holmes made him feel physically sick. He was eventually persuaded to resurrect the fictional detective when his other books failed to sell – and because people were shouting "MURDERER!" at him on the street.

3. Orson Welles
   Said he hated all of his films because he was a perfectionist and he always wanted to change or improve them.

He especially disliked *Citizen Kane* because it was the only film that anyone ever wanted to talk to him about.

4. Bela Lugosi
   The actor had a love-hate relationship with Dracula, the part that made him famous, because typecasting destroyed his career. He was even buried in the cape, although that wasn't his idea; it was his wife and son's. Later, the increasingly typecast Christopher Lee also grew to hate the role. According to Lee, Hammer Films guilt-tripped him into the part paying him well below his going rate or else fellow crew members could lose their jobs.

5. Agatha Christie
   Despite writing eighty-seven stories around him, Christie was not fond of her fictional Belgian detective Hercule Poirot, describing him as "a detestable, bombastic, tiresome, ego-centric little creep". Unlike Conan Doyle, she knew what her public wanted and resisted the temptation to have him bumped off.

6. The Beatles
   It was supposed to be the album that would bring them back together, but the Fab Four hated *Let it Be* so much that it broke up the band. Paul blamed Phil Spector and his "Wall of Sound" production but John placed the blame squarely at their own door and gave Spector some credit. "Given the shittiest load of badly recorded shit with a lousy feeling to it, ever, he made something out of it." Everyone except Paul hated the track "Maxwell's Silver Hammer" from the *Abbey Road* album, dismissing it as "granny music".

7. Christopher Plummer
   Don't mention *The Sound of Music* to Plummer. He

disowned the character he played, Captain Georg von Trapp, as "weak" and has been known to disparage the film musical he starred in as "S&M" or "The Sound of Mucus", describing it as "awful, sentimental and gooey". Which of course it was.

8. Alec Guinness
Guinness appeared in cinematic classics such as *The Bridge on the River Kwai*, *Great Expectations* and *Lawrence of Arabia* before agreeing to play Obi-Wan Kenobi in *Star Wars* in 1977, a film he described as "banal" and "mumbo-jumbo".* Guinness said it was his idea to get Obi-Wan killed off to make his part smaller. Ironically, *Star Wars* made him rich, because he was the only actor able to get a cut of the profits.

9. Ian Fleming
The author was so unhappy with his "experimental" ninth James Bond novel *The Spy Who Loved Me* that he tried to suppress it wherever he could. He blocked the publication of a paperback edition in the UK and only gave permission for the title to be used when he sold the film rights to Harry Saltzman and Albert R. Broccoli, requiring the film producers to write an entirely new story. Only the character of Jaws is loosely based on one of the characters in the book.

10. Led Zeppelin
The three living band members reunited in 1988 but fell out over "Stairway to Heaven", which Robert Plant

---

* Guinness always threw away *Star Wars*-related fan mail unopened and in his autobiography recalled a small boy who approached him and said that he'd seen *Star Wars* a hundred times. Guinness told the boy he'd give him an autograph if he promised to never watch the film again; the boy burst into tears.

called "that bloody wedding song". Jimmy Page meanwhile derided "Living Loving Maid (She's Just a
Woman)" as "filler". The song offended his girlfriend,
allegedly.

11. Radiohead
    The distinctive guitar crunch in their first hit song
    "Creep" resulted from guitarist Jonny Greenwood
    intentionally trying to sabotage the song during record-
    ing because he hated it so much; the band felt it improved
    the song so they kept it in. Eventually they all grew to
    hate "Creep" because people were turning up at concerts
    just to hear it, then walking out after it was played. Thom
    Yorke wasn't fond of the Radiohead classic "High and
    Dry" either: he said, "It's not bad . . . it's very bad."

12. Noel Gallagher
    The brains in Oasis described their third album, *Be Here
    Now,* as "the sound of a bunch of guys on coke in the
    studio not giving a fuck" and said the single "Roll With
    It" was "appalling". Unsurprisingly, brother Liam begs
    to differ. He rather likes *Be Here Now,* but says of
    "Wonderwall": "I can't fucking stand that fucking song.
    Every time I have to sing it I want to gag."

10 TV-RELATED DEATHS

1958: British actor Gareth Jones collapses and dies between scenes of a live television play, *Underground*, at TV studios in Manchester. The director, improvising around Jones's absence, continues the play to its conclusion. Coincidentally, Jones's character was supposed to have a heart attack, which is exactly what finished him off.

1984: magician and comedian Tommy Cooper suffers a fatal heart attack during a performance on the TV variety show *Live From Her Majesty's*. For several minutes the audience assumes that his sudden collapse is part of the act.

1990: Bo Diaz, a thirty-seven-year-old former baseball player, is killed at his home in Caracas when a satellite dish that he is adjusting on the roof of his home falls on him, crushing his neck and head.

1999: Abdel-Nasser Nuredeen from Cairo strangles his wife when she refuses to make him a cup of tea because she was busy watching the televised solar eclipse.

1999: entertainer Rod Hull, right-hand man of Emu, adjusts his TV aerial during the Champions League quarter-final, Internazionale v Manchester United. After asking his son Oliver to watch the screen and give him a shout when the picture improves, Hull climbs a ladder to the roof and falls to his death through the greenhouse, landing on concrete.

2000: a Greek ferryboat sinks after hitting a reef near the island of Poros, resulting in the deaths of eighty-two people. At the time of the collision, not a single crew member was on watch; they had placed the ship on autopilot so they could view a football match on TV.

2002: a man who is unhappy with his new widescreen TV storms the Rembrandt Tower in Amsterdam armed with two guns and explosives to protest against the TV manufacturers Philips Electronics. After taking eighteen hostages during a seven-hour siege, he realizes that he's got the wrong building and shoots himself in the head.

2006: the body of a woman is found wedged upside-down behind a bookcase in the home she shared with her relatives. They had spent nearly two weeks looking for Mariesa Weber, who had fallen head-first into the space behind the unit while adjusting the TV plug. Family members scoured her room for clues but found nothing, although they did notice a strange smell. He mother explained, "She's such a little thing."

2006: two Thai men are shot dead in a Bangkok restaurant while they are watching the Italy v Ghana World Cup match on TV. The gunman shoots dead the two fans at point-blank range after they ignore his request to keep the noise down.

2007: A man from Russia's Keralia region bludgeons his eighty-one-year-old grandmother to death in an argument over who has charge of the TV remote control. He says later he was drunk at the time and can't remember what it was, exactly, he wanted to watch.

FOUL FABLES:
10 X-RATED FAIRY TALES

1. In an early version of *Rapunzel*, the heroine is impregnated by the handsome prince, who runs off into the forest, leaving her with twins.

2. In the traditional version of *The Frog Prince*, the kindly princess kisses the frog and he turns into a handsome prince. In the original, the creepy frog tricked the princess into making a deal with him, followed her home, then tried to climb into bed with her, until finally she hurls him against the wall: this action somehow transforms him into a prince. In another even more violent version she cuts his head off.

3. In an 1800s Scottish version of *Cinderella*, the heroine survives by eating ear wax. In the original Brothers Grimm version, the stepsisters ensure that the glass slipper fits by amputating parts of their own feet; the blood pooling around their shoes gives them away. In the end they have their eyes pecked out by doves.

4. In medieval accounts of *Little Red Riding Hood*, the girl is raped and eaten by the wolf. In most versions the woodsman cuts Red Riding Hood and her grandmother out of the wolf's belly, finding them apparently none the worse for being *eaten* alive. In a later version, the girl escapes the hungry wolf by pretending that she needs to go outside to shit in the woods.

5. In the original serialized novel that the Disney film *Pinocchio* was based on, Jiminy Cricket is brutally murdered and Pinocchio has his feet burned off and dies gruesomely, hanged by villagers.

6. In the original Brothers Grimm version of *Sleeping Beauty*, the comatose heroine is raped and gives birth to twins. Their father later eats the babies.

7. In the early nineteenth century, *Goldilocks* was an old hag who was caught, tortured and impaled on a spike by the three bears. In another variation, the bears find Goldilocks, then rip her apart and eat her.

8. The 1989 Disney version of *The Little Mermaid* ends with the mermaid being changed into a human and enjoying a wonderful wedding with Eric. In Hans Christian Andersen's original, the mermaid sees the prince marry a princess and, in despair, after considering stabbing the prince to death, she opts for suicide by jumping into the sea.

9. In the 1812 Brothers Grimm version of *Snow White*, the evil queen is the actual mother, not the stepmother, of the heroine. She asks the huntsman for proof of her daughter's death – i.e. her liver, lungs and other internal organs – which she intends to eat. In another version she asks for a bottle of her daughter's blood, stoppered with her toe. The story concludes with a torture: the step-mother is forced into a pair of red-hot iron shoes and made to dance in them until she falls down dead.

10. In the modern version of *The Pied Piper of Hamelin*, the eponymous hero offers to rid the townsfolk of their vermin in exchange for money. When they refuse to cough up, he draws their children to a cave out of the

town until they change their mind, and then sends the children back. In the darker and possibly paedophilic original, the piper leads the children to a river where they all drown, except for a disabled boy who couldn't keep up.

10 DRAMATIC STAGE EXITS

1872: one-armed lion tamer Thomas McCarte makes his final performance in Bolton. A lion called Tyrant attacks him, prompting the three other lions to join in, ripping him apart in front of an audience of around 600. It is fifteen minutes before McCarte is extricated from the cage: he dies shortly afterwards.

1911: Sigmund Neuberger, aka the German magician "The Great Lafayette", has a much loved dog called Beauty, a terrier gifted to him as a pup by fellow performer and admirer Harry Houdini. Beauty dies four days before the opening of a show at the Empire Palace Theatre in Edinburgh. Neuberger arranges for the dog to be buried in the local cemetery. The local council agrees, on the condition that when the time comes Neuberger is also buried in the same plot. Four days later he is performing one of his signature illusions at the Empire Palace Theatre when fire breaks out on the stage. He rushes to escape through the small door leading from the stalls into the wings, having forgotten that he had ordered it locked to prevent interlopers spying on his stage tricks. Overcome by fumes, his body is reportedly found charred beyond recognition and sent to Glasgow for cremation. Two days after the fire, workers clearing the under-stage area find another body identically dressed as Lafayette. The body at the crematorium is that of the illusionist's stage body double. The urn containing The Great Lafayette's ashes is eventually laid to rest in the paws of his stuffed dog Beauty at Piershill Cemetery.

1918: William Elsworth Robinson, an American who performs as "Chung Ling Soo, the marvellous Chinese conjuror", is shot through the chest while performing his famous bullet-catching trick. His last words are: "Oh my God. Something's happened. Lower the curtain." It's a double shock for the audience, the first and last time that the enigmatic fake Chinaman had spoken English in public.

1925: circus strongman Zishe Breitbart demonstrates that he can drive a spike through five one-inch-thick timber planks using only his bare hands. He pierces his knee by accident, leading to fatal blood poisoning.

1926: escapologist Harry Houdini proudly claims that he can withstand any blow to the stomach. He is assailed by university student J. Gordon Whitehead in Montreal but does not have time to prepare himself to receive the blow. He dies of acute peritonitis caused by a ruptured appendix.

1971: while Frank Zappa is performing at the Rainbow Theatre, London, a fan rushes onto the stage and pushes him into the concrete orchestra pit. The fall almost kills Zappa, who sustains a crushed larynx, fractures, head trauma and injuries covering his entire body. The man who attacked him says he thought Zappa was eyeing his girlfriend.

1972: Les Harvey, guitarist for blues-rock band Stone the Crows, dies onstage in front of 1,000 fans when he is electrocuted by a poorly grounded microphone while tuning up for a show in Swansea, south Wales.

1990: soul legend Curtis Mayfield is permanently paralysed from the neck down when a lighting rig falls on his head during a performance in Brooklyn, New York.

1998: at the end of a show in Canterbury, England, ska and reggae musician Judge Dread says, "Let's hear it for the band," before collapsing with a heart attack. According to one account, the ambulance that subsequently arrived wouldn't start, and, when the Judge's fans began pushing it to the hospital, police accused them of trying to steal it.

2003: a crowd at Western Michigan University waiting to see the legendary Righteous Brothers singer Bobby Hatfield is informed that the show will not be taking place due to "a personal emergency of an unspecified nature". In fact, Hatfield had been found dead in his hotel room half an hour before he was scheduled to perform with cocaine-induced heart failure.

12 FREAK SHOW PERFORMERS WHO WERE BIGGER THAN THE ELEPHANT MAN*

1. Daniel Cajanus "The Swedish Giant"
   Born in Finland (then part of Sweden) in 1704, his adult height was variously estimated at up to ten feet ten inches (3.30 m), but medical research suggests his true height was around seven feet eight inches (2.34 m). Cajanus exhibited himself all over Europe, attracting the curiosity of scientists and royalty alike. He died aged forty-five, leaving a large sum to pay for his funeral and a burial with the intention of safeguarding his remains from grave robbers. Despite his precautions, various bits of his skeleton found their way into museums, where some parts of him still remain.

---

* Joseph Merrick was born in Leicester, England, in 1862 and dubbed the "Elephant Man" because of a tusk-like growth on his face. A circus promoter dreamed up the story that Merrick's mother had been trampled by an elephant while pregnant, resulting in her son's deformities. Medical science provides a more probable explanation. For many years it was thought he had neurofibromatosis type one, but doctors now think that he had the condition Proteus Syndrome, or possibly a combination of both. He voluntarily became a sideshow attraction in 1884 and was treated well, but, on a tour of Belgium, Merrick was robbed by his road manager and abandoned. After his "rescue" from his life as a sideshow freak by the London physician Frederick Treves, Merrick was still an object of curiosity for the rest of his short life, studied, prodded and examined by the Victorian medical establishment. He died aged twenty-seven in 1890.

2. Daniel Lambert "The Human Colossus"
   Weighing fifty stone (318 kg) and measuring five feet eleven inches, Lambert (1770–1809) was in his lifetime the heaviest person in recorded history. Despite crippling shyness and sensitivity about his bulk, he put himself forward as a freak show exhibit after losing his job as a prison warden in Leicester. In 1806 he set himself up at 53 Piccadilly, London, where for five hours a day visitors paid a shilling a time to enter his home and sit and watch him going about his daily business. His venture was hugely successful, drawing around 400 paying visitors a day, and he returned to Leicester a wealthy man. When he died aged thirty-nine, probably from fatty degeneration of the heart, his coffin had to be mounted on wheels to move it and it took twenty men to lower it into his grave. His fame was such that a waxwork likeness of Lambert toured America soon after his death.

3. Juan Baptista dos Santos "The Man With Two Penises"
   Born in Faro, Portugal, around 1843, equipped with two penises, three legs and three scrotums. His career as an exhibitionist was largely confined to medical circles; he turned down several lucrative offers to be touted across Europe as "The Three Legged Man". He was, however, very gracious with his time for the medical establishment and didn't mind exhibiting himself to royalty. Perhaps the most unusual aspect of his condition was that both of his penises functioned perfectly. A contemporary reported, ". . . the sight of a female is sufficient to excite his amorous propensities. He functionates with both of the penes [*sic*], finishing with one, then continues with the other."

4. Myrtle Corbin "The Four Legged Girl"
   Born in Tennessee in 1868, Myrtle's extra legs resulted from a rare form of conjoined twinning known as

dipygus, which gave her two complete bodies from the waist down, including an extra set of slightly smaller legs: she could move the smaller legs but they were too weak for walking. As she was also born with a clubbed foot, technically, the Four Legged Girl only had one good, usable leg. Her father began showing her to curious neighbours for a dime when she was just one month old and at fourteen she became a star attraction with P. T. Barnum. A flyer describes her as "gentle of disposition as the summer sunshine and as happy as the day is long". She had a brief but very lucrative career earning up to $450 a week and she spawned several fake imitators. She retired when she was eighteen and went on to have four daughters and a son.

5. Mary Ann Bevan "The World's Ugliest Woman"
Born Mary Ann Webster in London in 1874, one of eight children. As a young woman she worked as a nurse and in 1903 she married a greengrocer, Thomas Bevan. In her early thirties she began to show symptoms of acromegaly, a form of progressive gigantism resulting in abnormal growth and distortion of the facial features. She had four children before her husband died in 1914. Unable to support her family, she turned to the Coney Island impresario Sam Gumpertz, who hired her as a sideshow freak and under whose employment she remained for the rest of her life. In the early 2000s her likeness was used on a birthday card sold by Hallmark Cards in the UK with a joke about *Blind Date*; the card was withdrawn following complaints.

6. Stephan Bibrowski aka "Lionel The Lion Faced Boy"
Born in Warsaw in 1890, Bibrowski suffered from hypertrichosis, a rare congenital condition as a result of which almost the entire body is covered with long hair. His mother gave him up to a German showman

called Sedlmayer when he was four and he began exhibiting him around Europe. In 1902 he went to America where he replaced "Jo-Jo the Dog Faced Boy", Barnum and Bailey's previous hairy man, and stayed with the circus for five years. According to Barnum's publicity, Lionel's condition came about because his pregnant mother saw her husband being mauled to death by a lion. Bibrowski was hugely successful and enjoyed the opportunities provided by his unusual hairiness. In 1904 in New York, the hotel he was staying at caught fire and he was the very first man out, terrified of having his furry faced singed. In 1928 he retired from his sideshow career and moved back to Germany where he died from a heart attack in 1932 aged forty-one.

7. The Tocci Brothers
Born in Locano, Italy, around 1876, Giacomo and Giovanni Battista Tocci were conjoined twins, joined from the sixth rib down, with four arms and two legs, separate hearts, lungs and stomachs and shared reproductive organs. The trauma of witnessing the birth of his first-born sons gave their father Giovanni a nervous breakdown, but he recovered sufficiently to take the twins to a Turin freak show where he became their manager. Despite their physical closeness the relationship wasn't always harmonious. One drank, the other was teetotal: one was highly talkative, the other quiet; they settled disputes with their fists. After twenty years touring America the Tocci brothers disappeared from the public eye in the 1890s, returning to Italy and setting up home in a secluded, high-walled home near Venice to keep gawkers at bay. What became of them afterwards is not known, although some sources claim they had a joint marriage to two sisters.

8. Prince Randian "The Snake Man"

His real name unknown, Randian was born in British Guiana in 1871 without arms or legs. In 1889 he was brought to America by P.T. Barnum, where he became a famous limbless sideshow performer, renowned for his amazing self-sufficiency; he could shave, paint, write and roll cigarettes with his lips. For his stage routine Randian wore a snug woollen "onesie", giving him the appearance of a caterpillar or a snake and he would move himself around the stage by wiggling his hips and shoulders. With his wife, known as Princess Sarah, he fathered four daughters and a son, and appeared in the 1932 film *Freaks*.

9. Fanny Mills "The Big Foot Girl"

Born in England in 1860, from an early age she displayed signs of Milroy's Disease, a condition characterized by gross swelling, fluid building and discolouring of the soft tissue in the lower extremities. Although Fanny was a petite lady, weighing in at a lithe 115 lb, her feet required size thirty shoes. Her footwear was said to be made from the skins of three goats and were slipped on over pillow-case socks. Unable to walk without assistance, she required a full-time nurse. In America her promoters offered a reward of $5,000 to any man prepared to marry the "Big Foot Lady". The challenge was taken up by droves of bachelors who paid their admission fee to take a look at her, but in fact she was already married to a man called William Brown. Ill health forced her retirement from the freak show circuit aged thirty-two.

10. Mortado "The Human Pincushion"

Little is known about his background; according to Mortado's biography he was born in Berlin and served in World War I before meeting a New York agent and signing a deal with the Dreamland circus. Mortado had holes bored through his feet and hands – not traditional piercings, actual large holes – into which he would place fake blood pellets and be "crucified" as the shocked public looked on. As an encore, he rigged a special chair that would shoot water out of the holes in his hands and feet. How Mortado got the idea for his bizarre act, let alone how he managed to create the holes, or even his eventual fate, remains unknown. Mortado disappeared from public view in the late 1930s.

11. Veronica Shant "The Geek"
    Geeks were among the most regular and most frightening features of the American circus sideshow culture. The Geek was typically a derelict drunk or drug addict with no other financial options who was put in a cage and billed as a "wild man" (or woman). His or her job was to warm up the audience by making various unpleasant noises and eat anything offered, usually a live chicken. Veronica Shant was the most famous and most impressive of the Geeks. She brought a new dimension to the job because she genuinely enjoyed her work and devoured chickens, field mice and various other furry rodents with relish, causing much vomiting among her audience.

12. Zip "The Pinhead"
    Billed as "the missing link" from the deepest jungles of Africa – "the last survivor of a dying race". In fact, Zip was a gentleman from Harlem with an oddly shaped head. William Henry Johnson's small, tapering cranium and heavy jaw made him an attractive draw at van Emburgh's Circus in Somerville, New Jersey, where he was visited by celebrities of the day including the Prince of Wales in 1860. During his sixty-seven years in show business, Zip was said to have entertained more than one hundred million people. When he died in 1926 at

the age of eighty-four, his last words were reportedly: "Well, we fooled 'em a long time, didn't we?" His pall-bearers were the Fat Girl, the Tattooed Lady, the Human Skeleton and Cliko the Bushman.

RADIO CA-CA:
10 SHOCK JOCKS

1. In 1995, three days after the fatal shooting of the Hispanic singer/songwriter Selena and the day before her funeral, WXRK "king of shock jocks" Howard Stern got stuck into her mourners. While playing gunshots over Selena's music he announced, with a mocking, fake Hispanic accent, "This music does absolutely nothing for me. Alvin and the Chipmunks have more soul . . . Spanish people have the worst taste in music. They have no depth." Having infuriated Hispanic communities across the country, a disorderly conduct arrest warrant was issued in his name in Harlingen, Texas. The following week, Stern apologized on air in Spanish.

2. In 2001, while on air at WXTB in Tampa, Florida, Todd "Bubba the Love Sponge" Clem slaughtered and barbecued a wild Florida boar. Added sound effects convinced listeners that the hog was in great distress. Clem and three others were charged with animal cruelty and acquitted. Clem acknowledged that the animal was castrated so that a colleague could eat the testicles raw but said he didn't kill the boar, he only broadcast the killing. Other Clem stunts include a segment called Drink Your Pee, and Milk Challenge, in which people in his studio drink milk until they throw up.

3. In 2001 Dallas shock jocks Kramer and Twitch told listeners to their KEGL-FM evening show that pop

singer Britney Spears and her then boyfriend Justin Timberlake had been killed in a car accident in Los Angeles. Panicked fans called police and fire departments in their hundreds. The hoax was then turned into a spoof version of a BBC News Online web page and the link was sent around the world by email. The spoof page was removed when the BBC lodged a protest: Kramer and Twitch were fired.

4. In 2002 North American DJs Gregg "Opie" Hughes and Anthony Cumia sponsored a contest inviting listeners to have sex in well-known public places. The contest Sex For Sam passed without a major outcry until a couple copulated in a vestibule at St Patrick's Cathedral in Manhattan. The Opie and Anthony Show was cancelled and the station was fined $357,500. Other "incidents" on the show include interviewing a man who admitted how much he'd love to rape Condoleezza Rice, and convincing a mayor's daughter that her father had died in a car crash as part of an April fool prank.

5. In July 2003 American radio station WABC fired DJ Michael Savage after he told a "sodomite" caller (actually Bob Foster, a PC technician and confirmed prankster): "Oh, you're one of the sodomites. You should only get AIDS and die, you pig. How's that? Why don't you see if you can sue me, you pig. You got nothing better than to put me down, you piece of garbage. You have got nothing to do today, go eat a sausage and choke on it. Get trichinosis. Okay, do we have another nice caller here who's busy because he didn't have a nice night in the bathhouse who's angry at me today? Get me another one, put another sodomite on . . ."

6. In 2004 Portland, Oregon duo Marconi and Tiny were axed for playing an audiotape of the beheading of

American Nick Berg by Iraqi militants several times on their morning show, overdubbed with comedy noises and a laughter track.

7. In 2005 British Radio DJ Tim Shaw propositioned glamour model Jodie Marsh live on-air on his Kerrang! FM show, announcing that he would leave his family for her. Shaw's wife retaliated by putting his Lotus Esprit on eBay for fifty pence; the car sold within five minutes. In 2004 he phoned his sister-in-law live on-air to boast that he fantasized about her during sex with his wife. Shaw has been sacked by thirteen radio stations in the UK.

8. In 2008 BBC Radio 2 host Russell Brand rang actor Andrew Sachs and left an answering machine message claiming that he had "fucked" his granddaughter. Having second thoughts, Brand called back and apologized, adding, "I used a condom." Having third thoughts, Brand resigned his job.

9. In 2009 on his morning breakfast radio show, Australian DJ Kyle Sandilands' Lie Detector segment featured a fourteen-year-old girl who, when asked by her mother if she had ever had sex, broke down and revealed that she had been raped at the age of twelve. Kyle told listeners that her mother meant "any intercourse other than rape". The show was suspended for one week. Three days after his suspension expired, Sandilands told listeners that the dieting TV presenter Magda Szubanski could have lost more weight in a concentration camp.

10. In 2012 Australian DJs Mel Greig and Michael Christian made a prank call to a hospital in London where the Duchess of Cambridge was being treated for morning

sickness. Pretending to be the Queen and Prince Charles, they asked for a condition report. Having failed to see through their low-quality impressions, nurse Jacintha Saldanha hanged herself three days later.

10 PERFORMANCE ARTISTS

1. When the fifty-three-year-old Japanese sculptor Hananuma Masakichi was diagnosed with tuberculosis in 1885 he thought he had only months to live, so he decided to create a life-size statue of himself as a gift for the woman he loved. Masakichi spared no detail in his efforts to make a perfect replica. He painted and lacquered the statue to match his skin tone, used his own hair and nails and even decorated the genitalia with his own pubic hair. Finally, he pulled out all of his teeth and placed them in his wooden statue. Inconveniently, his expectation of impending death was premature: he lived for another ten years and died a pauper.*

2. In 1965 the German artist Joseph Beuys painted himself in gold, strapped a ski to one foot and sat in an exhibition space while whispering in the ear of a dead hare he was cradling in his arms. He called the piece *How to Explain Pictures to a Dead Hare.*

3. The abstract expressionist Millie Brown paints by swallowing dyed soy milk in a mixture of colours, which she then pukes onto a white canvas. Although some critics find the Londoner's work hard to swallow, she has received positive recognition from some, comparing her

---

* The Masakichi sculpture was acquired by the showman Robert Ripley and became one of his most prized exhibits until it was seriously damaged during the 1996 California Earthquake. It has since been sitting in a Ripley's warehouse waiting for someone to restore it.

work to that of Jackson Pollock, who was known for his "splatter" painting.

4. The work of Austrian artist Rudolf Schwarzkogler usually involved pain and self-mutilation. When he died in 1969, it was widely reported that he had killed himself by cutting off his own penis during a performance. Disappointingly, Schwarzkogler's reputation was exaggerated: he actually died after falling from a window.

5. In 1971 American Chris Burden allowed a friend to shoot him in the left arm with a .22 rifle, to show, he explained, that "I want to be taken seriously as an artist". The work was caught on video, a piece entitled *Shoot*. Burden recovered and went on to have himself nailed to a Volkswagen.

6. In 1975 the Dutchman Bas Jan Ader set out from Cape Cod in a small sailing boat to cross the Atlantic as part of a performance piece titled *In Search of the Miraculous*. His broken boat was found 150 miles off the coast of Ireland: it was empty.

7. In 1988 artist Rick Gibson ate a canapé made from donated human tonsils in Walthamstow High Street, London. A year later, he ate a slice of legally purchased human testicle in Lewisham High Street, London. In 1989 he attempted to eat another slice of human testicle in Vancouver, Canada, but was stopped by the police. When the charge was eventually dropped, he celebrated by eating a testicle hors d'œuvre.

8. In 2007 Chilean artist Marco Evaristi hosted a dinner party at which he served agnolotti pasta topped with a meatball cooked in the artist's own fat; he had it removed earlier in a liposuction operation.

9. In 2012 Japanese artist Mao Sugiyama had his genitals surgically removed. He then cooked them for five paying dinner-party guests. He charged around £170 per head to be fed his piping-hot genitalia, garnished with mushrooms and parsley. Sugiyama had initially considered eating them himself but decided to make some money out of it instead. Japanese police charged him with indecent exposure.

10. In 2013 naked performance artist Pyotr Pavlensky nailed his testicles to the ground in Red Square, Moscow, to denounce Vladimir Putin's police state.

7 GREAT WRITERS WHO DIED IN POVERTY

1. Thomas Paine
   The greatest pamphleteer in history and hero of the American and French revolutions died a penniless drunk in Manhattan. Only half a dozen people turned up for his funeral; a popular nursery rhyme at the time of his death went:

   Poor Tom Paine! There he lies:
   Nobody laughs and nobody cries
   Where he has gone or how he fares
   Nobody knows and nobody cares.

2. François Rabelais
   The great French renaissance writer noted in his will: "I owe much. I possess nothing. The rest I leave to the poor." In France, the expression *le quart d'heure de Rabelais* means it is time to pay the bill. It recalls his artful attempts to get out of paying a tavern bill when he had no money.

3. Heinrich Heine
   Died in poverty in a squalid Parisian garret, deserted by his former friends. A writer to the end, his last words were, "Write . . . write . . . pencil . . . paper."

4. Edgar Allan Poe
   Although *The Raven* was hailed as a great success in 1845 and established Poe as a literary genius, it didn't

bring financial security and he ended up writing to magazine editors begging for money. He died penniless in 1849, days after being found wandering the streets drunk and rambling, wearing clothes that weren't his.

5. Herman Melville
    Recognition for the author of *Moby Dick* did not begin until thirty years after his death, when his epic whaling novel was finally recognized as a literary masterpiece. He had long since abandoned any hopes of living off his writing, instead working as a customs inspector for nineteen years. He died of a heart attack in 1891, broke and almost unknown.

6. Oscar Wilde
    Known for his extravagant spending habits, after his release following his imprisonment for gross indecency, he was forced to live on a small annual allowance from the estate of his deceased wife. Living in poverty in Paris, he spent what little cash he had mostly on alcohol. When the doctor attending to him during his final days asked for payment, Wilde joked that he would die as he had lived, beyond his means.

7. Karl Marx
    He conceived of his history of capitalism, *Das Kapital*, in the late 1840s, but the first volume wasn't completed until 1867, well behind schedule and he never got round to finishing parts two and three. He died destitute and only eleven mourners turned up for his burial at Highgate Cemetery in London.

A SPOONFUL OF SUGAR:
12 DISNEY FACTS

1. Walt Disney sketched out the original idea for Mickey Mouse; however, the actual cartoon was done by an employee. Walt wasn't very good at drawing and rumour had it that he couldn't even reproduce his famed signature.

2. Pocahontas was a nickname given to the famous Native American girl by her tribe because of her precocious nature around men. It translates as "little slut".

3. The Academy Award-winning 1958 Disney film *White Wilderness* propagated the myth that lemmings commit suicide. Filmed on location in Alberta, Canada, it contains a scene showing a mass lemming migration, which ends with the lemmings leaping to their death into the Arctic Ocean. The entire sequence was staged: as there are no lemmings in Alberta, the filmmakers imported a few dozen trapped lemmings then herded them over a cliff into a river.

4. Until 2001 Disneyland workers weren't allowed to wear their own underwear when they were in character. Cast members were issued company briefs, which they had to hand in at the end of every day to be washed with their costumes.

5. Walt was a ruthless ringleader for Hollywood's

anti-communist witch-hunt in the 1940s. In 1947 he testified before the House Un-American Activities Committee that former animators of his were Communist sympathizers. He was also anti-union and claimed the 1941 strike by the Screen Cartoonists Guild was a ploy by Communists to gain influence in Hollywood.

6. Disney's film *Dumbo* was an initial disaster at the box office. Its finale of a dive-bombing elephant was considered deeply inappropriate because of the Japanese bombing of Pearl Harbor within weeks of its release.

7. A fifteen year old, Mark Maples, was the first person killed at Disneyland. In May 1964 he took off his protective harness and tried to stand up on the Matterhorn Bobsleds; he lost his balance and was thrown to the track below. Since then there have been twelve deaths in Disneyland California, twelve at Disney World Florida and at least one at Disneyland Paris.

8. The first movie to use the word "vagina" on film was the 1946 Disney animated film *The Story of Menstruation*.

9. Walt's animator Art Babbitt claimed that Disney attended meetings of the German American Bund, a pro-Nazi organization, in the 1930s. In 1938, a month after the Nazi campaign to round up all the Jews began, he invited Nazi propagandist and filmmaker Leni Riefenstahl to his studio and gave her a tour.

10. In 2004 a thirty-eight-year-old Disney employee dressed as Pluto was killed at the Magic Kingdom when he was run over by the Beauty and the Beast float in the Share a Dream Come True Parade.

11. In 2010 a woman from Pennsylvania sued the Disney Corporation, claiming that Donald Duck had groped her during a photo session. Disney settled the lawsuit with the claimant for an undisclosed amount; it was the twenty-fourth alleged assault by a costumed Disney character reported since 2004.

12. Every year, someone asks for permission to have a family member's ashes scattered over Disneyland. The answer is always no, but stealthy scatterings of human remains still occur. The most popular place for it is the Haunted Mansion.

10 HARD ACTS TO FOLLOW

1. Sid Ellis was one of the most popular music-hall turns of the 1920s. He entertained by lying on his back while his twenty-five stone wife played a piano balanced on his chest. While Mrs Ellis played the accompaniment, Sid sang "Ireland Must Be Heaven Because Mother Comes from There".

2. In 1961 one man died of cardiac arrest and five more were treated for shock when eighty-one-year-old inmate Gladys Elton performed a striptease at the Haslemere Home for the Elderly in Great Yarmouth. The following year there were three more deaths when eighty-seven-year-old resident Harry Meadows dressed up as the Grim Reaper and appeared looking through the window brandishing a scythe.

3. Messalina, wife of the Roman Emperor Claudius, once took part in a competition with Rome's most notorious prostitute. She defeated her by having sexual intercourse with twenty-five men in a night and a day.

4. Priscilla "Priss" Fotheringham was one of seventeenth-century London's most famous prostitutes. The young Priss was a beauty, but by her thirties she had lost her looks thanks to smallpox and years of drinking neat gin. Her solution to the resulting drop in income was a novelty act known as "chucking". Held up by two male volunteers, she stood on her head, knickerless with her legs astride, while patrons took turns to throw

half-crown coins into her vagina. Miss Fotheringham's "commodity" could hold a princely sixteen half-crowns, making her enough cash to set up and run her own brothel, until she died of syphilis in 1663.

5. In nineteenth-century Paris, one of the most expensive prostitutes was Caribbean-born Blanche Dumas, who possessed two vaginas, three legs and four breasts.

6. Jumbo the African elephant arrived at London Zoo in 1863 and went on to become its most famous ever attraction. When Jumbo reached adulthood, however, London's favourite pet became an unmanageable lust-crazed monster with a four-foot erection. The Zoo decided to sell its prize asset for £2,000 to P.T. Barnum; his new owners kept him under control by feeding him with biscuits soaked in bourbon. In September 1885 Jumbo was being led across a railway line in Ontario, when he was startled by an oncoming train, and charged headlong into it, crushing his skull. In 1975 the building housing his stuffed body caught fire and Jumbo was immolated. Some of his ashes were preserved, but they didn't prove such an attraction; It may have been the vessel they were contained in – a peanut butter jar.

7. In the 1970s Rita Thunderbird, "The Human Cannonball" from Battersea, London, thrilled audiences around the UK with her explosive circus act and trade-mark gold lamé bikini. During a performance in 1977, the charge went off, but Miss Thunderbird remained lodged inside the barrel: her bra was shot across the River Thames.

8. In 1970 a performance of the opera *Rigoletto* was halted when the star, baritone Louis Quilico, swallowed a pigeon feather and fainted.

9. In January 1983 police interrupted a performance of *Snow White and the Seven Dwarfs* at the Shaftesbury Theatre, London, when they dashed onstage and arrested one of the dwarfs, Raymond McCray, in connection with a bank robbery in Ilford. McCray had avoided detection by CCTV cameras during the raid because he was shorter than the counter.

10. The English actor John Bindon, who specialized in playing villains and appeared in *Get Carter* with Michael Caine and *Performance* with Mick Jagger, once entertained Princess Margaret at a party in Chelsea by balancing several beer glasses on his penis.

CHAPTER SIX

All Things Bright and Beautiful

20 FACTS ABOUT THE ANIMAL KINGDOM THAT ARE UNLIKELY TO COME IN USEFUL IN A PUB QUIZ

1. Cockroaches fart every fifteen seconds and account for 20 per cent of all the world's methane emissions.

2. Earwigs have cannibalistic tendencies and like to eat their brothers and sisters. They take into account the size and weight of other earwigs and whether or not they are related to them, before killing and eating them. The male *Diplatys flavicollis* earwig has two double-barrelled penises.

3. Armadillos carry more diseases than any other living mammal. A third of all Americans who suffer from gonorrhoea or leprosy catch it from an armadillo.

4. Duck droppings are a reindeer's favourite food.

5. Studies show that ugly guppy fish make the best fathers. The sperm of a good guppy is less effective at inseminating females than that of their less handsome colleagues.

6. Due to a genetic mutation, fruit flies with the "Ken and Barbie" gene have no genitalia.

7. Male Nile hippopotamuses have a territorial ritual; they square up, backside-to-backside, and then shower each other with shit.

8. Some female penguins are prostitutes. They will mate with males who are not their usual partners in exchange for gifts of rocks, which they then use as nesting material.

9. An adult African elephant can defecate up to 100 lb of shit a day. The food passes so swiftly through it that 60 per cent emerges much the same as it went in.

10. The Sami people of northern Finland have a unit of measurement called Poronkusema. It is the distance a reindeer can travel before it needs to urinate.

11. One-fifth of all road accidents in Sweden involve an elk.

12. The bush cricket (also known as katydid) has the largest testicles in the animal kingdom relative to size. If human testicles were as large, proportionate to body size, as those of *Platycleis affinis*, they would weigh about 14 lb each.

13. The Candiru is a type of tiny catfish found in South America, typically less than an inch long, and has a habit of swimming up the urethra of men's penises. It settles in there by anchoring its short spines into the surrounding tissue, which can cause inflammation, haemorrhage and death. The only way to remove it is surgically.

14. As an aid to digestion, rabbits eat up to 80 per cent of their own faeces.

15. Hawk moths have the kinkiest alarm system in the animal kingdom: they rub their genitals to frighten away bats.

16. After dining on rotting corpses, turkey vultures use their own urine to clean themselves. When they encounter a predator and are too full to fly they throw up to empty their stomachs.

17. Male cane toads enjoy sex with dead females.

18. In the early 1990s, a lone bottlenose dolphin called "Freddie" was semi-resident in and around Amble Harbour, Northumberland, England. It liked to tow bathers through the water by hooking his large penis around them.

19. The wombat is unique in the animal kingdom for producing cube-shaped turds.

20. In Brazil, there is a type of cockroach that eats eyelashes. It prefers those of young children and feeds on them while they are sleeping.

14 NATURALISTS WHO WERE NOT DAVID ATTENBOROUGH

401 BC: the Greek Ctesias says that India is inhabited by several types of monster, including dog-headed men and primates with three-foot-long ears. He also describes a unicorn as a "fleet and fierce wild ass with a white body, purple head and a straight horn, a cubit long, with a white base, black middle and red tip".

c. AD 70: in his book *Natural History*, Pliny the Elder says the orang-utan is a "marvellously cunning" ape that uses snares to catch birds and has been known to play draughts. He explains that the hippopotamus walks backwards to confuse anyone trying to track it and describes a little-known African tribe, in which parents are ritually eaten by their children and women use human skulls as bras.

c. AD 500: Timothy of Gaza says that weasels give birth through their ears, though some say through their mouths.

c. AD 600: the Spanish scholar St Isadora of Seville says that bees are generated from decomposed veal.

c. 1250: Albertus Magnus writes: "The lioness giveth birth to cubs which remain three days without life. Then cometh the lion, breatheth upon them, and bringeth them to life."

c. 1280: according to *The Book of Beasts*, "the elephant's nature is such that if he tumbles down he cannot get up again. Hence it comes that he leans against a tree when he wants to go to sleep, for he has no joints in his knees. This is the reason why a hunter partly saws through a tree, so that the elephant, when he leans against it, may fall down at the same time as the tree."

c. 1500: Leonardo da Vinci notes: "When the beaver is pursued, knowing this to be on account of the virtue of its testicles for medicinal uses, not being able to flee any farther it stops and in order to be at peace with its pursuers bites off its testicles with its sharp teeth and leaves them to its enemies."

1530: the Elizabethan writer William Horman says: "there is so much hatred between the dragon and the elephant that one will kill the other" and "the ostrich is the greatest of all birds and eats and digests iron".

1584: while wandering down the Amazon, Sir Walter Raleigh encounters a tribe of men he calls the Ewaipanoma, describing them as having "eyes in their shoulders, and their mouths in the middle of their breasts, and that a long train of hair groweth backward between their shoulders".

1676: the Frenchman Gabriel de Foigny describes Australia as a "merry land", inhabited by eight-foot-tall red-skinned "frolicking hermaphrodites" who strangle all of the single-sex children at birth.

1683: Izaak Walton, in *The Compleat Angler*, writes that eels are created from the "action of sunlight on dewdrops". A learned bishop disagrees and says that eels come from the thatched roofs of cottages.

1735: the godfather of plant and animal classification Carl Linnaeus describes several mythical beasts and "monstrous humans", including the "wild man" *Homo ferus*, who walked on all fours, and *Homo caudatus* – "man with a tail".

1859: the meteorologist Robert Fitzroy, a rabid opponent of Darwin's *On The Origin of Species*, writes letters to *The Times* explaining that giant animals such as the Mastodon did not survive the biblical flood because they were too big to fit into Noah's Ark.

1933: the Nazi race theorist Professor Hermann Gauch notes that "birds can be taught to talk better than other animals is explained by the fact that their mouths are Nordic in structure".

20 ANIMAL RIGHTS ABUSES

1559: at her coronation, Queen Elizabeth I has a cat burned in a wicker basket to symbolize the releasing of demons.

1560: Ivan the Terrible's pet elephant, the first ever brought to Russia, has been trained to bow before the Czar. When it is brought to the Kremlin, surrounded by thousands of people who come to see it, the terrified animal fluffs his lines; the furious Czar Ivan orders his soldiers to hack it to pieces.

1650: German scholar Athanasius Kircher proposes a "cat piano". You play it by sticking pins into cats, selected for the different pitches at which they mew.

1652: in County Tyrone, Ireland, Oliver Cromwell's soldiers disembowel a Scottish man and a dog to see "whether a dog's or a Scotchman's guts were longest".

1720: a Sumatran elephant is put on display in London for the first time but is dead within a year because the public give it dozens of pints of beer every day.

1726: the king of Poland, Augustus "the Strong", hosts an animal-tossing event in Dresden. In all, 647 foxes, 533 hares, 34 badgers and 21 wildcats are tossed and killed.

1826: an elephant called Chunee, an attraction at a London menagerie, starts to go wild when it reaches sexual maturity. When Chunee kills his keeper in a fit of sexual frustration, his owners call in the army to shoot him. The soldiers line up outside the elephant's cage and shoot endless volleys into his thick hide, but fail to finish him off. In the end, Chunee is stabbed to death with bayonets.

1861: on his latest trip to Africa, British explorer John Hanning Speke's pet donkey, the one that had carried him to discover Lake Victoria three years earlier, is beaten to death by hostile locals.

1870: the prostitute Cora Pearl, said to be the most fashionable woman in Paris, dyes her dog blue to match her outfit. It dies shortly afterwards.

1916: Mary, a performing elephant in Sparks World Famous Circus, Tennessee, turns on circus employee Red Eldridge, throwing him to the ground and stamping on his head.* After erroneous newspaper accounts claim that "Murderous Mary" has killed at least eight men, circus owners face a customer boycott and agree to a public lynching by crane. The first attempt to string Mary up is thwarted by a broken chain, but at the second attempt the animal struggles for several minutes before death by strangulation. The spectacle is watched by 3,000 people, including local children who were given time off school to watch.

1940: the very first bomb dropped on Berlin by the Allies kills the only elephant in Berlin Zoo.

1941: Hollywood actor Errol Flynn is upset by the discovery that his dog Arno has fallen overboard from his yacht and drowned. Gossip columnist Jimmie Fidler accuses him of negligence. Flynn encounters Fidler in a nightclub and beats him up, while Fidler's wife joins in and stabs the star in

---

* A post-mortem on the elephant revealed that the attack on Eldridge was probably triggered by a jaw infection.

the ear with a fork. Flynn's form with animal welfare is spotty; he once reportedly glued a dog's eyes shut and clipped his parrot's wings then put it in a hot tub to watch it dance.

1970: the Royal Canadian Mounted Police pioneer the use of gerbils to sniff out drugs in Canadian prisons. Despite a high success rate, the project is abandoned due to (a) the high number of suspicious deaths among the gerbils while sniffing around the drug-dealing prisoners and (b) the lingering smell of gerbil urine.

1974: makers of the horror flick *The Texas Chain Saw Massacre* take dead dogs and cats from a pet cemetery. The set makeup artist is instructed to pump them full of formaldehyde so they will last long enough to film.

1987: Spanish animal lovers unite to outlaw the practice of donkey squashing. Their petition calls for the end of a Mardi Gras fiesta in Villanueva de la Vera, in which the town's fattest man rides an old donkey to its death. Ropes are tied around the animal's neck and, when it falls or trips, revellers yank it to its feet. When the donkey can no longer walk, youths join the fat man and jump on it until it dies. Petitioners also seek bans on other fiesta events including hurling drunken bulls off cliffs, stoning roosters, slashing bulls with scissors and darts and decapitating live chickens.

1997: Canadian Peter Lerat is arrested after threatening to hit a two-month-old racoon on the head with a rock if Toronto pedestrians don't hand over their cash. Lerat was arrested earlier after he walked into a local doughnut shop carrying a Canada goose and threatened to break its neck unless someone gave him money. The bandit released the goose after a customer stumped up.

1999: stung by public outrage, KLM Royal Dutch Airlines apologizes for using a shredding machine to kill 440 Chinese squirrels shipped illegally to the Netherlands.

2000: at a museum in Denmark, Chilean artist Marco Evaristti displays an exhibit featuring ten Moulinex Optiblend 2000 blenders containing live goldfish. Visitors are invited to turn on the blenders. The museum director is charged with animal cruelty, but acquitted when a court rules that liquidizing goldfish is not a crime.

2010: Charlie, the smoking chimp, dies at Bloemfontein Zoo, South Africa. The ape picked up his twenty-a-day habit from visitors who would throw lit cigarettes to him through his bars.

2012: the British Army admits to routinely shooting live pigs with high-velocity weapons to give their medics something to practise on for battlefield surgery. The exercise is called Operation Danish Bacon.

ROCK 'N' ROLL TAXONOMY: 12 SPECIES NAMED AFTER MUSICIANS

1. Lizard *Barbaturea morrisini*
   (Jim Morrison)

2. Trapdoor spider *Aptostichus bonoi*
   (Bono)

3. Spider *Heteropoda davidbowie*
   (David Bowie)

4. Horsefly *Scaptia beyonceae*
   (Beyoncé)

5. Parasitic crustacean *Gnathia marleyi*
   (Bob Marley)

6. Wasp *Aleiodeas gaga*
   (Lady Gaga)

7. Hermit crab *Medoparapylocheles michaeljacksoni*
   (Michael Jackson)

8. Crustacean *Cirolana mercuryi*
   (Freddie Mercury)

9. Extinct marine arthropod *Aegrotocatellus jaggeri*
   (Mick Jagger)

10. Mite *Funkotriplogynium iagobadius*
    (James Brown)

11. Gall wasp *Preseucoila imallshookupis*
    (Elvis Presley)

12. Colombian tree frog *Hyla stingi*
    (Sting)

DEAD PIG WALKING:
10 ANIMAL TRIALS

AD 146: the Greek historian Polybius reports that he and Scipio Aemilianus, who destroyed Carthage in AD 146, saw two man-eating lions being crucified as a deterrent to other lions.

AD 864: the Council of Worms passes the death sentence on a swarm of bees that has stung a man to death.

1394: a court in Orne, France, sentences a pig to death for blasphemy after it wanders into a church and helps itself to the Holy Wafers.

1457: in Savigny-sur-Etang, France, a sow and her six piglets are caught in the act of killing a five-year-old boy; all seven pigs are imprisoned and tried for the murder. The sow is found guilty and sentenced to be hanged by her hind legs from a gallows tree, but her offspring are pardoned, owing to their youth and the bad example set by their mother.

1474: in front of a large crowd, a cock is burned at the stake in Basle "for the heinous and unnatural crime of laying an egg" that, if hatched, would yield a basilisk (an egg useful in witchcraft).

1544: a flock of swallows is sentenced to death in Germany for disrupting churchgoers with their chirping and in particular for annoying Egbert, Bishop of Trie; the birds "sacrilegiously defiled his head and vestments with their droppings when he was officiating at the altar".

1610: several rabid dogs attack and kill a Franciscan novice. In spite of a plea by the defence council of mitigating circumstances – i.e. their insanity – they are sentenced to death.

1926: while working as a police officer for the British colonial government in Burma, George Orwell passes the death sentence on a domestic elephant that went "rogue" and killed a man by stepping on him. Orwell later describes the incident in his essay "Shooting an Elephant" noting, "The friction of the great beast's foot had stripped the skin from his back as neatly as one skins a rabbit."

1924: Pep, a Labrador retriever, is accused of killing Pennsylvania Governor Gifford Pinchot's cat. The dog is tried without the assistance of defence counsel in a proceeding led by the Governor himself. Governor Pinchot finds Pep guilty and sentences the dog to life imprisonment in the Philadelphia State Penitentiary. Pep dies in prison of natural causes six years later.

1925: in Indiana, local authorities arrest a chimpanzee for smoking a cigarette in public. The chimp is found guilty and fined five dollars.

RAINING CATS AND DOGS: 10 PEOPLE KILLED BY FALLING ANIMALS

455 BC: the Greek playwright Aeschylus is hit on the head by a falling tortoise, dropped by an eagle. He had been staying outdoors to avoid a prophecy that he would be killed by a falling object.

162 BC: Eleazar Maccabeus is crushed to death in battle by a war elephant that is thought to be carrying the enemy leader King Antiochus V. Maccabeus nips underneath the animal and spears its belly; it promptly falls dead on top of him.

1131: Crown Prince Philip of France is thrown while riding through Paris when his horse trips over a black pig running out of a dung heap. The horse topples onto the prince, crushing him to death.

1834: in the Rockies, short-sighted Scottish botanist David Douglas stumbles into a hole dug to trap wild animals; a bull falls in after him, trampling Douglas to death.

1991: South African jogger Victor Villenti dies when an 8 lb leg of frozen lamb, placed on a third-storey window ledge to defrost, drops on his head. He and his entire family were vegetarians.

2002: Seventeen-year-old warehouse worker Paul Langfield

is unable to jump out of the way in time when a ton of frozen chicken topples off a forklift truck in South Yorkshire.

2008: a man from Massachusetts is found dead from carbon monoxide poisoning in his home. It transpires that a dead racoon had fallen down the chimney flue and blocked it, allowing poisonous gases to build up.

2011: an abattoir worker from Paisley, Scotland, dies when a dead cow falls on him. Alexander McCrae has worked at the abattoir for only one month when a carcass slips from a hook on a conveyor system and strikes him on the head.

2011: in Pennsylvania a woman is killed when a deer, struck by another vehicle, flies through her windscreen. Seventy-year-old Rosemary Bower is heading east when a westbound car strikes a deer that has run onto the road; the impact cuts the animal in half, catapulting the head and shoulders into the car, killing the driver.

2013: Joao Maria de Souza is in bed with his wife Leni when a cow plummets through the ceiling of their home in Caratinga, southeast Brazil. The cow had escaped from a nearby farm and climbed onto the roof of the couple's house, which backs onto a steep hill, only for the corrugated roof to give way sending the one-and-a-half-ton animal onto Mr de Souza's side of the bed.

15 CELEBRITY PETS

1. When he wasn't drinking burgundy from a human skull or consorting with choirboys, Lord Byron dealt with the tedium of undergraduate life at Cambridge by keeping a pet bear in his room.

2. King George IV had a giraffe, a diplomatic gift from Mehmit Ali, Pasha of Egypt. The giraffe was permanently crippled by her journey from Egypt, carried on the back of a camel with her legs lashed together under the camel's body. At Windsor Castle she was doted on and fed cow's milk, but she struggled to walk, so a huge triangular structure on wheels was constructed into which the giraffe was strapped each day and trundled round her paddock with her hooves just touching the ground. Despite the kindness, two years after her arrival in England, the giraffe died. The king, who was said to be obsessed with his giraffe, was distraught and commissioned the taxidermist John Gould to stuff it.

3. The philosopher Jeremy Bentham had a cat called the Reverend Sir John Langbourne that he fed macaroni. When the cat died, Bentham gave it a good burial in his garden, unlike his own body which he donated to science and invited his friends round to watch it being dissected.

4. Rembrandt had a pet monkey called Puck. When it died Rembrandt was heartbroken and immortalized Puck by painting his corpse into the portrait of a family he was

working on. His patrons protested and threatened to withdraw the commission unless Rembrandt removed the offending dead monkey. Rembrandt refused and kept the painting, monkey included.

5. D. H. Lawrence had a favourite horse called Aaron. When it died the author had it made into a duffel bag.

6. Charles Dickens had a pet raven called Grip. When Grip died in 1841, Dickens couldn't bear to part with it so he had him stuffed and mounted in a glass case to display in his study.

7. The Nazi Luftwaffe chief Hermann Goering had a pet lion called Caesar. It was allowed to roam freely around his home and often urinated on the floor, which Goering found highly amusing.

8. The Ethiopian ruler Haile Selassie had a favourite Pekingese dog called Lulu that urinated on the shoes of visiting dignitaries. It stopped doing this when one of the Emperor's other dogs, a German shepherd, broke Lulu's neck.

9. The Satanist Aleister Crowley killed his cat to see if it had nine lives. He recalled in his book *Confessions*, "I administered a large dose of arsenic, I chloroformed it, hanged it above the gas jet, stabbed it, cut its throat, smashed its skull and, when it had been pretty thoroughly burnt, drowned it and threw it out of the window that the fall might remove the ninth life."

10. Winston Churchill had many pets but one of his favourites was a green parakeet named Toby. When Churchill was writing his memoirs, he was often seen at his desk with Toby on his head. During a trip to Monte Carlo in

1960, Toby flew out of an open window and was never seen again.

11. Andy Warhol had several Siamese cats, all named Sam.

12. Salvador Dalí had a pet ocelot called Babou, who often accompanied the artist on trips to restaurants. One day an alarmed female diner berated Dalí for taking a wild animal into the restaurant. He told her that the ocelot was, in fact, a cat and that he had painted it to make it look "op-art". Reassured, she got on with her meal.

13. The actress Sarah Bernhardt had a pet alligator named Ali-Gaga, but it died after she fed it too much milk and champagne. She also had a boa constrictor but she shot it when it ate her cushions.

14. Sigmund Freud had a beloved chow called Lün. Freud smoked up to twenty cigars a day and it gave him mouth and jaw cancer, for which he underwent a series of painful operations. By 1939 his rotting jawbone created such a terrible smell that, to his great distress, his dog refused to go near him.

15. Princess Anne had a bull terrier called Dotty. She was fined after it bit two children in a park: it was destroyed after it attacked and killed the Queen's favourite corgi.

DOGS' DINNERS: 5 PEOPLE WHO BECAME PET FOOD

1. In the Old Testament, Jezebel was the daughter of Ethbaal, King of the Phoenicians, and one of the wives of Ahab, King of North Israel. For transgressions against God, she was thrown out of a window by members of her own court and was eaten by stray dogs. All that was left was her skull, feet and hands.

2. The Canadian actress Marie Prevost began her acting career as a bathing beauty in Mack Sennett comedies, but her career began to slide after a series of forgettable films. She started to gain weight and hit the bottle. In 1937 workers broke into her apartment after hearing her dog barking incessantly for two days and found her lifeless body. She had been partially eaten by her dachshund, Maxie.

3. In 1999 in Greenville, Tennessee, a dachshund ate three of his owner's toes while he slept. Charles Golden woke up to find he was missing his big left toe and the two adjoining toes. Golden didn't have much feeling in his feet because he was diabetic.

4. In 2002 Ronald Huff's fascination with lizards came to a grisly end when police found his cold-blooded pets feasting on his corpse in Newark, Delaware. Huff, who

kept seven Nile monitor lizards, was killed by a single bite from a Komodo dragon that he allowed to roam free in his apartment.

5. In 2009 a Florida couple Jaren Hare and her boyfriend Charles Darnell found Hare's two-year-old daughter Shaianna dead in her cot with their albino Burmese python, Gypsy, coiled tightly around her and its fangs embedded in her forehead. The serpent, eight foot six in length, hadn't been fed for a month.

CHAPTER SEVEN

The Wonder of You

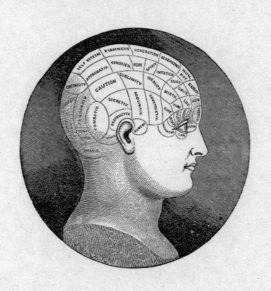

BECAUSE YOU'RE WORTH IT: 12 HISTORIC BEAUTY TIPS

1550 BC: to give their hair volume and bounce, Egyptians apply honey and crushed donkey teeth daily. The menstrual blood of a female dog will remove unwanted hair and crushed dog genitals will stop your hair turning grey.

400 BC: crocodile dung is good for giving women's faces a bright and shining complexion. Some dealers deceitfully sell the droppings of starlings fed on rice as a cheap imitation.

c. 330 BC: Aristophanes offers this advice to ladies about pubic hair maintenance: "Pluck and trim your doorways like good spiders and the flies will come walking in."

c. AD 70: to make black hair dye, says Pliny the Elder, drown a dozen or more leeches in red wine, then let them rot for forty days.

1582: get rid of persistent warts – trap a live mole, punch it in the face and allow blood from its nose to drip onto the affected areas.

1586: Italian Gaspare Tagliacozzi, considered the "father of modern plastic surgery", creates a "virtual" nose for syphilis sufferers. Beware, however: it can fall off if the user blows too hard.

1598: Christopher Wirtzung's health book★ tells ladies to remove unsightly body hair by drowning twenty green frogs in wine. Leave them in the warm sun for forty days, strain through a cloth and apply liberally.

1664: Samuel Pepys notes in his diary that his wife is using the fashionable cosmetic of the day, "puppy water", made from the urine of a young dog. Good for removing wrinkles, tightening and lightening the skin and eradicating blemishes, it works best when blended with "a pint of fasting spittle", i.e. saliva collected from a person or persons who has not eaten for several days.

1693: ladies, to keep the man in your life keen, wash your genitals then use the water to make him a drink of hot chocolate.

1837: a Victorian beauty therapist warns young ladies to avoid reading books, especially "difficult" or "masculine" titles, or they will risk losing their looks.

1842: American girls eat paper to acquire fashionably pale skin. Travel writer James Buckingham reports: "Many sheets are sometimes eaten in a day . . . this is persisted in till the natural appetite for wholesome food is superseded by a depraved and morbid desire for everything but that which is nutritious."

1962: breast implants grow in popularity, especially among

★ Snappily titled *The General Practise of Physick. Containing All inward and outward parts of the body, with all the accidents and infirmities that are incident unto them, even from the crown of the head to the sole of the foot. Also by what means (with the help of God) they may be remedied: very meet and profitable, not only for all physicians, chirurgions, apothecaries, and midwives, but for all other estates whatsoever; the like whereof as yet in English hath not been published.*

showgirls who inject their breasts with liquid silicone, despite dangerous side effects, such as amputation of the breast due to infection and guaranteed "pendulous" breasts by the time they reach forty. It is a technique first used in Japan in the early 1900s to plump out legs withered by polio.

SEEING RED:
12 DISTURBING FACTS
ABOUT GINGERISM

1. In ancient Egypt, redheads were buried alive as sacrifices to the god Osiris.

2. Judas Iscariot, the Apostle who betrayed Jesus for thirty silver coins, was often portrayed in medieval paintings with flaming hair and a red beard. It was probably only done to make the traitor stand out from the other Apostles in paintings, but it contributed to several centuries of discrimination against "untrustworthy" redheads.

3. The ancient Greeks believed that redheads would turn into vampires after they died.

4. According to a French proverb, "redheaded women are either violent or false, and usually are both." A Russian proverb warns that "there was never a saint with red hair".

5. In the Middle Ages, a child with red hair was assumed to have been conceived through "unclean sex" or during menstruation.

6. In Scotland during the reign of King James VI, women could be condemned as witches and burned at the stake simply for having red hair. Flame-coloured hair was evidence that its owner had stolen the fire of hell.

7. According to George Chapman's 1613 play *Bussy D'Ambois*, the perfect poison is made from the fat of a red-haired man.

8. In the seventeenth century, doctors advised against breast-feeding if the woman had red hair because "their milk is hot, sharp and stinking" and "of an ill taste".

9. The nineteenth-century Italian expert on criminology Cesare Lombroso said that red hair was associated with crimes of lust; he claimed that 48 per cent of "criminal women" were redheads.

10. In November 2008 Facebook had a "Kick a Ginger" group, which aimed to establish a "National Kick a Ginger Day" on 20 November; it acquired almost 5,000 members.

11. After several complaints from customers, in December 2009 Tesco withdrew a Christmas card that showed a child with red hair sitting on the lap of Santa Claus and the words: "Santa loves all kids. Even ginger ones."

12. In September 2011 one of the world's largest sperm banks, Cryos International, stopped accepting donations from ginger men because of low demand from women seeking artificial insemination from ginger donors.

16 FASHION STATEMENTS

c. 1450 BC: on special occasions, the Egyptian Queen Hatshepsut wears her false beard to emphasize her manliness.

1323 BC: Egyptian ruler King Tutankhamen is buried with 145 pairs of underpants.

60 BC: like many Romans of the day, the great orator Cicero washes his clothes in urine, collected in jars left around the city for people to pee in. Consequently, he always smells faintly of piss.

c. 1042: Harold Godwinson, later King Harold II of England, has the first of several tattoos. They come in useful for identifying his badly mutilated body after the Battle of Hastings in 1066.

1514: King Henry VIII shows off his new massive codpiece. A courtier notes that it is "lined with red and hung open like a maidenhead at full stretch".

1547: Italian sculptor Silvio Cosini flays a corpse for study, then makes himself a new waistcoat from the discarded skin.

1601: Isabella, daughter of King Phillip II of Spain, vows that she will not change her underwear until the siege of Ostend ends. Unfortunately, the siege lasts over three years, by which time her white shift had turned brown.

1654: the French mathematician Blaise Pascal wears stockings soaked in brandy to keep his feet warm; curiously, this does not appear to harm his reputation as a philanderer.

1672: the French King Louis XIV, who was only five feet three inches tall, wears red high heels around Versailles. Soon, red high heels are a symbol of status across Europe.

1800: King John VI of Portugal has a favourite coat, which he refuses to change even when it wears out: his chamberlains have to sew repairs on his body while he sleeps in it.

1850: fashionable Victorian gentlemen wear tie pins made from badgers' penises.

1867: Queen Alexandra, wife of Edward VII, is left slightly lame in one leg after an illness. It quickly becomes the fashion among ladies at court to imitate her limp.

1889: Sarah Bernhardt shows off her new hat featuring a stuffed bat.

1890: at his inaugural ball, the new governor of Wyoming, Dr John Eugene Osbourne, sports a pair of leather winklepicker shoes, made from the skin of hanged stagecoach robber George "Big Nose" Parrott. Osborne is, however, disappointed that Parrott's nipples weren't on the tips of the toes, as he'd requested.

1919: Adolf Hitler's close associate Ernst Hanfstaengl tells Adolf that his toothbrush moustache is passé. Hitler replies: "It might not be the fashion now, but it will be later because I'm wearing it."

1931: Nazi chief Heinrich Himmler asks fellow Nazi Hugo Boss to design his soldiers a uniform that will inspire fear in men and "success with girls". Hugo comes up with a natty black uniform, set off nicely with a silver death's-head hat motif. By 1938 the Hugo Boss label is working exclusively for the German military machine and using slave labour to meet the high demand.

PLUMBING THE DEPTHS
10 TOILET TRIVIA CLASSICS

1. The earliest-known guidelines on human waste disposal came from Moses in the Old Testament. Although it didn't make it into the Ten Commandments, he advised his people to bury their shit well away from the campsite.

2. Most British toilets flush in the key of E flat.

3. The Cretan Palace of Knossos has been described as "a plumbers' paradise". From around 1650 BC it had an extensive system of drains, fresh water pipes and settling tanks. Sadly, this technology was lost for thousands of years and Crete is much less well equipped today.

4. Medieval monks wiped their arses with shards of pottery; King Louis XIV used lace.

5. In 1596 Queen Elizabeth I's godson Sir John Harrington installed his new invention, a flushing loo with a cistern, in her palace at Richmond. Harrington was ridiculed for his "offensive" invention and didn't make another one.*

6. Hitchcock's *Psycho* was the first studio movie to show a

---

* It was another 200 years before someone thought of putting an S-shaped pipe underneath the basin to keep out the smell of shit.

flushing toilet. It provoked an outcry among filmgoers who complained it was "indecent".

7. John Nevil Maskelyne was a stage magician, plate-spinner, escapologist and inventor. His patents included a cash register and a typewriter and, in 1892, the coin-operated lock for public lavatories. The first public conveniences in the UK were opened in London in 1852, on 2 February in Fleet Street, for men, and on 10 February in Bedford Street, for women. Inconveniently, it was another thirty-one years before A. Ashwell of Herne Hill, London, patented the Vacant/Engaged sign.

8. Before toilet paper, sailors used the frayed end of a rope; they all used the same rope.

9. Neither Shakespeare nor Jane Austen used the word lavatory. However, Longfellow, in his *Hyperion*, produced the memorable line: "On a lavatory below sat a cherub."

10. Adolf Hitler's lavatory seat was liberated in the dying days of World War II by an American soldier, Sergeant Ragnvald Borch. It was removed from the Führer's Berghof residence en-suite, so it probably saw action from the dictator on a daily basis.*

---

* This is not the only toilet memento from the Turd Reich. Greg Kohfeldt, a garage owner in New Jersey, claims to be in possession of an entire toilet taken from Hitler's private yacht.

8 DODGY DIVINATION TECHNIQUES

1. Phrenology: character reading by the shape of your skull. Created by the German physician Franz Joseph Gall, it was very popular in nineteenth-century Europe and in the United States. In 1852 James W. Redfield published his *Comparative Physiognomy* illustrated with 330 engravings showing "Resemblances between Men and Animals". For example, "Germans to Lions", "Negroes to Elephants and Fishes", "Chinamen to Hogs", "Yankees to Bears" and "Jews to Goats".

2. Gastromancy: fortune-telling by listening to noises made by the stomach.

3. Metoposcopy: interpretation of facial wrinkles, especially those on the forehead. The technique was invented by sixteenth-century mathematician Girolamo Cardano, who identified about 800 facial wrinkles each associated with astrological signs and qualities of temperament and character. Long, straight furrows indicate nobility of character, three curved furrows on the forehead indicate a "dissolute simpleton".

4. Omphalomancy: a form of divination in which the number of knots in a newborn's umbilical cord are counted to foretell the number of children the mother will have.

5. Moleosophy: fortune-telling by the position of moles on your body. A mole on the right-hand side of the forehead is said to be indicative of talent and success; on the left it indicates stubbornness and an extravagant personality. A mole on the right knee predicts a happy marriage; on the left knee it means a bad temper. Moles on the buttocks indicate a lack of ambition. Bad news if you have a mole on the back of the throat; it signifies that you will be beheaded.

6. Onychomancy: fortune-telling by examining fingernails.

7. Rumpology: fortune-telling or character reading by examining buttocks. According to rumpologists, your left and right buttocks reveal your past and future respectively and the crack of your behind corresponds to the division of the two hemispheres of the brain. An apple-shaped, muscular bottom indicates someone who is charismatic, dynamic, very confident and often creative. A pear-shaped bottom suggests someone very steadfast, patient and down-to-earth. A flat bottom suggests the person is rather vain and is negative and sad.*

8. Mammarism: fortune-telling or character assessment from the crinkles around nipples. It was invented around 1940 by an Irish-American "Professor" Patrick Cullen who claimed he could "read" women's breasts by patting them, a technique he perfected in the brothels of Shanghai during a twenty-six-year career in the army.

---

* The American rumpologist Jackie Stallone, mother of Sylvester, predicted the outcome of Presidential elections and Oscar awards by reading the bottoms of her two pet Doberman Pinschers. The blind German rumpologist Ulf Buck meanwhile claims he can read people's futures by feeling their naked buttocks.

Female clients who were uncomfortable with the process could opt to take the readings themselves in the back room of his studio in Brighton while Cullen kept in touch by two-way radio and a peep-hole in wall. He also developed the "silhouette method" of determining whether a woman was a virgin, another art he claimed to have learned in the Far East. This involved holding a sheet against a woman's naked body while it was silhouetted against a bright light.

10 FLATOLOGICAL FACTS*

1. According to St Augustine, writing in the fifth century, men used to "have such command of their bowels, that they can break wind continuously at will, so as to produce the effect of singing". We lost this ability because Adam and Eve sinned.†

2. The ancient Romans thought that a stifled fart was a health hazard because the vapours went straight to your brain. In AD 41, Emperor Claudius made it lawful to break wind at the table, either silently or noisily, after hearing about a man who had almost died by holding one in.

3. Farting was blamed for the deaths of thousands of people in first-century Jerusalem. A Roman soldier let one rip to express his disgust at the Jews and it triggered a riot that left about 10,000 dead.

4. The first appearance of a fart in English literature was in an anonymously written poem about the arrival of summer, written around 1250. *The Cuckoo Song* features the line "the bull leaped, the stag farted".

5. Richard Jobson, explorer of the Gambia River in the early seventeenth century, reported that members of the

---

* Flatology is the scientific study of farting.
† St Augustine claimed to have known someone who had such great control over his wind that he could fart poetry.

Ashanti tribe were always careful never to break wind in company. He reported that an old man of the tribe accidentally farted as he bowed to the chief and was so embarrassed by his breach of etiquette that he went away and hanged himself.

6. Vaginal flatulence is otherwise known as a queef. Unlike rectal gases, vaginal farts are odourless.

7. Queen Victoria and Adolf Hitler both suffered from chronic flatulence. Empress Eugenie, wife of the French leader Napoleon III, was incapable of suppressing her farts in company. The French leader General Charles de Gaulle blamed his frequent farting on his love of offal dishes.

8. In January 2011 the Malawi government tried to pass a law making it illegal to fart in public.*

9. If you work in an office, on a daily average you will inhale one litre of other people's farts.

10. In 2009 a *Britain's Got Talent* contestant failed to progress to the next stage by farting in tune to "The Blue Danube". Simon Cowell described him as "a vile, disgusting creature".

---

* The government minister who made the announcement backed down in the face of much mockery by the Malawi press.

THE ORIGIN OF FAECES: 10 SHIT FACTS

1. Sterculinus was the Roman god of manure.

2. Human excrement in a dried, powdered form known as poudrette was inhaled as snuff by the noble ladies of the eighteenth-century French court.

3. Two US presidents, Thomas Jefferson and James K. Polk, died from diarrhoea.

4. Seventeenth-century followers of the Dalai Lama worshipped his faeces, which were put in golden boxes and treated as holy relics.

5. Christian Franz Paullini, a seventeenth-century German physician, compiled a stool recipe book for treating digestive ailments. He advised pregnant women to prepare for childbirth by eating "the excrements of her husband, warm and smoking".

6. The seventeenth-century King of Bhutan was so revered by his subjects that they used his dried turds as a condiment with meat dishes.

7. Mozart Amadeus Mozart was obsessed with shit. There are more than two dozen letters he sent to his wife, his father and other members of his family in which he

mentions faeces, including these lines sent to his cousin
Maria:

> *Well, I wish you good night*
> *But first shit into your bed and make it burst.*
> *Sleep soundly, my love*
> *Into your mouth your arse you'll shove.*

8. Stool examination was once an important diagnostic
   tool used by doctors and was still popular well into the
   late 1900s.* London's Wellcome Library has an engrav-
   ing of a doctor examining a bedpan and a maid asking
   him if he'd like a fork.

9. The religious reformer Martin Luther ate a spoonful of
   his own faeces every day for his health. He said he was
   impressed by the generosity of a God who gave away
   such important medicine freely.

10. Burglars often defecate at the scene of their crimes.†
    The ritual isn't reported very often because the victims
    often don't want to talk about it.

---

* The perfect stool is log-like and S-shaped, not broken up into pieces.
The secret of achieving the ideal turd shape is to eat fibre, which lends
bulk to the stool and acts as a glue to keep it together.
† In one documented incident in 1908, a burglar named Demeter
Radek was re-arrested after breaking and entering, defecating inside
and wiping himself with his own parole papers.

10 BAD HAIR DAYS

692: the Pope bans wigs because God's blessing can't get through the hairpiece and into the head.

1305: the French physician Bernard de Gordon warns men against excessive lovemaking, as it will overheat the skull and cause rapid hair loss.

1567: Hans Steininger of Branau, Austria, sports a beard that's four foot six in length; he usually keeps it rolled up in a leather pouch. However, while escaping from a fire, he dies after tripping over his extravagant whiskers and breaking his neck.

1610: King Christian IV of Denmark sports a Polish plait – a crusty, oily mass of filthy, matted hair held together by dried blood, dirt and dead lice. He trains it into the shape of a pigtail down the left side of his head: it soon becomes *de rigueur* in his court to follow suit.*

1833: Texan settler Josiah P. Wilbarger is one of a party of four who are attacked by Comanches. Scalped and left for dead, Wilbarger makes a miraculous recovery and, although his skull never heals, leaving him with a partly exposed brain,

---

* Generally, Polish plaits were the result of neglect, but they could also be brought on by lice infestations, in which the spent eggs would act as a kind of mortar. This condition was especially common among the Polish peasantry, who superstitiously believed it brought good health. Peasants would spread fat on their plaits, which they tucked under woollen hats.

he lives a full and normal life for another eleven years, right up to the day he bangs his head on a low beam in his house.

1905: German hairdresser Karl Nessler develops a new type of permanent wave using diluted cow urine and an electric heating device. He practises his technique on his wife, Katharina. The first two attempts completely remove her hair, leaving scalp burns.

2002: a mother is charged with first-degree murder, accused of leaving her children to die inside her sweltering car while she goes to have her hair done. The two children, ten months and three years old, are left alone in her black unventilated car for more than three hours.

2003: a man working in an amusement park dies when his long hair gets caught in a roller coaster, pulling him 40 ft in the air then dropping him onto a fence. Doug McKay is spraying lubricant on the tracks of the Super Loop 2 at the Island County Fair in Langley, Washington, when he is scalped by a car full of fairgoers.

2009: the world's longest ear hair, sported by Indian grocer Radhakant Baijpai, measures 9.8 inches (25 cm). Considered by Radhakant to be a symbol of luck and prosperity, he notes: "God has been very kind to me."

2010: Jenny Mitchell, a nineteen-year-old hairdresser, is killed when her car explodes. Fumes caused by chemicals mixing with hydrogen peroxide leaking from a bottle of hair bleach ignites when she lights up a cigarette.

7 STEPS FOR MAKING A SHRUNKEN HEAD*

1. Remove the head of your victim.

2. Open the skin up from the base of the neck to the crown.

3. Remove the skull.

4. Dip the skin into a vegetable extract.

5. Sew up the skin along the neck to restore the head to its original form.

6. Fill the neck cavity with hot sand or pebbles and leave to dry out. Turn the head for several days so that the drying process is uniform until the finished head is about the size of a man's fist.

7. Sew the lips shut with a series of long cotton cords. The exact pattern of this stitching will vary according to your locality.

---

* According to *National Geographic*, October 1921.

12 TOILET HABITS

1. The Roman Emperor Elagabalus always defecated into a golden goblet.

2. The Italian composer Carlo Gesualdo had himself beaten daily by his servants, but employed a special servant whose duty it was to beat him "at stool".

3. The French Bourbon kings routinely held audiences while using the toilet. Louis XIII had a commode under his throne; his court jester noted that, while the king preferred to eat in privacy, he chose to shit in public.

4. Queen Elizabeth I's commode was a basic box with a lid. She had it covered in crimson velvet trimmed with lace.

5. In the Georgian royal court of England it was fashionable to squat over a "bourdaloue" – a small jug like a gravy boat that you clenched between your thighs.* Privacy was not essential; the French ambassador's wife annoyed her hosts with "the frequency and quantity of her pissing which she does not fail to do at least ten times a day amongst a cloud of witnesses". But if the queen didn't give you permission to go, you just had to cross your legs.

6. Rather than allow her staff to buy toilet paper, Queen

---

* Possibly named after the preacher Louis Bourdaloue, who was famous for his very long sermons.

Victoria ordered all the free magazines and newspapers sent to her various palaces to be cut up into squares.

7. The poet W. H. Auden only ever allowed his house guests one sheet of toilet paper each.

8. China's Mao Zedong disliked flushing toilets. He preferred to wander through the gardens of his Beijing compound and defecate on the grass. The Chinese leader frequently suffered from painful constipation: after finally relieving himself after a nine-day blockage, there was national rejoicing and widespread chants of "the chairman's bowels have moved!"

9. The Italian tenor Mario Lanza was famous for urinating in public; on the set, or in the wings, or on one occasion, in a bucket in full view of the audience.

10. The *Carry On* films actor Kenneth Williams always insisted on taking his own personal toilet paper with him when he went to the theatre. He made his house guests use the nearby public toilet at Tottenham Court Road tube station.

11. Whenever the Queen is on a royal visit, for example during the construction of a new building, special lavatorial arrangements are made in case she is caught short. She doesn't like other people to overhear her, so engineers are summoned to drain the offending water and replace it with straw, so she can pee and flush in silence.

12. Prince Charles has a servant to fold down his toilet seat. It is just another everyday chore he never need worry about. The Prince's servants also squeeze his toothpaste onto his brush for him, pick up his discarded

clothes from the floor and hold the specimen bottle when the Prince has to produce a urine sample. Unlike Henry VIII, however, he doesn't have someone to wipe his arse.

PENISES: 10 HARD FACTS

1. Only one man in every 400 is flexible enough to perform fellatio on himself.

2. Smoking can shorten the penis by up to a centimetre. It calcifies blood vessels, which in turn impedes erectile circulation.

3. Men who have been hanged can get a "death erection" also known as "angel lust".

4. On average, a man will ejaculate 7,200 times during his lifetime. The average speed of ejaculation is twenty-eight miles per hour.

5. A man has an average of eleven erections per day and nine at night.

6. There are at least forty-two kinds of bacteria living on the skin of the penis.

7. Doctors can grow skin for burn victims using the foreskins of circumcised infants. One infant foreskin can produce 23,000 square metres of human flesh.

8. The most common cause of penile rupture is excessively vigorous masturbation.

9. Iceland has the world's only penis museum. It houses 280 specimens from ninety-three species; the largest is a

five-foot-seven penis of a sperm whale; the smallest is a hamster penis measuring less than 2 mm.

10. English euphemisms for "penis" include anaconda, bacon bazooka, baloney pony, bell on a pole, cock, chopper, cum gun, deep V diver, dick, ding-a-ling, disco stick, Excalibur, fanny battering ram, fuck pole, jimmy, joy stick, lamb cannon, love muscle, meat stick, mutton bayonet, pink cigar, pink oboe, pork sword, prick, schlong, skin flute, spit stick, third leg, trouser snake, spam javelin, wang, wick, yard and yogurt gun.

CHAPTER EIGHT

God's Mysterious Ways

13 THINGS YOU WON'T LEARN ABOUT IN BIBLE CLASS

1. The Old Testament Lord says (Deuteronomy 23:1), "He whose testicles are crushed or whose male member is cut off shall not enter the assembly of the Lord." Rabbis were expected to prove their parts were in working order before they could work in a temple.

2. In the Old Testament (I Samuel 18) Saul sent his prospective son-in-law David to bring him a hundred Philistine foreskins before he consented to his daughter's hand in marriage. David busts a gut and collects 200.

3. In the Old Testament, puking is a sign of innocence in criminal proceedings.*

4. In some countries, nativity scenes feature a caganer – a small figure with his trousers down, showing a bare backside and in the process of having a shit.† Apparently, this is very popular in parts of Spain, France, Italy and Portugal.

5. God hates baldness. The Old Testament contains

---

* Except for Oscar Pistorius, who threw up in court when he saw what his dum dum bullets had done to his girlfriend.
† The name "El Caganer" literally means "the crapper" or "the shitter".

countless references as to how He will make Israel's enemies lose their hair. According to Revelations, at the end of the world, God will render select groups of evil people bald.

6. The Dead Sea Scrolls were written by a Jewish sect who were so holy they didn't believe in defecating on the Sabbath.

7. In Ezekiel 4:12–15, God offers a cookery tip to Ezekiel; He tells him to use human excrement as fuel to cook bread, rather than the usual animal dung mixed with straw. When Ezekiel protests, God generously allows him to use cow dung instead.

8. The Old Testament mentions unicorns, satyrs (men with goat legs), cockatrices (rooster-serpents that kill when you look at them) and a race of giants who survived the Great Flood; Noah made room for all of them on the Ark.

9. The Old Testament outlined various ways in which women and girls could be sold into sexual slavery. For example, a Hebrew is allowed to sell his daughter to another Hebrew, but that man, in turn, was not allowed to re-sell her to a foreigner.

10. God had several face-offs with other gods, which of course He won hands down. For example, in His triumph over the god Baal, there is a contest in which the winner is the first god to set fire to a pile of wood. His pile goes up in flames first of course, despite it being drenched with water.

11. According to Deuteronomy, it is okay to rape a Hebrew girl provided you then purchase her for fifty shekels

(about £360) from her family and take her as a wife; then you can rape her for as long as you like. Deuteronomy lays out strict rules about capturing a virgin and forcing her to be your wife: she's allowed to mourn her dead parents for a whole month before you rape her.

12. The word "buttocks" occurs only three times in the King James Bible: once each in the Second Book of Samuel, the First Book of Chronicles and the Book of Isaiah. There are no buttocks in the New Testament.

13. In Deuteronomy 23:10–13, the Israelites are instructed to cover up their faeces outside their encampment, because God is inclined to stroll around at night and He doesn't want to step in any of their poo.

20 DEAD POPES

1. Peter I (*c.* 68): crucified upside by the Roman Emperor Nero.

2. Callixtus I (223): murdered by a rioting mob and thrown down a well.

3. Anastasius II (498): "sent down his intestines" while defecating.

4. Martin I (654): died in exile of "malnutrition and related causes".

5. Steven II (752): had a stroke three days after his election.

6. John VIII (882): poisoned then beaten to death with a hammer.

7. Steven VI (896): strangled during a prison riot.

8. Leo V (903): after reigning for just a month, murdered in prison by his successor.

9. John X (928): suffocated with a cushion.

10. John XII (964): either beaten to death by a jealous husband who caught him in bed with his wife or died of a stroke during sex, aged twenty-seven.

11. Benedict VI (974): thrown into prison and later strangled by order of Boniface VII.

12. Lucius III (1145): stoned to death.

13. John XX (1277): crushed to death when the ceiling of the new study he had just had built in the Vatican collapsed on him.

14. Nicholas V (1455): having survived attempted murder, died of complications caused by gout.

15. Pope Paul II (1471): died of a stroke after gorging himself on three watermelons.*

16. Innocent VIII (1492): despite following doctor's orders and drinking several cups of warm fresh blood supplied by three local youths, expired from an unspecified chronic illness.

17. Leo X (1521): died after an anal abscess was dressed with a poisoned bandage.

18. Clement VII (1534): died after eating a death cap mushroom.

19. Urban VII (1590): contracted malaria the day after his election and died twelve days later.

20. Gregory XIV (1591): killed by a huge gallstone said to weigh 70 g.

---

* Many prefer the rumour that he was being sodomized by a well-endowed servant.

12 THINGS NO ONE EXPECTED FROM THE SPANISH INQUISITION

1. Many think of the Spanish Inquisition as *the* Inquisition, but it was only a branch operation. The Inquisition and the hunting down of heretics by the Catholic Church was already nearly 250 years old when the Spanish Inquisition was chartered by the Pope in 1478.

2. The very first victims of the Inquisition were dissident Christians known as the Cathars, who called themselves "Good Christians" and regarded themselves as more authentic than the friars who tortured and burned them. Only when a Jew (or a Muslim) formally converted to Christianity did he or she come under the scrutiny of the Inquisition, on the assumption that most or all of them were still secretly practising their old faiths. A Jewish convert who changed her underwear on Saturdays or a Muslim convert who ordered a plate of couscous in a public tavern were both regarded as suitable for burning at the stake as heretics.

3. In 1483 Pope Sixtus IV appointed Tomás de Torquemada as Grand Inquisitor of Spain. Torquemada was a fan of various forms of torture including foot roasting, the garrucha and suffocation. He invited Spain's Jews to leave the country; those who didn't take up his offer were likely to be arrested and could find out about his

new torture manual first-hand. Evidence that was used to identify a Jew included the absence of chimney smoke on Saturdays (a sign the family might secretly be honouring the Sabbath), buying of too many vegetables before Passover or the purchase of meat from a converted butcher. Suspected Jews were ordered to "confess" and those who refused were brutally tortured by order of Torquemada, who, as it turns out, was from a Jewish family.

4. Officially, the Inquisition never burned witches. In fact, it ruled that witchcraft did not exist and that all people calling themselves witches were simply mad; the Inquisition also denounced witch-hunters. Unfortunately, this did not stop local authorities and groups of angry villagers from rounding up "witches" and burning them anyway.*

5. The Inquisition invented the "Dunce's Cap" – headgear to identify the heretic on his/her way to the stake. It lived on in schools as standard punishment for the classroom nonconformist.

6. Despite rumours of the Spanish Inquisition burning people left, right and centre all over Europe, it was never deployed overseas. Heresy was, however, a convenient excuse in the Netherlands and other countries to remove various politically troublesome individuals.

7. Although there was a list of banned texts, the Inquisition wasn't into book burning. In fact, Torquemada wanted to *save* the books and documents taken in the Conquest of Mexico and South America.

---

* *Malleus Maleficarum*, the definitive guide for witch-hunters written in 1486, described women who stole dozens of penises, then hid them in a tree where they lived like birds in a nest.

8. The phrase "the third degree" is a legacy of the Inquisition. Inquisitors subjected an accused heretic to questioning under torture according to a scale that measured five degrees of severity. The first degree consisted of stripping off his or her clothing and then displaying the instrument of torture to the naked victim. The second degree called for torture to be sustained for a period no longer than it took for the inquisitor to recite a single Ave Maria or Paternoster. The third degree allowed the torturer to torment his victim in earnest and without any time limits. By the fifth degree, the victim was likely to be suffering from broken bones, severe loss of blood and perhaps a limb torn from his or her body.

9. Jane Bohorquia of Seville was put on the rack for discussing Protestantism with a friend. She was pregnant and a week later she died. The Inquisition reported: "Jane Bohorquia was found dead in prison; after which, upon reviewing her prosecution, the Inquisition discovered her innocent. Be it therefore known that no further prosecution shall be carried on against her."

10. The number of victims burned at the stake during the Spanish Inquisition is disputed because many of the records were destroyed or lost. According to Juan Antonio Llorente, secretary to the Inquisition from 1481 to 1517, at least 13,000 were burned alive, 8,700 were burned in effigy (that is, having been previously strangled in prison) and 17,000 condemned to various other punishments. Estimates vary wildly. The Inquisition was formally abolished in 1834, by which time according to some estimates a total of 341,021 had been condemned to death, although some authorities think this was a gross exaggeration and the total was no more than 3,500.

11. The last person to be put to death by the Inquisition on charges of heresy was a schoolteacher who was strangled to death in 1826, and buried in a wooden barrel painted with flames to simulate an *auto de fe* (act of faith). The Spanish Inquisition, however, was not formally dismantled until 1834.

12. Strictly speaking, the office of the Inquisition still exists, although it has been renamed several times over the centuries and is now known as the Sacred Congregation for the Doctrine of the Faith. The cardinal who until recently directed its affairs, Joseph Ratzinger, became Pope Benedict XVI in 2005.

THE DEVIL YOU KNOW: 10 TELLTALE SIGNS OF A WITCH*

1. Indecent dancing

2. Excessive eating

3. Making love diabolically

4. Atrocious acts of sodomy

5. Blasphemery (*sic*)

6. A smoker's cough†

7. Avenging themselves insidiously

---

* According to Pierre de l'Ancre (1553–1631), a French judge from Bordeaux who conducted a massive witch-hunt in Labourd. In less than a year he had seventy people burned at the stake including several priests. De l'Ancre wasn't satisfied: he estimated that some 3,000 witches were still at large (10 per cent of the population of Labourd in that time). He went on to become a leading expert on witches and wrote three books on the subject.

† De l'Ancre said that smoking tobacco directly linked accused witches in Europe with the "diabolical" Indians in the Old World. For him and several other witch-hunters, tobacco was "an inversion of the Christian sacrament".

8. Keeping toads, vipers, lizards and all sorts of poison as precious things

9. Passionate lovemaking with a stinking goat

10. A Devil's Teat★

★ The mark, anywhere on a woman's body, from which it was believed that demons would suckle. During witch-hunts, suspects would be examined by "witch prickers" who looked for the Devil's Teat. It was believed that a true devil's teat would have no feeling or blood when stabbed. Many innocent women were so traumatized by the experience of having their bodies probed by a strange man that they became numb and could feel nothing, thus giving the appearance of guilt.

15 THINGS BANNED BY THE BIBLE*

1. Burning yeast or honey in offerings to God (2:11).

2. Failing to include salt in offerings to God (2:13).

3. Eating fat (3:17).

4. Letting your hair become unkempt (10:6).

5. Tearing your clothes (10:6).

6. Going to church within sixty-six days after giving birth to a girl (12:5).

7. Eating, or touching the carcass of, weasels, rats, any kind of great lizard including geckos, monitor lizards and wall lizards, skunks or chameleons (11:29).

8. Sex with a woman during her period (18:19).

9. Reaping to the very edges of a field (19:9).

10. Picking up grapes that have fallen in your vineyard (19:10).

---

* The Book of Leviticus.

11. Eating, or touching the carcass of, eagles, vultures, kites, ravens, owls, gulls, hawks, cormorants, ospreys, storks, herons, hoopoes or bats. (11:13–19).

12. Trimming your beard (19:27).

13. Eating or touching the carcass of flying insects with four legs, unless those legs are jointed (11:20–22).

14. Getting a tattoo (19:2).

15. Sitting in the presence of the elderly (19:32).

CHAPTER NINE

Musical Miscellany

THE BANNED PLAYED ON:
10 SONG LYRIC CONTROVERSIES

1620: the popular English folk song The Crabfish features the lines "Up start the Crabfish, and catch her by the cunt".

1895: music hall's Marie Lloyd sings "She Sits Amongst the Cabbages and Peas". Following complaints, she is hauled before local magistrates and ordered to perform the song, so she changes it to: "She Sits Amongst the Cabbages and Leeks". They let her off because the bench doesn't get the joke.

1891: the Barrison Sisters, one of the biggest vaudeville acts of the day, are promoted as The Wickedest Girls In the World. During their act they raise their skirts slightly above the knee and sing "Would you like to see my pussy?" Petticoats are raised higher and higher until eventually revealing a black kitten poking out of their underwear.

1937: George Formby falls foul of BBC censors with his song "With My Little Stick of Blackpool Rock" which includes the lines: "With my little stick of Blackpool Rock, along the promenade I stroll, In the ballroom I went dancing each night, No wonder every girl that danced with me, stuck to me tight." The Controller of Sound Broadcasting notes: "No one is more alive than I to the need to buttress the forces of virtue against the unprincipled elements of the jungle."

1958: Link Wray, the guitarist credited with inventing "fuzz" guitar after punching a hole in a speaker giving him a distorted guitar sound, has a big US hit with his single "Rumble" despite it being banned on several radio stations, on the grounds that it glorifies juvenile delinquency – a rare achievement for a song with no lyrics.

1964: the governor of Indiana bans the Kingsmen's "Louie Louie" for being "obscene". The FBI spend the next two years investigating the song's lyrics, playing it at different speeds, getting in different experts to try to work out what the Kingsmen were singing, but fail to come up with anything. The official report concludes: "It is his belief that only those who want to hear such things can read it into the vocal."

1966: eighteen-year-old singer France Gall has a big hit with the song "Les Sucettes" written for her by French heavy-breather Serge Gainsbourg (of "Je T'Aime Non Plus" fame). The teenage Gall is under the impression she is singing about aniseed-flavoured lollipops, unaware that the song was actually about the joys of performing fellatio.*

1971: the BBC fail to spot the Rolling Stones' less than enlightened attitude to the fairer sex on "Brown Sugar", a story about a white man having sex with a young slave girl who has just got off the boat and been sold at market. They ban the B-side instead – "Bitch".

1988: members of the rap group NWA receive a letter from the FBI pointing out that the agency does not appreciate the song "Fuck The Police". Law enforcement groups all over the country agree.

---

* Rough translation:

Annie likes lollipops,
Aniseed lollipops . . .
Give her kisses
An aniseed taste.

2004: Python Eric Idle is fined $5,000 for saying 'fuck' on an American radio station. He responds by writing a Noel Coward pastiche, "Fuck You Very Much".

10 UNFINISHED SYMPHONIES

1750: work on Johann Sebastian Bach's *The Art of Fugue* ends abruptly after he undergoes an operation to restore his failing eyesight. Although the operation is successful he dies within weeks; the cause of his death is probably a stroke, complicated by pneumonia.

1791: Mozart doesn't get round to completing his *Requiem*. Bedridden and suffering from swelling, pain and vomiting, he dies aged thirty-five. His symptoms are consistent with trichinosis, a worm infestation caused by eating undercooked pork.

1808: Josef Haydn gives up on his sixty-eighth and final string quartet, but lingers on, sinking into senility.

1827: Ludwig van Beethoven's *Symphony No. 10* remains incomplete when he slips into unconsciousness and dies, cause of death disputed; alcoholic cirrhosis, syphilis, infectious hepatitis, lead poisoning, sarcoidosis (chronic lung disease) and Whipple's disease have all been proposed.

1828: the combined effects of tertiary syphilis and mercury poisoning prevent Franz Schubert from completing his *Symphony No. 8 in B minor*, his Unfinished Symphony.

1893: Pyotr Ilyich Tchaikovsky's *Symphony in E Flat* remains incomplete when the composer dies, reportedly from cholera after he drinks a glass of unboiled water in a restaurant.

1911: no sooner has Gustav Mahler sketched out the first draft of his *Symphony No. 10* than he suddenly succumbs to a fatal streptococcal throat infection.

1935: Alban Berg stops work on his opera *Lulu* when he dies from an infected insect sting.

1967: the Beach Boys abandon their ambitious follow-up to the acclaimed *Pet Sounds* album, due to Brian Wilson's deteriorating mental health and increased friction among band members.

1970: Jimi Hendrix fails to complete his eagerly awaited album *First Rays of the New Rising Sun* after inhaling his own vomit while overdosing on barbiturates.

THE NEXT BIG KING:
6 ELVIS IMPERSONATORS*

1. The original Elvis impersonator was sixteen-year-old Jim Smith who began his act in 1956, shortly after Elvis became famous. He appeared several times on American TV but had to mime because he could neither sing nor play a guitar.

2. Dr Jukka Ammondt, a Finnish professor, is the only Elvis impersonator known to sing his songs in Latin, including "*Nunc Hic Aut Numquam*" ("It's Now Or Never").

3. In 1996 Elvis Herselvis, a lesbian Elvis impersonator, was invited to take part in the Second International Elvis Presley Conference held at the University of Mississippi in order "to test the limits of race, class, sexuality and property". She was banned from the event after a protest by sponsors of Elvis Presley Enterprises.

4. Bill Haney holds the distinction of being the only Elvis impersonator the King himself ever saw perform. Haney met Elvis after the show at the Levee Lounge in Memphis, 1976, recalling: "He looked overweight. I was told not to mention anything about his weight."

---

* There are now at least 85,000 Elvises around the world compared to only 170 in 1977 when he died. At this rate of growth, experts predict that by 2020 Elvis impersonators will make up a third of the world population.

5. In 1990 Elvis impersonator Michael Conley was sentenced to life imprisonment for shooting dead, then robbing Charles Koroluk, a Toronto tourist in Fort Lauderdale. During his three-week trial, Conley irritated some bailiffs and delighted others by singing a variety of Elvis hits.

6. Dana MacKay, considered by many to be a king among Elvi, was the first impersonator to play Elvis in the Legends in Concert show and once portrayed the King in a factual TV documentary. He and his girlfriend Mary Huffman, a beauty pageant winner, lived in his sprawling Las Vegas home, which MacKay called mini-Graceland. In 1993 they were both gunned down in their home in an unsolved mob-style double murder.

8 MOST VIOLENT NATIONAL ANTHEMS

1. Algeria
   Sample:
   We swear by the lightning that destroys,
   By the streams of generous blood being shed
   When we spoke, nobody listened to us
   So we have taken the noise of gunpowder as our rhythm
   And the sound of machine-guns as our melody.

2. Tunisia
   The blood surges in our veins
   We die for the sake of our land
   For the flag, For our country
   To die is a fine thing! Our past cries out to us:
   Have a disciplined soul! To die is a fine thing!

3. Albania
   Only he who is a born traitor
   Averts from the struggle.
   He who is brave is not daunted,
   But falls – a martyr to the cause.

4. Armenia
   Everywhere death is the same
   Everyone dies only once
   But lucky is the one
   Who is sacrificed for his nation.

5. Hungary
   But no freedom's flowers return
   From the spilled blood of the dead
   And the tears of slavery burn
   Which the eyes of orphans shed.

6. Italy
   Let us join in the cohort
   We are ready to die!
   We are ready to die!
   Mercenary swords, they're feeble reeds.
   The Austrian eagle has already lost its plumes
   The blood of Italy and the Polish blood
   It drank, along with the Cossack. But it burned its heart.

7. Turkey
   The bloody flag is raised, the bloody flag is raised.
   Do you hear in the countryside, the roar of these savage
      soldiers?
   They come right into our arms, to cut the throats of
      your sons!
   May a tainted blood irrigate our furrows!

8. Vietnam
   Our flag, red with the blood of victory, bears the spirit of
      the country
   The distant rumbling of the guns mingles with our
      marching song
   The path to glory is built by the bodies of our foes
   For too long have we swallowed our hatred. Be ready for
      all sacrifices!

KNOCKIN' ON HEAVEN'S DOOR: 10 MUSICAL DEATHS

1066: the first casualty at the Battle of Hastings is William of Normandy's jester Taillefer; he rides out ahead, singing the "Song of Roland" while juggling a sword, and is promptly cut down by an English warrior. The Normans omit this detail from the Bayeux Tapestry out of embarrassment.

1823: at the battle of Nasamkow, Brigadier-General Sir Charles MacCarthy leads a 500-strong British force against 10,000 Ashanti tribesmen. He instructs his men to stand to attention while his band strike up "God Save The Queen", as this will scare the Ashanti into running away. It doesn't and he and his men are massacred.

1942: British composer Felix Lloyd Powell commits suicide while wearing the uniform of the Peacehaven Home Guard by shooting himself in the heart with his own rifle. He was most famous for writing the music for the wartime classic "Pack Up Your Troubles in Your Old Kit Bag and Smile, Smile, Smile", once described as "perhaps the most optimistic song ever written".

1966: singer/songwriter Bobby Fuller is best known for his hit single "I Fought The Law". Within months of it reaching the charts, Fuller is found dead in the front seat of his car parked outside his Hollywood apartment, beaten, bloodied and drenched in petrol; the coroner records a verdict of suicide.

1975: R&B singer Jackie Wilson has an onstage stroke and keels over in the middle of singing his signature tune "Lonely Teardrops". The audience, convinced that this is part of the act, applauds and cheers wildly. Wilson slips into a coma from which he never recovers, dying eight years later.

1983: Tom Evans becomes the second member of the band Badfinger to hang himself, following the example set by his colleague Pete Ham in 1975. Their deaths were linked to a dispute over lost royalties, especially from their most lucrative song, "Without You". It includes the line "I can't live, I can't live any more".

1979: soul singer/songwriter Donny Hathaway likes to lean out of the window of his seventeenth-floor Chicago apartment and sing to passers-by, a habit that also got him barred from several hotels. During a break in recording with his singing partner Roberta Flack, he is found dead on the pavement outside his New York hotel. No one knows if he was pushed, jumped or fell from the window of his fifteenth-floor room.

1992: the singer Dead is found dead from a self-inflicted gunshot wound, having left a note that reads, "please excuse all the blood". His body is discovered by Euronymous, a fellow member of the Norwegian band Mayhem, who takes pictures of the scene. One of the photos turns up as the cover for a bootleg "Dawn of the Black Hearts" several years later.

2000: a policeman shoots himself dead in the toilets during a performance by The Cure in Prague. A member of the audience describes the mood of the concert as "gloomy".

2003: a twenty-five-year-old Filipino man is stabbed to

death while singing a Frank Sinatra classic out of tune at a birthday party. The victim, Casimiro Lagugad, is singing "My Way" badly, much to the annoyance of Julio Tugas, who silences him with a stab in the neck.

ROCK 'N' ROLL
BAD BEHAVIOUR:
11 DEFINING MOMENTS

1956: Elvis Presley appears live on *The Steve Allen Show* performing "Hound Dog". The show's host hits on the novel idea of having twenty-one-year-old Elvis wear a tuxedo and sing to an actual basset hound, which is sitting on a stool. It goes well until halfway through the song when the basset hound urinates on the studio floor.

1958: Jerry Lee Lewis steps off a plane in London for his UK tour arm-in-arm with his wife Myra, whom he reveals is also his cousin and "about thirteen". A tabloid newspaper furore ensues when it turns out that the rocker is also a serial bigamist who first married when he was fourteen. The tour is cancelled and Jerry Lee is banned from playing in Britain.

1965: manager Andrew Loog Oldham's sleeve-note for the Rolling Stones' second album encourages Stones fans to mug blind people in order to raise the money to buy their new record. He succeeds in his aim of arousing widespread indignation.

1966: John Lennon tells the *London Evening Standard*: "Christianity will go. It will vanish and shrink. We're more popular than Jesus now; I don't know which will go first, rock 'n' roll or Christianity. Jesus was alright, but his disciples were thick and ordinary."

1975: Revd Charles Boykin of Tallahassee, Florida, organizes the burning of Rolling Stones records, claiming they are sinful. Boykin is acting on a recent survey that claims 984 out of 1,000 local unmarried mothers had sex when listening to rock music.

1976: The Sex Pistols and a gang of safety-pinned hangers-on make an unscheduled appearance on Thames Television's prime-time *Today* TV show, replacing Queen, whose lead singer Freddie Mercury was still recovering from a trip to the dentist. Presenter Bill Grundy, hoping to inject some tension into a hitherto dull interview, quips, "You've got another ten seconds, say something outrageous." Guitarist Steve Jones takes up the offer, noting that Grundy is a "dirty bastard", a "dirty fucker" and a "fucking rotter". This causes a man called James Holmes, a forty-six-year-old lorry driver, to kick in his TV set.

1982: at a gig in Des Moines, Iowa, Ozzy Osbourne warms up his audience by pelting them with 25 lb of pig intestines and calves' livers. One fan returns the favour by tossing a real bat on stage. Stunned by the lights, the bat lies motionless and Ozzy, believing it is a rubber prop, bites into its neck. He is rushed to hospital and tested for rabies.

1993: US singer-songwriter "GG" Allin (born Jesus Christ Allin because his dad wanted him to have the best possible start in life) dies of an accidental heroin overdose. The troubled front man of several US "scum punk" bands, including the Scumfucs, the Disappointments and the Murder Junkies, rewrote the rulebook on audience participation. Described by one critic as "so vile that he makes Marilyn Manson look like a Sunday-school teacher", during one live performance Allin defecated onstage, smeared excrement on his body and ate it before flinging the rest of it at the crowd. Most of his shows ended prematurely and often in arrest.

1996: at the Brit Awards, as Michael Jackson performs "Earth Song" with a group of children, Pulp front man Jarvis Cocker invades the stage, lifts his shirt and then shows Jacko his bottom. Meanwhile, almost unnoticed by the media, Liam Gallagher demonstrates his contempt for the occasion by miming the insertion of a trophy up his nether regions, calls media ubiquity Chris Evans "ginger bollocks" and refers to Blur's "Park Life" as "Shite Life".

2002: metal band Dillinger Escape Plan open at England's prestigious Reading Festival. To warm things up DEP vocalist Greg Puciato defecates on stage, puts the mess in a bag and throws it at the audience, announcing, "This is an example of shit on stage, which is all you're gonna get here today."

2003: rapper Big Lurch is convicted of the murder and partial consumption of his roommate while under the influence of PCP.

FINAL MOVEMENTS:
10 CLASSICAL MUSIC DEATHS

1. Henry Purcell achieved an extraordinary amount in his short life before dying at thirty-six in 1695. There might have been a lot more if he hadn't spent another late night out with his mates; as a result, his wife locked him out of their house in Westminster for hours in the rain and he contracted a fatal bout of pneumonia.

2. In 1777 the Czech composer and close friend of Mozart, Josef Myslivecek, died after a botched attempt by a Munich doctor to cure his advanced tertiary syphilis by burning off his nose.

3. In 1791 the Czech composer Frantisek Kotzwara was in London working at the King's Theatre when he took time out from his busy schedule to visit a brothel in Vine Street. After drinking a lot of brandy, he gave a prostitute called Susannah Hill two shillings and asked her to cut off his testicles. When she declined to do so, Kotzwara asked her if she wouldn't mind hanging him with a rope while they had sex instead. Not wanting to lose a paying punter, Hill obliged, but, by the time the deed was done, Kotzwara was stone dead, the first recorded death from erotic asphyxiation. Hill was charged with murder, but acquitted. Fearing a slew of copycat cases, the judge

ordered the court records of the trial be destroyed, but a copy got out anyway, and was published in a pamphlet a few years later, *Modern Propensities; or, An Essay on the Art of Strangling.*

4. In 1888 the Jewish composer and virtuoso pianist Charles-Valentin Alkan was found dead in his home. For many years it was believed that he had been crushed by a falling bookcase while reaching for a volume of the Talmud, which he had placed on the top shelf. In fact, the frail seventy-four-year-old died after being trapped beneath a fallen umbrella stand.

5. In 1893 Pyotr Ilyich Tchaikovsky fell ill just days after conducting the premiere of his Sixth Symphony, the *Pathéthique.* According to official reports he had taken a "fateful sip of unboiled water" and contracted a fatal bout of cholera. It is widely believed, however, that the Russian composer had been having an affair with a young nobleman he was tutoring and had committed suicide rather than live with the scandal.

6. In 1897 Hugo Wolf began to show signs of mental derangement brought on by his syphilis, forcing him to stop composing altogether. After an attempt to drown himself, he admitted himself into an insane asylum, where he died in 1903. His unfaithful wife Melanie, tortured by the fact that her infidelity was the cause of her husband's illness, killed herself three years later.

7. In 1899 French Romantic composer Ernest Chausson went for a bicycle ride near his house in Limay. He lost control on a downhill slope and crashed into a brick wall headfirst.

8. The life and career of fifty-year-old Viennese composer Alban Berg was terminated when a lone bee sting became septic. His wife tried to operate on it with a pair of scissors and the resultant blood poisoning killed him on Christmas Eve, 1935.

9. Austrian composer Anton von Webern left Vienna during World War II, thinking he would be much safer in the town of Mittersill. In September 1945, while standing on his veranda lighting up a cigar, he was shot dead by a trigger-happy American GI.

10. Arnold Schoenberg suffered from triskaidekaphobia – fear of the number thirteen. The Austrian composer even changed the title of one of his songs so that it wouldn't have thirteen letters. On Friday, 13 July 1951 Schoenberg stayed in bed all day, sick with anxiety, because it was his seventy-sixth birthday (7 + 6 = 13). He died of unknown causes, it was estimated, at thirteen minutes before midnight.

DIVAS AND DESPOTS: 10 STARS WHO PERFORMED FOR DICTATORS AND THEIR FAMILIES

1. James Brown – sang for President Mobutu of Zaire (1974)

2. Bob Marley – Robert Mugabe, President of Zimbabwe (1980)*

3. Nelly Furtado – Libyan leader Muammar Gaddafi (2007)

4. Maria Carey – Muammar Gaddafi (2008) and President José Eduardo dos Santos of Angola (2013)†

5. Usher – Muammar Gaddafi's family (2009)

6. Sting – Gulnara, daughter of Uzbekistan President Islam Karimov (2009)‡

7. Beyoncé – Muammar Gaddafi (2010)

---

* Bob wasn't Mugabe's first choice. The Zimbabwean ruler requested Cliff Richard.
† After earning around $1million for the Gaddafi gig, she claimed that she wasn't aware at the time exactly who she was playing for.
‡ Karimov has been accused of boiling his enemies alive.

8. 50 Cent – Muammar Gaddafi's family (2011)

9. Seal – Chechen President Ramzan Kadyrov (2013)

10. Jennifer Lopez – Turkmenistan President Gurbanguly Berdimuhamedow (2013)

8 MUSIC TALENT SCOUTS

1954: Jim Denny, Manager of "Grand Ole Opry", tells Elvis Presley, "You ain't goin' nowhere, son. You ought to go back to drivin' a truck."

1956: Columbia Records head Mitch Mitchell passes on Buddy Holly, describing him as "unmusical".

1962: Decca A&R man Dick Rowe tells the Beatles manager, "Guitar music is on the way out, Mr Epstein."

1965: the BBC reject David Bowie as "amateurish and out of tune".

1965: the BBC reject The Who: "Overall, not very original and below standard."

1968: the BBC turn down the artist now known as Sir Elton John as a "dull performer with a thin voice", adding, "he writes dreary songs and he sounds like a wonky singer."

1969: the BBC dismisses Led Zeppelin as "derivative", "old-fashioned" and "unsuitable for daytime radio".

1969: the same judges reject Marc Bolan: "Crap, and pretentious crap at that."

SETTLING SCORES:
12 CLASSICAL PUT-DOWNS IN
140 CHARACTERS OR LESS

1. "A composer for one right hand."
   Richard Wagner on Frederic Chopin

2. "Monsieur Wagner has good moments, but awful quarters of an hour."
   Gioachino Rossini on Richard Wagner

3. "After the last notes of *Gotterdammerung* I felt as though I had been let out of prison."
   Pyotr Ilyich Tchaikovsky on Richard Wagner

4. "What a giftless bastard."
   Tchaikovsky on Johannes Brahms

5. "A tub of pork and beer."
   Hector Berlioz on George Frideric Handel

6. "Berlioz composes by splashing his pen over the manuscript and leaving the issue to chance."
   Frederic Chopin on Hector Berlioz

7. "The work of an idiot."
   Giacomo Puccini, after the world premiere
   of Stravinsky's *The Rite of Spring*

8. "If he'd been making shell-cases during the war it might have been better for music."

> Maurice Ravel on Camille Saint-Saens

9. "He'd be better off shovelling snow than scribbling on manuscript paper."

> Richard Strauss on Arnold Schoenberg

10. "Written by a deaf man and should only be listened to by a deaf man."

> Thomas Beecham on Ludwig van Beethoven

11. "Listening to the Fifth Symphony of Ralph Vaughan Williams is like staring at a cow for forty-five minutes."

> Aaron Copland on Vaughan Williams

12. "I would like to hear Elliott Carter's *Fourth String Quartet,* if only to discover what a cranky prostate does to one's polyphony."

> James Sellars on Elliott Carter

THE FOREVER 27 CLUB: 40 MUSICIANS WHO DIDN'T REACH THEIR 28TH BIRTHDAY

Robert Johnson (blues guitarist/singer, 16 August 1938)

Rudy Lewis (The Drifters, 20 May 1964)

Malcolm Hale (Spanky And Our Gang, 31 October 1968)

Dickie Pride (singer, 26 March 1969)

Brian Jones (Rolling Stones, 3 July 1969)

Alexandra (singer, 31 July 1969)

Al "Blind Owl" Wilson (Canned Heat, 3 September 1970)

Jimi Hendrix (guitarist/singer, 18 September 1970)

Janis Joplin (singer, 4 October 1970)

Arlester "Dyke" Christian (Dyke And The Blazers, 13 March 1971)

Jim Morrison (The Doors, 3 July 1971)

Linda Jones (soul singer, 14 March 1972)

Leslie Harvey (Stone The Crows, 3 May 1972)

Ron "Pigpen" McKernan (Grateful Dead, 8 March 1973)

Roger Lee Durham (Bloodstone, 27 July 1973)

Wallace Yohn (Chase, 12 August 1974)

Dave Alexander (The Stooges, 10 February 1975)

Peter Ham (Badfinger, 24 April 1975)

Gary Thain (Uriah Heep, 8 December 1975)

Cecilia (singer, 2 August 1976)

Helmut Kollen (Triumvirat, 3 May 1977)

Chris Bell (Big Star, 27 December 1978)

D Boon (The Minutemen, 22 December 1985)

Pete de Freitas (Echo & The Bunnymen, 14 June 1989)

Mia Zapata (The Gits, 7 July 1993)

Kurt Cobain (Nirvana, 5 April 1994)

Kristen Pfaff (Hole, 16 June 1994)

Richey Edwards (Manic Street Preachers, declared missing 1 February 1995, officially presumed dead 23 November 2008)

Stretch (rapper, 30 November 1995)

Fat Pat (rapper, 3 February 1998)

Freaky Tah (Lost Boyz, 28 March 1999)

Rodrigo Bueno (singer, 24 June 2000)

Sean Patrick McCabe (Ink & Dagger, 28 August 2000)

Maria Serrano (Passion Fruit, 24 November 2001)

Jeremy Ward (The Mars Volta, 25 May 2003)

Bryan Ottoson (American Head Charge, 19 April 2005)

Valentin Elizalde (singer, 26 November 2006)

Orish Grinstead (702, 20 April 2008)

Lily Tembo (Musician, 14 September 2009)

Amy Winehouse (singer, 23 July 2011)

CHAPTER TEN

R.I.P.

15 IRONIC DEATHS

c. 100 BC: the Greek Agamemnon is hailed a great hero when he returns from the Trojan War, unscathed. Shortly afterwards, while he is relaxing in his bathtub, his wife Clytemnestra strikes him twice with an axe.

1774: Dr William Hewson, surgeon and pioneer anatomist, cuts his thumb while dissecting a decomposing corpse and dies of blood poisoning.

1794: after years of braving Africa's perils while tracing the origins of the Blue Nile, Scottish explorer James Bruce returns home and dies after falling down his stairs.

1857: while on a field survey in North Carolina, the American geologist Elisha Mitchell loses his footing and falls to his death in Mitchell Falls, which he had himself named twenty-two years earlier.

1939: aviation pioneer Lady Mary Heath, the first woman to fly solo from South Africa to England, dies after a fall from a London bus.

1950: Charles Drew, the African-American doctor who pioneered the use of blood banks during World War II, bleeds to death in a car accident.

1965: Hollywood starlet Linda Darnell, who lit up the screen in more than fifty films, has a lifelong fear of dying in a fire. While staying with friends, she dies in a house blaze after falling asleep with a lit cigarette while watching one of her old films.

1981: convicted murderer Michael Sloan cheats the electric chair when a retrial clears him of the sexual assault and murder of twenty-four-year-old Mary Elizabeth Royem. Six years later, Sloan dies on another electric chair: while sitting naked on a metal toilet seat, he bites through an electric cable while trying to repair some earphones.

1983: Dennis Wilson, founding member and drummer of The Beach Boys and allegedly the only one who can actually swim, drowns while retrieving four kilos of cocaine from under his yacht.

1985: a party thrown by city lifeguards in Los Angeles is marred when a guest, thirty-one-year-old Jerome Moody, is found dead at the bottom of the pool. The lifeguards are celebrating their first drowning-free swimming season in living memory.

1993: mountaineer Gerard Hommel, veteran of six Everest expeditions, falls off a ladder and dies after cracking his head on a sink while changing a light bulb in the kitchen of his home in Nantes, France.

2005: Richard "Doc" Brown, world expert on roller coaster safety and designer of more than sixty white-knuckle rides including the groundbreaking Back To The Future ride at Universal Studios, dies from a head injury after falling over in his driveway.

2007: a Vietnamese man, Nguyen Van "Electric" Hung, appears on national TV to show off his amazing ability to resist electric shocks while inserting his fingers into electrical sockets. Soon afterwards, he is electrocuted at home when he tries to repair his generator and forgets to turn off the power supply.

2012: Cynthia Jean Gillig-Stone, better known as porn star Echo Valley, dies near Leakey, Texas in a car accident as a result of her inability to wear her seatbelt because of her enormous breasts.

2013: Lee Halpin, a twenty-six-year-old filmmaker from Newcastle-upon-Tyne, freezes to death while making a documentary about sleeping rough. Speaking on a YouTube video, he says the project is part of an application for an investigative journalism course and that he wanted to "immerse" himself in the lifestyle of a homeless person.

AIRLINE BLACK BOX TRANSCRIPTS: 12 LAST WORDS

1. "Skipper's shot. We've been shot. I was trying to help."
   Pacific Air Lines, flight 773, 7 May 1964

2. "Ma I love you."
   Pacific Southwest Airlines flight 182, 25 September 1978

3. "Actually, these conditions don't look very good at all, do they?"
   Air New Zealand flight 901, 28 November 1979

4. "No need for that, we are okay, no problem, no problem."
   Saudi Arabian Airlines flight 163, 19 August 1980

5. "What? There's what? Some hills, isn't there?"
   VASP flight 168, 8 June 1988

6. "Watch out for those pylons ahead, eh. See them? Yeah, yeah, don't worry."
   Air France flight 296Q, 26 June 1988

7. "That's it, I'm dead."
   Surinam Airways flight 764, 7 June 1989

8. "A bit low, bit low, bit low."
   Martinair flight 495, 21 December 1992

9.   "Hang on. What the hell is this?"
                    US Air flight 427, 8 September 1994

10. "Uh, smoke in the cockpit . . . smoke in the cabin."
                    Valujet flight 592, 11 May 1996

11. "Mountains!"
                    Vnokovo Airlines flight 2601, 29 August 1996

12. "Fuuuuuuckkkkkk!"
                    Polish Air Force flight 1549, 4 April 2010

CHECKING OUT:
10 CELEBRITY HOTEL
DEATHS NOT INVOLVING
DRUGS OR ALCOHOL*

1. Oscar Wilde: died aged forty-six at the Hotel d'Alsace in Paris, in November 1900. He was still recovering from a fall in prison, which caused an infection in his right ear, possibly leading to cerebral meningitis. This was where he was supposed to have uttered a couple of his most famous witticisms to visiting friends: "I am dying beyond my means" and "my wall paper and I are fighting a duel to the death. One or other of us has got to go." The latter is apocryphal. He never said it but wrote something very similar in a letter to a friend. "I seem to be fighting a death battle with this wall paper. The wall paper is winning."

2. Dan Andersson: in 1920 the Swedish author was staying at Hotel Hellman in Stockholm, when the hotel staff forgot to fumigate his room after using hydrogen cyanide against bed bugs. He died of cyanide poisoning.

3. Warren G. Harding: the twenty-ninth President of the

---

* Honourable mention. The actor Richard Harris lived at the Savoy hotel in London. When he was finally carried out on a stretcher in 2002, he told passers-by, "It was the food."

United States expired in room 8064 of the Palace Hotel, San Francisco on 2 August 1923. The fifty-six-year-old took to his bed with food poisoning, but the exact cause of death is not known because his First Lady refused to allow an autopsy. This gave way to rumours that she had poisoned her husband to protect him from possible impeachment; she was overheard sitting next to her husband's open casket in the East Room of the White House the night before the funeral, saying, "No one can hurt you now, Warren."

4. Nikola Tesla: the tragically under-appreciated electrical genius, inventor and eccentric gave up the ghost alone and in poverty in room 3327 of the New Yorker Hotel in January 1943. His emaciated corpse was later found by maid Alice Monaghan after she had entered Tesla's room, ignoring the "do not disturb" sign he had had placed on his door two days earlier.

5. Eugene O'Neill: the playwright who wrote *The Iceman Cometh* and *A Long Day's Journey into Night* was sixty-five, broke and depressed when he shuffled off the mortal coil in Suite 401 of the Shelton Hotel in Boston in 1953. His last words were: "I knew it. I knew it. Born in a hotel room and God damn it died in a hotel room." O'Neill was born in a Broadway hotel room, in New York.

6. Coco Chanel: the eighty-seven-year-old designer croaked in the Ritz Carlton Hotel in Paris in 1971, death by natural causes. It was the same hotel that another style icon, Princess Diana, left by car for her appointment with death in 1997.

7. Vladimir Nabokov: in 1977 the Russian-American author of *Lolita* succumbed to a virus infection in his

sixth-floor suite at the Palace Hotel in Montreux, Switzerland, where he and his wife, Vera, had lived for the last eighteen years. According to his son, Dmitri, he expired "with a triple moan of descending pitch".

8. Margaret Thatcher: although said to be adored by her family and millions of supporters, she breathed her last, alone, in her room in The Ritz, London, aged eighty-seven, while convalescing after an operation to remove a growth in her bladder in 2013.

9. Adam Faith: the singer turned actor, who topped the UK singles charts with his 1959 single "What Do You Want?", died of a heart attack in 2003, aged sixty-two, while having sex with his girlfriend who was forty years his junior, in a Stoke-on-Trent hotel. His last words were: "Channel Five is all shit, isn't it? Christ, the crap they put on there. It's a waste of space."

10. Gene Pitney: the American singer was found dead in a Hilton hotel in Cardiff by his manager during a UK tour in 2006. Cause of death – cardiovascular disease. His sole UK number one hit was a duet with Marc Almond, "Something's Gotten Hold Of My Heart".

DEATH AND TAXIS: 10 FAMOUS PEOPLE (AND ONE DOG) KILLED BY CABS

1. Robert "Romeo" Coates, known as "the world's worst actor". Crushed between a cab and a private carriage on 15 February 1848 while leaving a concert in Drury Lane, London.

2. Octavius Sturges, the physician who coined the medical term "chorea". Knocked down by a cab on 26 October 1894 while crossing the road in Cavendish Square, London, "the approach at which with India-rubber tyred wheels he had not heard, being somewhat deaf".*

3. Lance-Sergeant Peter Kelly of the Berkshire Regiment was killed at the Battle of Maiwand in 1880, but his dog Bobbie, the regimental mascot, survived and was awarded a medal by Queen Victoria. A year later Bobbie was run over and killed by a taxi in Gosport.†

4. Henry H. Bliss, a sixty-eight-year-old New York City real estate broker, stepped in front of a cab at 74th

---

* *Oxford Dictionary of National Biography.*
† Bobbie was stuffed and put in a museum.

Street and Central Park West on 14 September 1899 –
the first American ever to be killed in an automobile
accident.

5. Eleanor Smith, wife of Edward Smith, captain of RMS
   Titanic. Knocked down by a taxi in Kensington, London
   on 28 April 1931.

6. Sir Stanley Jackson, England cricketer and Tory MP.
   Having survived several assassination attempts in India,
   he was run over by a taxi while hailing one outside the
   Hyde Park Hotel, London, on 9 March 1947.

7. "Diamondfield" Davis, American prospector and
   gunslinger. Pardoned for the 1896 Deep Creek Murders
   in Idaho, he got lucky when he struck it rich in Nevada
   and established several mining towns. His luck ran out
   when he was run over by a cab in Las Vegas in 1949.

8. Eddie Cochran. While touring in the UK, the twenty-
   one-year-old singer was killed when his taxi hit a
   lamppost on Rowden Hill, Chippenham, Wiltshire, on
   17 April 1960. His current hit at the time was "Three
   Steps to Heaven".*

9. Stiv Bators, forty-year-old veteran of the New York City
   punk scene, was struck by a cab while crossing a street
   in Paris on 3 June 1990. He was taken to a nearby hospital, but discharged himself before receiving any
   treatment; he died that night in his sleep.

10. Steve "Asbestos" Duplantis, American pro golf caddy,

---

* The taxi driver was convicted of dangerous driving, fined £50,
disqualified from driving for fifteen years and sent to prison for six
months.

stepped off a kerb in Del Mar, California, and was hit by a taxi on 23 January 2008.

11. Kōji Wakamatsu, Japanese film director, was run over by a taxi cab in Tokyo on 17 October 2012, on his way home after a budget meeting to discuss his next project, a movie about the Japanese nuclear lobby.

9 MORBID OBSESSIONS

1. King Carlos II "the Hexed" of Spain insisted on having relatives' graves opened so he could have a look at their corpses.

2. After her husband Albert's death in 1861, Queen Victoria remained in official mourning for the rest of her life, dressed from head to toe in black "widow's weeds". Every morning, she insisted that servants set out Albert's clothes, brought hot water for his shaving cup, scoured his chamber pot and changed his bed linen. The glass from which he took his last dose of medicine remained by his bedside, untouched, for nearly four decades.

3. Victoria Woodhull, the first woman in American history to run for presidential office in 1872, was terrified that she would die if she went to bed. She spent every night of the last four years of her life sitting in a chair.

4. The actress Sarah Bernhardt made frequent visits to the Paris morgue to look at corpses of derelicts dredged from the River Seine. She persuaded her mother to buy her a rosewood coffin with white satin lining: she often slept in it and was eventually buried in it.

5. The poet John Donne had his portrait painted while posing in a winding sheet with his body and hands arranged like those of a corpse. The work completed, Donne had it placed beside his bed as a constant reminder of his own mortality.

6. When the poet Ralph Waldo Emerson's first wife Ellen died of tuberculosis in February 1831 he was distraught and visited her grave daily. In his diary over a year later Emerson wrote, "I visited Ellen's tomb and opened the coffin".

7. Abraham Lincoln had his dead son Willie exhumed twice so he could have a look at and hold the body.

8. The composer Anton Bruckner had a thing for dead composers' skulls. When Franz Schubert's coffin was opened in 1888, Bruckner was overcome with awe. He reached in and grabbed his skull with both hands, only letting go when he was physically pulled away. He had done the same thing a few months earlier to Beethoven's corpse.

9. After Elvis's death the *National Enquirer* paid his cousin Billy Mann $18,000 to secretly photograph the corpse.

20 POST-MORTEM ADVENTURES

1. The first Chinese Emperor Qin Shi Huang died while he was on a journey to seek the elixir of life in 210 BC. Two of his closest advisers and supporters of his ruthless regime were fearful that they would be executed as soon as the news got out, so they hatched a plan to conceal the old emperor's death from the world. They arranged for the imperial carriage to take him home to the palace, closely followed by a cartload of rotting fish to disguise the stench of his decomposing body. The conspirators succeeded in reaching the capital without the emperor's death being discovered. They carried on without him for four years before they quarrelled and his death became public knowledge.

2. The seventh book of Pliny's *Natural History* contains a section on the signs of death for his fellow Romans. Pliny listed several, but his advice didn't turn out to be entirely reliable. The consul Acilius Aviola and the praetor Lucius Lamia both woke up on their flaming funeral pyres – too late for their attendants to save either from horrible deaths.

3. The ancient Egyptian practice of mummification of the dead continued throughout the Ptolemaic period and centuries of Roman occupation. When Octavian visited Alexandria in AD 30 he viewed the mummy of Alexander the Great, but, when he touched it, part of the nose fell off.

4. When Genghis Khan died, his four legitimate sons were so paranoid about keeping the location of his grave a secret, to avoid its being despoiled, that they ordered the slaughter of everyone the funeral cortege came across – perhaps more than 20,000 people. Leaving nothing to chance, they then got their soldiers to kill the slaves who excavated the tomb, then had those soldiers executed in turn. It was a complete success, because Genghis Khan's grave was never found.

5. In 1890 the *Gloucester Citizen* reported that a man from Orenburg in Russia had lapsed into a coma and was presumed dead. A few days later he roused and somehow managed to climb out of his coffin, only to be clubbed to death by villagers who thought he was a zombie.

6. By the time Charles Dickens died of a stroke in 1870 his fame had reached international proportions, but in his will he requested a simple, low-key funeral in the cemetery of Rochester Cathedral⋆ – "and on no account to make me the subject of any monument, memorial, or testimonial whatever". The great man's wishes were completely ignored; the Dean of Westminster wanted a spectacular new burial for Poets' Corner so Dickens found himself buried in the Abbey.

7. In 1913 a one-legged black hobo Anderson McCrew died after falling off a moving freight train in Marlin, Texas. The morning after his death, he was taken to a funeral parlour and embalmed. When no one came forward to claim the body, a travelling carnival purchased it and displayed McCrew as "The Amazing Petrified

---

⋆ Rochester Cathedral featured in Dickens' first work, *The Pickwick Papers*, and he also knew the head verger William Miles, thought to have inspired the character of Mr Tope in *The Mystery of Edwin Drood*.

Man – The Eighth Wonder of the World". When the troupe disbanded fifty-five years later, McCrew remained in storage until Elgie Pace, a widow from Dallas, discovered him. She wanted to give him a decent burial but couldn't afford one, so she nicknamed him Sam and kept him in her basement. Sixty years after his death, an undertaker volunteered to give McCrew a funeral.

8. Every night, Chairman Mao's body in his crystal coffin goes down into an earthquake-proof vault in an elevator and every morning it is brought back up again.

9. The US President Franklin Delano Roosevelt was specific about his funeral arrangements, which he detailed in a four-page document: he wanted a simple service in the East Room of the White House; no lying-in-state; a gun carriage carrying a simple casket made of dark wood; no embalming or no hermetic sealing of his corpse; no brick, cement or stone linings for his grave. He placed his instructions in a private safe where, unfortunately, they were only discovered after his funeral. In the event, Roosevelt was embalmed and placed in a hermetically sealed coffin made of fine bronze-coloured copper and then was carried in a Cadillac hearse to a cement-lined vault.

10. The Victorian inventor George Bateson patented a device for preventing premature burial – a popular fear of the era. The Bateson Life Revival Device, or Bateson's Belfry as it was known, was a casket with a bell mounted in a miniature bell tower on the lid. Attached to the bell was a rope connected to the presumed corpse's hand through a hole in the coffin lid to alert an attentive gravedigger to the rescue. Despite some sales success and being awarded a medal by Queen Victoria for

services to the dead, Bateson didn't trust his own apparatus.* He built a series of increasingly complicated alarm systems for his own coffin, then changed his mind and rewrote his will, requesting cremation. Anxiety that his directions would not be followed drove him mad. In a fit of depression he doused himself with linseed oil and set himself ablaze in his workshop; he chose premature cremation rather than risk the horror of premature burial.

11. In the Victorian era, photography was still relatively new and expensive and the difficulty in staying still long enough for a high-quality photo meant that most poor people only had their picture taken after they had died. The photos were sent to distant relatives, many of whom might never have met a young child who died. Quite often, members of the family would pose with the dead in family portraits.

12. Many people muse that, come the day, they will "go out with a bang": some people actually do. In 1998 a French court ordered an eighty-two-year-old widow to pay £13,000 to a crematorium that was wrecked when a heart pacemaker exploded during the cremation of her husband's body; the deceased man's doctor was also ordered to pay another £26,000 in damages for failing to warn the crematorium that the body contained the

---

* He was right not to do so. A person enclosed in a normal-sized airtight coffin would perish within sixty minutes because of lack of oxygen, so any coffin that lacked a fresh-air supply would become a death trap no matter how many bells it was fitted with. However, putrefaction of a corpse is accompanied by swelling of the abdomen and contracture of the arms and legs. This would have set off many of Bateson's alarm mechanisms, no doubt leading to many heart-stopping scenes in local cemeteries.

device.* A recent survey found that half of crematoria workers in the UK had experienced a body exploding during cremation as a result of a carelessly overlooked pacemaker.

13. The dangers of premature burial were graphically illustrated by the tale of Lawrence Cawthorn, a butcher from Newgate Market in London, who fell ill in 1661. At the time, the apparent absence of a heartbeat or breath were considered proof of death, and, as few people were seen by a doctor in their final illness, it was often left to lay people to pronounce someone deceased. Lawrence's landlady, eager to inherit his belongings, saw to it that her lodger was promptly declared dead and then buried. During Cawthorn's funeral, mourners were horrified to hear a muffled cry and a frenzied clawing at the coffin walls. He was quickly dug up, but it was too late to save him. Cawthorn's lifeless body showed signs of a terrible struggle: the shroud was torn to pieces, his eyes were hideously swollen and his head was battered and bleeding.

14. In 1937 nineteen-year-old Angelo Hays from the French village of St Quentin de Chalais was thrown from his motorcycle and hit a brick wall, head first. Hays was declared dead and three days later was buried. In nearby Bordeaux, an insurance firm, suspicious that Hays' father had recently insured his son's life for 200,000 francs, sent an inspector to investigate. He demanded exhumation of the body to confirm the cause of death and, when Hays was dug up, his body was still warm: the head injury had caused him to slip into a coma. He was

---

* Chemicals in a pacemaker's battery can explode with the force of two grams of TNT – enough to fire a 16 lb artillery shell at a speed of 60 mph.

taken to hospital and after a long period of rehabilitation made a complete recovery.

15. Some human corpses turn partly or completely into soap – a process known as saponification. The fatty tissue of the body, along with other liquids from putrefaction form into lumps of adipocere, also known as grave wax. It is especially common in obese people with large fat deposits.

16. Five years after D. H. Lawrence's death and burial in France, his widow Frieda arranged to have his body exhumed, cremated and taken to Taos, New Mexico, where Lawrence had dreamed of establishing a utopian community. Angelo Ravagli, Frieda's lover at the time, was to accompany the ashes to Taos. Ravagli later confessed he had dumped the author's ashes in France to save on travel expenses. The remains he delivered to Frieda were some ashes he found in New York.

17. In 1955, three years after Eva Perón died, her embalmed corpse was removed by the Argentinean military in the wake of a coup that deposed her husband, President Juan Perón. For a while it was stowed behind a cinema screen in Buenos Aires. The owner's daughter, thinking it a store dummy, played with Eva for days.

18. In 1992 an eighteen-year-old girl, declared clinically dead, regained consciousness to find herself being raped on a slab by a mortuary attendant in Bucharest. The shocked rapist was arrested, but the girl's parents declined to press charges because their daughter "owed her life to him".

19. The American Russ Columbo was a famous screen and radio presence in the early 1930s. In 1934 the

twenty-four-year-old actor was visiting a close friend who owned a pair of antique duelling pistols. The friend used the pistols to strike matches, but one of them still had some gunpowder and an antique bullet in the chamber. The bullet ricocheted off the desk and hit Columbo in the left eye, lodging in the back of his brain: he died six hours later. His sixty-eight-year-old mother had a heart condition and her doctors advised the family that the bad news could be fatal. She was told that her son had married his girlfriend Carole Lombard and had left for Europe for a honeymoon. So began a bizarre conspiracy that lasted for a decade. There were fake postcards, telegrams and an elaborate story about a European tour that kept getting extended. Newspaper reports of Lombard's marriage to Clark Gable were carefully edited before they reached the family home. Mrs Columbo died in 1944, outliving her son by ten years, without ever knowing that he was dead.

20. In 2011 Fagilyu Mukhametzyanov, forty-nine, from Kazan, Russia, died from a heart attack brought on by the shock of waking up at her own funeral. Mourning relatives were filing past her open coffin when the supposedly dead woman suddenly woke up and started screaming as she realized where she was.

I DON'T LIKE MONDAYS: 10 SUICIDAL THOUGHTS

1. Monday is the most popular day for committing suicide. Saturday is the least popular. March, April and May have the highest suicide rate, around 5 per cent higher than the average for the rest of the year. Suicides at Christmas are below the average.

2. There are seven suicides in the Bible. The first was Abimelech, who lived in the twelfth century BC. He tried to kill his seventy half-brothers so he could become king. In his last battle he was severely injured when a woman dropped a millstone on his head. He ordered his sword bearer to finish him off so it could never be said that a woman killed him.

3. In America someone attempts suicide every minute and successfully completes a suicide once every seventeen minutes. Worldwide, about 2,000 people kill themselves every day.

4. Ancient Germanic tribes used to pin down the bodies of suicide victims in bogs. They did it to prevent the spirits of the dead from haunting the living.

5. Until the early nineteenth century in England, suicide victims were often buried at night at a crossroads with a stake driven through the heart. Crossroads represented the sign of the cross and the steady traffic over the grave

kept the person's ghost down. The last suicide to get this treatment was Abel Griffiths, a twenty-two-year-old law student. He was dragged through the streets of London and buried at a crossroads in only his drawers, socks and a sheet in June 1823.

6. In ancient Rome, the most common methods of suicide employed razors, scalpels and daggers. Hanging was seen as unclean and shameful. More rarely, Romans set themselves on fire – immolation. Roman gladiators would sometimes stick wooden sticks or spears down their throats or force their heads into the spokes of moving carts so that they could choose their own time of death rather than be defeated in contest.

7. Hanging is the leading method of suicide worldwide, but there are national preferences for types of suicide. The English and Irish are more likely to use poison, whereas Americans prefer firearms. Nearly 10 per cent of all fatal police shootings in the US are a result of "suicide by cop".

8. More than 2,000 young Japanese Kamikaze suicide pilots died during World War II. The number of ships they sank, however, is disputed and may be as low as thirty-four.

9. Twenty per cent of people who commit suicide leave behind a note.

10. Doctors are twice as likely to kill themselves as the general population. Female physicians are more likely to do it than their male counterparts. Psychiatrists, anaesthetists and ophthalmologists are at greater risk for suicide, with paediatricians having the least risk.

BURIED ALIVE:
15 PREMATURE OBITUARIES

1816: while dining in a London hotel, Samuel Taylor Coleridge overhears a man reading a newspaper report about the poet's suicide by hanging. The man notes: "Extraordinary that Coleridge should have hanged himself just after the success of his play ... but he always was a strange mad fellow."

1888: Swedish-born arms manufacturer Alfred Nobel reads his obituaries, erroneously published when he was confused with his late brother Ludwig. "The merchant of death is dead," reports one French paper, adding that Nobel "became rich by finding ways to kill more people faster than ever before".

1897: while Mark Twain is in London, a rumour that he is dead reaches the editor of the *New York Journal*, who cables his London correspondent: "If mark twain dying in poverty in london send 500 words." Another follows this order: "If mark twain has died in poverty send 1000 words." Twain responds: "The report of my death was an exaggeration." This is widely misreported as: "The rumours of my death are greatly exaggerated."*

---

* In 1907 Mark Twain was given up for dead again, this time by the *New York Times*, presumed lost at sea when his ship vanished in thick fog. Twain turned up a few days later and said he'd look into it. "If there is any foundation for the report, I will at once apprise the anxious public." He died definitively three years later.

1916: *The Times* mourns the death of writer Robert Graves, left for dead at the Battle of the Somme. He recovers from his injuries and dies of natural causes in his ninetieth year.

1922: as the Pope lies dying of pneumonia, a New York newspaper prints their morning edition with the headline POPE BENEDICT XV IS DEAD. Realizing their error, they run their evening edition with the headline POPE HAS MIRACULOUS RECOVERY.

1938: "Cockie" Hoogterp, second wife of Swedish aristocrat Baron Blixen, reads about her death in the *Daily Telegraph*. She returns her subscription bills marked "Deceased" and orders the *Telegraph* to print, "Mrs. Hoogterp wishes it to be known that she has not yet been screwed in her coffin." The paper had confused her for the Baron's third wife, who died in a car crash.

1940: after suffering a stroke, the Jamaican nationalist leader Marcus Garvey reads his obituary in a Chicago newspaper, which describes him as "broke, alone and unpopular". Garvey is so put out by the criticism that he suffers a second stroke and dies.

1969: as a rumour sweeps the US that Paul McCartney has died in a road accident and secretly been replaced by a lookalike, his American publicist phones him to ask if he is okay. McCartney replies: "Yes I am. Now fuck off."

1979: India mourns the death of elder statesman Jayaprakash Narayan after Prime Minister Morarji Desai informs Parliament that he has died in a Bombay hospital. After Desai's moving eulogy Parliament is adjourned and flags are lowered to half-mast. The entire Indian sub-continent is shaken by the news, none more so than Mr Narayan who is in bed convalescing. "Sorry about that," Desai remarks later.

1985: *The Times* errs again, publishing an obituary of BBC sports commentator Rex Alston, aged eighty-four. It is an unpleasant surprise for Alston, who has spent the night in a Westminster hospital, having collapsed at dinner the previous evening. He recovers and remarries the following year, becoming the only person to have his death and his marriage announced in *The Times* in that order.

1993: upon hearing that rehearsals are being made for her funeral, the Australian press reports the death of Elizabeth, the Queen Mother. In fact, rehearsals for her funeral had already been going on every six months for a couple of decades. They went on being rehearsed, right up to the new millennium and her eventual demise aged 101, making it the least spontaneous funeral ceremony ever.

1999: Dave Swarbrick, the folk musician, reads about his death in the *Daily Telegraph* while recuperating in a Midlands hospital. "It's not the first time I've died in Coventry," he muses.

2001: actress Dorothy Fay, wife of "the singing cowboy" Tex Ritter, finds herself in the *Daily Telegraph* obituary column. A nurse at the Motion Picture Hospital returned after a holiday to find that Fay was not in her usual room. When told that she had "gone" the nurse phoned one of Fay's friends, a regular contributor to the *Telegraph* obituaries desk. She had gone – to another hospital room.

2003: CNN accidentally reveals dozens of pre-prepared obituaries on its website. The news organization had been working on a design makeover and many details were transposed. Some followed the template of the obituary of the

Queen Mother shown the previous year; the site noted the Pope's "love of racing" and described Dick Cheney as the "UK's favourite grandmother".

2013: US President George Bush Senior spends Christmas in hospital with bronchitis. Adding insult to illness, the German news magazine *Der Spiegel* publishes his obituary online, describing Bush as a "colourless politician".

BOYS IN THE HOOD:
10 CELEBRITY CAR CRASHES

1931: F. W. Murnau, the German-born film director of *Faust* and *Nosferatu*, dies when his car leaves the road on a stretch of Californian coastline. The driver was his fourteen-year-old Filipino houseboy, Garcia Stevenson: it was said that Murnau was giving his servant a blowjob at the time.

1945: a Cadillac does to General George S. Patton what two world wars failed to, when the car he is a passenger in collides with a truck in Germany. Although the impact is minor, the sixty-year-old general hits his head on the metal partition between the front and back seats and he dies in hospital from an embolism.

1955: while out driving his beloved Porsche Spider, nick-named "Little Bastard", on his way to a race in Salinas, California, James Dean collides head-on with a driver who has just turned left onto the highway. Almost decapitated with multiple fractures to his jaw and massive internal injuries, Dean, twenty-four, is pronounced dead on the spot.*

1956: after leaving a massive imprint on the art world, Jackson Pollock fatally leaves his mark on a tree with his

---

* After Dean's fatal car crash, his smashed Porsche was privately exhibited around Los Angeles. Fans were charged twenty-five cents to view the death car and fifty cents to sit behind the bloodstained steering wheel. The car was later broken up and pieces were auctioned off.

Oldsmobile convertible – less than a mile from his home in Springs, New York.

1967: film actress Jayne Mansfield is on her way back from a local nightclub in a 1966 Buick Electra, driven by night-club chauffeur Ronald Harrison, when the car rear ends a trailer spraying for mosquitoes. She and Harrison are killed instantly but her three children, who were sleeping in the back of the car, all survive.

1973: American actor and rapper Lamont Bentley runs a stop sign in California at high speed, goes through a chain-link fence and rolls down an embankment. Although ejected through his sunroof, he is run over by five other vehicles.

1982: Princess Grace of Monaco, formerly Grace Kelly, Hollywood starlet, is driving through the principality when her Rover 3500 careers through a retaining wall and into 120 ft of trees and branches. Grace is killed instantly; her passenger, daughter Stephanie, survives with multiple inju-ries but doesn't find out about her mother's passing until two days after her funeral.

1997: Princess Diana and her companion Dodi Al Fayed attempt to sidestep paparazzi stationed outside the Ritz hotel, Paris. Slipping through a back entrance, they are led to a Mercedes sedan driven by Henri Paul, with Diana's bodyguard Trevor Rees-Jones in the front passenger seat. As the car enters the Pont de l'Alma tunnel, Paul loses control and the vehicle slams into an interior wall of the tunnel, then into the dividing pillars. Rees-Jones is the sole survivor.

2002: member of R&B group TLC Lisa "Left Eye" Lopes, known for the patch she wears over her left eye, careers off a highway in La Ceiba, Honduras. Seven other people are in the vehicle with Lopes but none of them sustains life-threatening injuries.

2011: Ryan Dunn, thirty-four-year-old star of MTV's *Jackass*, hits speeds of over 130 mph before his Porsche 911 wraps around a tree and is quickly engulfed in flames. Dunn's remains are identified by his tattoos and hair.

ESPRIT DE CORPSE:
12 FUNERAL PRACTICES

1. In nineteenth-century Britain people employed "sin-eaters" to eat the sins of the dead. They were usually poor people or beggars paid to eat bread and drink beer or wine over a corpse, in the belief they would take on the sins of the deceased. A relative would place a loaf of bread on the chest of the deceased and pass a cup of ale to the sin-eater across it.

2. Following the death of a Wari tribesman of Brazil, family members wait for several days until the corpse of their loved one begins to decompose, then they cut it into small pieces – first the brains, heart and liver – then roast and eat it, the choice cuts going to the parents and elders. The Wari believe they are eating the "animal essence" of their loved ones, which in turn gives them strength.

3. Undertakers in the US earn air miles every time they ship a corpse.

4. In Scotland funeral-goers were encouraged to handle the body before it was interred to avoid the possibility of being haunted. Traditionally, the corpse of a murdered man would not decay until it had been ceremoniously "touched".

5. In most Western cultures a man's status at death can be measured by the expense of his funeral. In India, until

the early nineteenth century, the status of Hindu men was gauged by the number of wives who accompanied them to the funeral pyre – a practice known as suttee. In British India in 1829 suttee was classified as "culpable homicide", punishable only by fine or imprisonment.

6. The churchyard used to be the final resting place for people whose social status did not entitle them to be buried within the Church itself. Even in the churchyard, your status could be judged by the position of your burial plot. The best sites were to the east, as close as possible to the altar wall, where the deceased could be assured the best view of the rising sun on Judgement Day. The next best plots were occupied by those buried parallel to the long axis of the church, head pointing west, feet to the east. People of lesser distinction were buried on the south side. The north was suitable only for stillborn children, bastards and outsiders unfortunate enough to have died while passing through the parish.

7. Until recently, in rural China, strippers were a common feature at funerals. Status was judged by the number of funeral attendees, so families who could afford it employed "warm-up acts" to attract a bigger crowd. In 2003 two hundred people showed up at a Chinese funeral at which five strippers were arrested by the local police.

8. According to an ancient tradition still alive in the highlands of western China, a young man who dies unmarried goes to his grave accompanied by a dead woman, who will serve as his wife in the afterlife. Often these women have died a natural death; occasionally they have not. In 2008 Chinese police arrested three men for killing two young women to sell their corpses as "ghost brides" for dead single men.

9. Coffin-makers in the US are now making extra-large casks because of the super-sizing of their customers.

10. In the nineteenth century there was a brief vogue for rubber coffins, which were said to slow down the rate of putrefaction. Unfortunately, despite the supposed impermeability of these rubber coffins, the bodies contained within them were generally found to be disappointingly rotten. The French pathologist Paul Brouardel tested one and noted: "The body is destroyed in three or four years, and there is formed a liquid greasy substance, like black axle-grease, which rolls about, and when the coffin is opened gives forth an abominable stench."

11. London's first public cemetery was opened at Kensal Green in 1832. It became *the* place to be seen dead for the wealthy and famous, thanks to the interment of Queen Victoria's favourite uncle, Augustus Frederick, Duke of Sussex, in April 1843. Kensal Green still boasts the largest number of royals buried outside Windsor and Westminster Abbey to this day.

12. In 2008, when the cemetery in the town of Sarpourenx, southwest France, became full, the local Mayor was frustrated when his planning permission to extend it was turned down. Gerard Lalanne had a contingency plan: he told the village's 260 residents: "all persons not having a plot in the cemetery and wishing to be buried in Sarpourenx are forbidden from dying in the parish." His warning concluded: "Offenders will be severely punished."

AFTERLIFE TYCOONS: THE 10 TOP-EARNING CELEBRITY CORPSES*

Michael Jackson, singer – $160 million over the year. Cause of death – overdose/homicide in 2009, aged fifty.

Elvis Presley, singer – $55 million. Heart attack, in 1977, aged forty-two.

Charles Schulz, cartoonist – $37 million. Colon cancer, in 2000, aged seventy-seven.

Elizabeth Taylor, actress – $25 million. Heart failure, in 2011, aged seventy-nine.

Bob Marley, singer – $18 million. Cancer, in 1981, aged thirty-six.

Marilyn Monroe, actress – $15 million. Overdose, in 1962, aged thirty-six.

John Lennon, singer – $12 million. Murdered, in 1980, aged forty.

---

* As of December 2013 according to *Forbes*, the American business magazine.

Albert Einstein, scientist – $10 million. Natural causes, in 1955, aged seventy-six.

Bettie Page, actress – $10 million. Natural causes, in 2008, aged eighty-five.

Theodor Geisel, author – $9 million. Natural causes, in 1991, aged eighty-seven.

12 UNUSUAL ROYAL DEATHS

c. AD 20: the Swedish King Fjolnir goes to bed after attending a banquet hosted by Frode of Leidre, when he is awoken in the night by the need to pee. On his way back to his room he slips and falls into a giant barrel of mead and drowns.

840: Louis "the Pious", King of the Franks, dies of fright after seeing a solar eclipse.

1190: the Holy Roman Emperor Frederick I drowns after falling face-down in his heavy armour into a shallow part of a river. His men pickle him in a barrel of vinegar to preserve his body.

1256: King Uzana of Burma is trampled to death by an elephant, the first of four Burmese royals to die in elephant-related circumstances. Crown Prince Minrekyawswa (1471) is also trampled to death; King Razadarit (1421) dies after becoming entangled in a rope while attempting to lasso one; King Tabinshweti (1560) is beheaded while searching for a "lucky" white elephant.

1498: Charles VIII of France bangs his head on a door lintel on his way to watch a tennis match. He never recovers from his coma.

1641: the French Bourbon prince Comte de Soissons leads an army of revolt in eastern France against Cardinal Richelieu. The prince wins a great victory at La Marfee, but at the moment of triumph accidentally blows his brains out while lifting his visor with his pistol.

1615: King Philip III of Spain falls ill with a "mortal fever", but is miraculously cured when the body of St Isadora is brought into the king's bedroom. Six years later he contracts another fever, the result of sitting too long near a hot brazier. The palace footman whose job it is to remove it isn't available – it never occurs to the king to move it himself.

1737: an unwell Queen Caroline, wife of George II, is attended by her physicians, when one of them leans too close to a candle and accidentally sets fire to his wig. The queen laughs so hard that her strangulated bowel bursts, killing her.

1880: Queen Sunandha of Thailand dies when the royal boat capsizes on the way to the palace. Dozens of onlookers, forbidden on pain of death to touch the queen, stand and watch as she drowns.

1934: the Belgian King Albert I is killed in a mountaineering accident in the Ardennes. His last words are: "If I feel in good form, I will take the difficult way up. If I do not, I will take the easy one. I will join you in an hour."

1935: Astrid, Queen of the Belgians, is pointing out something on a map to her husband King Leopold when their car goes off the road, down a steep slope and slams into a pear tree. Queen Astrid's body is ejected from the car and collides with the trunk of the tree, while the car slams into a second tree.

1982: Sobhuza II, King of Swaziland, calls his advisers for a routine cabinet meeting. After half an hour he suddenly adjourns the meeting and asks everyone to leave except his minister for health. "I am going," the king informs his minister. "Where?" the minister enquires. The king smiles, waves goodbye and dies.

10 STEPS FOR PREPARING A CORPSE FOR SHIPMENT*

1. Thoroughly clean and embalm the remains.

2. Pack all external orifices.

3. Place the remains in a plastic coverall.

4. Partially dress the remains using underclothing, pyjamas or a hospital gown, then wrap in a clean sheet.

5. When shipping by carrier, wrap the shrouded body in a sheet of plastic. Do not place one hand over another, as this might not be the desired position.

6. When shipping casketed remains, place a very heavy layer of cotton around the head and face to protect the casket and clothing from any purge. Turn the pillow over for shipping to prevent soilage from purge or cosmetics.

7. Secure the body on a cot if shipping within the container; if casketed, place the bed of the casket in the lowest position and move the feet to the furthest end; secure the head end so the body will not slide.

---

* According to *Embalming: History, Theory, & Practice* by Robert Mayer.

8. Document the condition of the body prior to, during and after embalming.

9. Send a copy of the embalming report with the remains.

10. Notify the receiving funeral director of any unusual conditions (e.g. trauma, obesity, oedema).

15 SPORTING TRAGEDIES

564 BC: Arrachion of Phigalia wins the pancration, a brutal triathlon event combining boxing, wrestling and general endurance. His opponent concedes, but not before jumping on Arrachion's back, breaking the victor's neck. It is only after Arrachion is declared the winner that the judges discover that he is in fact dead – the only deceased person in history to win an Olympic event.

1017: on Christmas Day, England's King Cnut has the noble Eadric Streona summarily beheaded; the king is annoyed because Streona beat him in a game of chess.

1159: King Henry II of France is taking part in a jousting match to celebrate a peace treaty between France and Spain when a lance fragment pierces Henry's eye and penetrates his brain. The king dies the following say, aged forty.

1844: William Crockford, owner of the Epsom Derby second favourite Ratan, dies following a fit of apoplexy, brought on by the poisoning of his horse a few days before the race. Crockford's untimely demise is bad news for his gambling friends, because he also has a heavily backed filly entered for the Oaks. If his death became public, the filly would be disqualified. They get around the problem by propping Crockford's body up at a window in his house overlooking the racecourse, where, clearly visible to the crowd, it discredits any rumours of his death. Crockford's filly wins the race and the punters collect their winnings before their ruse is discovered.

1897: Turkish wrestler Yousouf Ishmaelo travels to the US and defeats reigning Greco-Roman champion Ernest Roeber. Ishmaelo converts all his winnings into gold coins, which he keeps in a belt around his waist at all times. Returning home, his ship *Le Bourgogne* collides with a British vessel. Ishmaelo goes overboard but refuses to abandon his money belt. Although a strong swimmer, he sinks to his death.

1912: at the Stockholm Olympics, Portuguese marathon runner Francisco Lazaro falls dead during the marathon. He had coated his body with several pounds of beeswax to prevent sunburn.

1932: the legendary, virtually unbeatable Australian race-horse Phar Lap is found dead just two weeks after winning the world's richest race in Mexico. Stable lad Tommy Woodcock claims a race-fixer, identified only as "the Brazilian", has poisoned his horse. Nearly sixty years later it emerges that Phar Lap was probably killed by an accidental overdose of arsenic administered by Woodcock himself.

1964: marathon runner Kokichi Tsuburaya, Japan's last hope to win a gold medal in a track event at the Tokyo Olympics, is so upset after his defeat that he commits hara-kiri. In his suicide note, he apologizes for having failed his country. He finished third in the race and won a bronze medal.

1982: Navy lieutenant George Prior dies from a severe allergic reaction to Daconil, a fungicide used on his local golf course in Arlington, Virginia. Prior had ingested the toxin through his habit of carrying a tee around in his mouth while he was playing.

1983: during a tennis match at the US Open, a serve from the Swede Stefan Edberg hits the linesman Dick Wertheim in the groin. The official keels over, hits his head on the floor and dies from blunt cranial trauma.

1983: while attempting a manoeuvre called "The Dive of Death" – a reverse three and a half somersault in the tuck position – Sergei Chalibashvili hits his head on the platform, falls into a week-long coma and subsequently dies. The judges record his score as 0.0.

1987: in front of 1,500 holidaymakers in Great Yarmouth, wrestler Mal "King Kong" Kirk expires beneath the belly of 26-stone Shirley Crabtree, aka "Big Daddy". Kirk suffers a fatal heart attack after Daddy performs his "splash down" manoeuvre on him. He'd told friends hours earlier: "If I have to go, I hope it is in the ring."

1992: while celebrating with a firework display at the end of the Barcelona Olympics, Brad Kim, a twenty-one-year-old member of the US kayak team, is decapitated while trying to light a rocket.

1996: while hunting for a lost ball at Dublin's Cradockstown golf course, David Bailey is surprised by a rat, which runs up his trouser leg and urinates on his leg. His friends encourage him to take a shower, but Bailey insists on finishing the round. Two weeks later he dies of kidney failure, a symptom of rat-borne Weil's disease.

2013: football fans in Maranhão in northern Brazil invade the pitch and decapitate the referee, then parade his head on a stake. Officials say the spectators were upset because the ref, Mr Octavio da Silva, stabbed a player, Josenir dos Santos, for refusing to leave the pitch after he was sent off.

TOP 15 NEWSPAPER OBITUARY EUPHEMISMS

1. "Tireless raconteur" (crashing bore).

2. "He/she tended to become over-attached to certain ideas and theories" (fascist).

3. "Larger than life" (bully).

4. "Noted raconteur" (terrible old bore).

5. "Gave colourful accounts of his/her exploits" (liar).

6. "A free spirit" (unemployable).

7. "She did not suffer fools gladly" (foul-tempered harridan).

8. "Vivacious" (drunk female).

9. "His door was always open" (alcoholic).

10. "His door was always open, at any time of the day or night" (alcoholic, with an eye for boys).

11. "He was good company" (convivial alcoholic).

12. "A bohemian character" (an alcoholic who lived in a disgusting flat).

13. "Confirmed bachelor" (homosexual).

14. "Burdened by occasional irregularities in his private life" (indecent exposure, adultery or cross-dressing).

15. "A colourful character" (a total cunt).

BLOOD ON THE TRACKS: 5 MOST POPULAR LONDON UNDERGROUND LINES FOR SUICIDE JUMPERS

1. Northern Line

2. Central Line

3. Piccadilly Line

4. District Line

5. Jubilee Line

The peak time for jumping for men is between 10 a.m. and 4 p.m. and for women 10 a.m. and 1 p.m. The high season for jumpers is spring. The highest number of incidents occurs at King's Cross, followed by Mile End and Tooting Bec.

BONES OF CONTENTION: 12 MISLAID BODY PARTS

1. Tutankhamen's willy

   The ancient Egyptian pharaoh was mummified with a fully erect penis. Photos taken by Howard Carter show it was still attached to King Tut's body when he was first unwrapped in 1922. The upright body part broke off some time after the discovery of his tomb and is still missing, possibly stolen.

2. Santa's bones

   In the Middle Ages, the body parts of saints were big business because of their supposed abilities to perform miracles. The remains of St Nicholas were said to leak myrrh, making him a particularly lucrative bag of bones. In 1087 the Italian town of Bari hired some pirates to steal St Nick from Myra, in present-day Turkey. The theft of Santa's bones is still celebrated in Bari with an annual parade and fireworks.

3. Dante's bones

   The Italian poet died of malaria and was buried in Ravenna in 1321, but Dante's birth city of Florence decided they wanted him back. Ravenna refused to cooperate, and to thwart Florentine corpse-nappers they secretly hid the poet's body in a wall. The location was forgotten until 1865, when a worker unearthed it during church renovations. While they were waiting to rebury Dante, several people helped themselves to pieces of the poet's body. In 1878 a local civic employee sheepishly returned a box of Dante's bones, stolen in 1865. Soon after, several more people returned pieces of the poet that they had nabbed.

4. Beethoven's ears and skull

Beethoven's body was exhumed twice: once in 1863 in order to preserve his remains better in a metal coffin, then again in 1888 when they were transferred to the Vienna Central Cemetery. During his original autopsy a doctor stole Ludwig's ear bones and several locks of hair. When the composer's body was examined a second time two large segments of his skull went missing, swiped by a doctor, Gerhard von Breuning, who wanted the shape of Beethoven's skull analysed to see if they offered up any clues about his personality. The skull segments changed hands several times until 1936, when, amid fears that they could be used as a Nazi propaganda tool, they were hidden in an unknown location. The pieces of skull resurfaced in 2005 and were loaned to San Jose State University Centre for Beethoven Studies, where they reside today.

5. Mozart's skull

When Mozart died in 1791 at the age of thirty-five, he was buried at Vienna's St Mark's Cemetery in a grave with four or five other bodies – a standard middle-class burial procedure in those times. The exact location of his final resting place is not known, but, according to tradition, a gravedigger attached a wire to the skull so that he could identify it when he went to retrieve it several years later. From there, the skull had several owners; it spent some time in the phrenological collection of one Dr Hyrtl, before ending up in the hands of the Mozarteum in Salzburg, Austria in 1902. DNA tests on the skull to prove authenticity have since proven disappointingly inconclusive, so the mystery of Mozart's whereabouts remains unsolved.

6. Thomas Paine's bones
    In 1819, ten years after the political activist's death in New York, journalist and Paine fan William Cobbett exhumed Paine's body and shipped it to England where he hoped to build an impressive memorial. Cobbett was unable to raise the money, so Paine stayed in a trunk in his attic. When Cobbett died, Paine's remains disappeared: according to legend, his bones were turned into buttons. Since then, people all over the world have claimed to own a part of Paine, including a woman from Brighton who says she has his jawbone.

7. Napoleon's bits
    The Little Corporal is widely scattered. His intestines were allegedly held in London until they were destroyed during a bombing raid during the Blitz. His penis meanwhile is believed to be in the possession of the daughter of John Lattimer, a New Jersey urologist, who bought it at auction in 1977 for $3,700. At the time it was sold it was one-and-a-half inches long. When it was put up for public display in Manhattan in 1927, *TIME* magazine remarked that it looked like a "maltreated strip of buckskin shoelace".

8. John Bellingham's head
    In May 1812 Britain's one and only prime ministerial assassin walked into the lobby of the House of Commons and shot dead the Tory PM Spencer Perceval. Although clearly unhinged, the witless killer refused to enter a plea of insanity and was hanged and dissected. Bellingham's skull was lost for more than fifty years until it turned up in a box in the basement of the anatomy department of St Bartholomew's Medical School. Someone had

thoughtfully written "Bellingham" in ink across the forehead.

9. Sarah Bernhardt's leg

   In 1905 the famous French actress injured her knee while leaping off a parapet during the final scene of a performance of *La Tosca* in Brazil. The injury never healed properly and by 1915 gangrene had set in and her leg had to be amputated above the knee. She continued to perform, sticking to roles best suited to a uniped. The circus mastermind P. T. Barnum reportedly offered Ms Bernhardt a large sum for the appendage but she turned him down. It went missing until, ninety-four years after it was amputated, staff members at Bordeaux University's medical school stumbled across the leg in a storeroom.

10. Mata Hari's skull

    Margaretha Zelle, the Dutch spy better known as Mata Hari, was executed by a French firing squad in 1917. As no family member stepped forward to claim her body, it went to the Museum of Anatomy in Paris where her head was severed, preserved in wax and placed in the museum's collection of notorious criminals. In 2000 the museum's archivists discovered that the skull was missing, presumed stolen. Whatever the explanation, the enigmatic Mata Hari is still at large.

11. Albert Einstein's brain

    After his death in 1955, Einstein's brain was removed and studied by pathologist Thomas Harvey in the hope that it might reveal some great insight into the nature of genius. Most of it was sliced and mounted on hundreds of slides, many of which are now lost.

12. John F. Kennedy's brain

    During JFK's autopsy at Bethesda Naval Hospital in

1963 the brain was placed in a stainless-steel container with a screw-top lid and stored in the National Archives. Three years later, it was discovered the brain had gone missing and it hasn't been seen since. Conspiracy theorists say the missing organ would have proved Kennedy was not shot from the back by Lee Harvey Oswald, but from the front – perhaps from the grassy knoll. A more plausible version has it that the president's brain was taken by his younger brother Robert, either to conceal the true extent of the President's illnesses or to hide evidence of the number of medications he was taking.

SPEAKING ILL OF THE DEAD: 12 POST-MORTEM OBSERVATIONS

1. "Posterity will ne'er survey
   a Nobler grave than this:
   Here lie the bones of Castlereagh:
   Stop, traveller, and piss!"

   > Lord Byron, on the death of British elder
   > statesman Lord Castlereagh

2. "How can they tell?"

   > Dorothy Parker, on hearing that American President
   > Calvin Coolidge had died

3. "Oh?"

   > Queen Mary, when informed of the
   > death of her son, King George VI

4. "Well, it only proves what they always say. Give the
   public something they want to see, and they'll come out
   for it."

   > Red Skelton, commenting on the big turnout for the
   > funeral of the Hollywood mogul Harry Cohn

5. "They say you mustn't say nothing but good about the
   dead. He's dead – *good*."

   > African-American comic Jackie "Moms" Mabley
   > celebrating the demise of her husband

6. "I'm amazed he was such a good shot."

> Noel Coward, upon hearing that his accountant
> had blown his brains out

7. "Nixon was so crooked that he needed servants to help him screw his pants on every morning."

> Hunter S. Thompson shortly after the
> death of Richard M. Nixon, US President

8. "Good career move."

> Gore Vidal upon the death of Truman Capote

9. "Fourteen heart attacks and he had to die in my week."

> Singer Janis Joplin when US President Dwight D.
> Eisenhower's death bumped her off the cover of
> *Newsweek* in 1969

10. "Elvis died when he joined the army."

> John Lennon, on hearing that Elvis Presley had died

11. "This guy was a pervert. He was a child molester, he was a paedophile, and to be giving this much coverage to him day in and day out, what does it say about us as a country?"

> Peter King, Republican state congressman
> for New York, on the death of Michael Jackson

12. "The publicity generated by his death was so much . . . it was good for F1. It was a shame that we had to lose Ayrton, but it happened."

> Formula 1 boss Bernie Ecclestone,
> reflecting on the death of Ayrton Senna, killed in
> an accident at the 1994 San Marino Grand Prix

12 DEAD POLITICIANS

121 BC: assassins execute the Roman Tribune Gaius Gracchus, out to receive a bounty on the weight of his head in gold. One of the co-conspirators, Septimuleius, decapitates Gaius, scoops his brains out and fills the cavity of his skull with molten lead. When the lead hardens, the head is taken to the Senate and weighed in on the scale at more than 17 lb; Septimuleius is paid in full.

1498: the chancellor of Mainz, Georg Pfeffer von Hell, stumbles in his privy, falls down the hole and drowns in the cesspit below.

1672: an angry Dutch mob turns on their Prime Minister, Johan de Witt, and his brother Cornelis, arrested on a trumped-up charge of plotting to assassinate Prince William III. They are beaten, stabbed and shot to death, then their fingers, ears and genitals are sliced off and sold as souvenirs. Other parts of their bodies were allegedly eaten by the mob: the first time in history that a crowd has snacked on burghers.

1777: British diplomat Simon Harcourt, the 1st Earl of Harcourt, drowns while walking on his estate in Oxfordshire after falling head-first into a well as he attempts to rescue his dog. Harcourt's body is found in the narrow well with only his feet protruding from the water. His dog survived by standing on the earl's feet.

1783: American revolutionary James Otis Jr tells friends

and relatives that he hopes death will come from a bolt of lightning. His wish is fulfilled when lightning strikes the chimney of a friend's house in whose doorway he is standing.

1816: American founding father Gouverneur Morris dies after poking a piece of whalebone through his urinary tract to relieve a blockage.

1923: Aubrey Herbert, Conservative MP for Yeovil, dies of blood poisoning after having all of his teeth removed in a strange bid to cure his blindness.

1967: the Australian Prime Minister Harold Holt goes for a dip on Cheviot Beach near Portsea, Victoria, and is never seen again, after telling his four friends, "I know this beach like the back of my hand."

1973: Peter Valyi, Hungarian finance minister, is on a routine official visit to a steel works when he steps forward to get a better look inside a blast furnace. He trips and falls in head-first.

1979: Japanese politician Nitaro Ito tries to inject some life into his flagging election campaign. He goes for the sympathy vote by staging a fake attack on himself. Having persuaded one of his employees to punch him in the face, Ito stabs himself in the leg, hits an artery and bleeds to death.

1994: MP Stephen Milligan, rising star in the Conservative Party and their "back to basics" moral crusade, is found dead in his London apartment by a cleaning lady. Lying on his living-room table, he is naked save for a pair of women's stockings and suspenders, with a plastic bag over his head and an electrical flex tied around his neck.

1998: French MP Andre Isoardo shoots himself five times before finally managing to kill himself. Police in Marseilles discover a suicide note; they also find 9 mm bullets lodged in his stomach, groin, wrist, throat and brain.

DEAD SERIOUS:
20 DECEASED PHILOSOPHERS

Thales of Miletus (*c.* 546 BC): originator of the phrase "know thyself" died from heatstroke and dehydration while watching the Olympic games on a very hot day.

Heraclitus (475 BC): according to one account, drowned in cow dung.*

Empedocles (430 BC): threw himself into the crater of Mount Etna to prove his immortality. Apart from a solitary bronze slipper spat out by the flames, there has been no sign of him since.

Zeno of Elea (*c.* 430 BC): stabbed to death during a fight with the tyrant Demylus, although he did manage to bite off his assailant's tongue and spit it back into his face.

Metrocles (325 BC): suicidally distraught after farting during a lecture rehearsal, took his own life by starving himself to death.

Plato (347 BC): allegedly died of a lice infestation.†

---

* According to another version Heraclitus suffered from dropsy, which he tried to cure by coating himself with cow dung and baking in the sun, believing that this would remove the fluid. He died a day later.
† He died either while being serenaded by a Thracian flute-playing girl, or at a wedding feast.

Diogenes (323 BC): died either from eating raw octopus, or from being bitten by a dog. Or by deliberately holding his breath. He asked to be buried face down, "because after a little time down will be converted into up".

Lucretius (52 BC): said to have committed suicide after being driven mad by a love potion.

Plotinus (270): death hastened by his refusal to treat a disease of the bowels with an enema.

Hypatia (415): the first great female scholar was murdered by a mob of angry Christians, who then tore her skin off with oyster shells.

Avicenna (1037): history's first recorded opium overdose, just after an overly energetic bout of sex.

Thomas of Aquinas (1274): died after banging his head against the bough of a tree.

Giordano Bruno (1600): burned alive at the stake by the Inquisition for pointing out that the universe was infinite.

Thomas Hobbes (1679): struck down by "acute pain" when urinating.

Jean-Jacques Rousseau (1778): died of massive cerebral bleeding, hastened by being bowled over by a giant Great Dane that was running through the streets of Paris.

Max Stirner (1856): was stung on the neck by an unidentified insect and died from an infection.

Friedrich Nietzsche (1900): collapsed into terminal insanity, probably neurosyphilis, after kissing a horse in the street in Turin.

Ludwig Wittgenstein (1951): died of prostate cancer the day after his birthday. His friend Mrs Bevan gave him an electric blanket saying, "Many happy returns." Wittgenstein replied: "There will be no returns."

Roland Barthes (1980): knocked down by a dry-cleaning van while walking home through Paris.

Gilles Deleuze (1995): threw himself from the window of his Paris apartment to relieve his suffering from emphysema.

11 PEOPLE WHO FELL TO THEIR DEATHS

c. 560 BC: the fabled Greek storyteller Aesop upsets his hosts in Delphi by criticizing their home; they respond by throwing him head-first from the Hyampeia rock.

1197: Henry II, Count of Champagne, falls to his death from an open first-floor window. One account says he was looking at a passing parade when he was startled by the arrival of some guests behind him; others reckon that he lost his balance while attempting a discreet nocturnal pee. Either way, he might have survived if his favourite dwarf, who tried to grab him as he fell, hadn't plummeted from the window and fallen on top of him.

1203: according to several chronicles, King John of England kills his nephew Arthur of Brittany by throwing him out of a castle window in Rouen, France.

1204: blind Byzantine ex-Emperor Murzuphlus is arrested for treason and dragged to the main square in Constantinople. The new Emperor Baudouin asks the mob what he should do with his prisoner; they decide that Murzuphlus should be forced to leap off a high marble column in the middle of the square in full view of everyone.

1419: an angry mob of Hussite peasant rebels storms the town hall on Charles Square in Prague and throws the judge, the mayor and several city council members out of the window. They all either die in the fall or are killed by the crowd outside.*

1452: in a fit of temper, King James II of Scotland stabs William, eighth Earl of Douglas twenty-six times then throws his body out of the window at Stirling Castle.

1871: Hans Christian Andersen dies from his injuries after falling out of bed.

1903: during a palace coup, King Alexander and Queen Draga of Yugoslavia are shot, disembowelled and then thrown from a second-floor window.

1993: lawyer Gary Hoy free-falls from the twenty-fourth floor of a Toronto tower block, after attempting to impress work colleagues by hurling himself against the office window to test the tensile strength of the glass.

2007: a "distance spitting" contest goes awry when a forty-three-year-old man in Brandenburg, Germany, falls from a balcony while apparently trying too hard to gain extra momentum to propel his saliva further and is carried over the railing. The newspaper *Der Spiegel* refers to the incident as a "tragic sports injury".

2013: a Cleveland stripper attempts a tricky manoeuvre during a lap dance on a second-floor balcony. Lauren Block is entertaining a customer at Christie's Cabaret when she

---

* The Czech people were fond of throwing people out of windows in times of crisis; since 1419 there has been at least one more Prague defenestration, in 1618.

tries a "jump-dance" move and accidentally flies head-first over the rail.

12 STRANGE SUICIDES

AD 131: the Roman Emperor Maxinimus II takes his own life by bashing his head against a rock until his eyes fall out.

1921: spiritualist Thomas Lynn Bradford from Detroit, Michigan, kills herself in an experiment to prove the existence of an afterlife. There have been no further communications from her since.

1925: the Russian poet Sergei Esenin writes an entire poem in his own blood. It also serves as his suicide note.

1959: blonde, blue-eyed Danish actress Gwili Andre, known as "the highest priced model in America" was signed as a "Garbo look-alike" by RKO Studio, earning $25,000 a year and dating Howard Hughes, but failed to live up to the hype (one critic called her a "stiff, colourless and completely talentless performer"). She is found sprawled on the bedroom floor of her apartment, burned to a crisp in a funeral pyre she has made out of her old press cuttings.

1987: Toronto prisoner Franco Brun takes his own life by shoving a small Bible down his throat. Earlier that day he was moved to a solitary windowless cell after he was seen masturbating at his cell window overlooking the street by a guard. The twenty-two-year-old is only serving a fifteen-day sentence.

1995: a thirty-nine-year-old man from Canberra, Australia, shoots himself three times with a pump-action shotgun. The first shot passes through his chest, but misses all of his vital organs. He reloads and shoots away his throat and part of his jaw. Breathing through the hole in his throat, he reloads and holds the gun against his chest with his hands and operates the trigger with his toes: this shot enters his heart, fatally.

1999: Saswati Mishra, nineteen, jumps to her death from the fifth floor of a building in Bhubanneswar, India, after two astrologers predict she will become a widow. Her suicide note says she has complete faith in astrology and is killing herself because she can't face losing her husband.

2000: Elisabeth Otto, thirty-one, falls 2,000 ft to her death when she disembarks from a California commuter airplane mid-flight. She was reportedly despondent after recently moving to the United States from Holland.

2008: a businessman decapitates himself in his sports car to get back at his younger wife for leaving him. Gerald Mellin, fifty-four, taunted his estranged wife Mirrielle, thirty-three, with threats of suicide and showed her the rope he was going to use, which he kept in the boot of his open-top Aston Martin DB7. He ties one end of the rope to a tree, then climbs into his Aston Martin and wraps the other end around his neck before speeding off in his £90,000 car into a busy main road.

2008: Nordin Montong, a cleaner at Singapore Zoo, is mauled to death when he enters an enclosure containing three white tigers and provokes them with his broom. It is the first recorded "death by tiger" suicide.

2009: after a run of family problems, depressed fifty-two-year-old Montenegran Milo Bogisic walks into a funeral parlour and pays cash for a new coffin. While puzzled staff look on, he writes out his own obituary, then jumps into the casket and shoots himself in the head. He survives when the bullet passes straight through his chin and nose missing his brain. Unfortunately, the undertakers refuse to give him a refund for the coffin. "He'll have to keep it. He'll get some proper use out of it one day," says a spokesman for Palma Funerals.

2013: a house-cleaning robot in Australia activates itself while its owners are out, shuffles across a work surface and hurls itself to its death on a stove hot plate, leaving only a heap of cinders. The world's first robot suicide does not think of leaving a note.

12 SUICIDE NOTES

1. "I feel certain that I am going mad again: I feel we can't go through another of those terrible times. And I shan't recover this time. I begin to hear voices, and can't concentrate."

    Virginia Woolf, author, d. 28 March 1941

2. "To my friends: My work is done. Why wait?"

    George Eastman, inventor, d. 14 March 1932

3. "Dear World, I am leaving you because I am bored. I feel I have lived long enough. I am leaving you with your worries in this sweet cesspool – good luck."

    George Sanders, British actor, d. 25 April 1972

4. "No More Games. No More Bombs. No More Walking. No More Fun. No More Swimming. 67. That is 17 years past 50. 17 more than I needed or wanted. Boring. I am always bitchy. No Fun for anybody. 67. You are getting Greedy. Act your old age. Relax. This won't hurt."

    Hunter S. Thompson, author, d. 20 February 2005

5. "To Harald, may God forgive you and forgive me too but I prefer to take my life away and our baby's before I bring him with shame or killing him, Lupe."

    Lupe Velez, actress, d. 13 December 1944

6. "I don't believe that people should take their own lives without deep and thoughtful reflection over a considerable period of time."

    Wendy O. Williams, punk rock singer, d. 6 April 1998

7. "Things just went wrong too many times."

    Tony Hancock, comedian and actor, d. 24 June 1968

8. "We made a death pact, and I have to accomplish my part of the deal. Please bury me next to my baby. Please bury me with my leather jacket, jeans and motorcycle boots. Goodbye. With love, Sid."

    John Ritchie aka Sid Vicious,
    Sex Pistol, d. 2 February 1979

9. "Excuse all the blood."

    Prer Ohlin aka Dead, Norwegian vocalist with black metal band Mayhem, before cutting his wrists, then shooting himself in the head with a shotgun; d. 8 April 1991

10. "Please leave immediately if you have a weak stomach or mind since I don't want to cause physical or mental distress."

    Pennsylvania State Treasurer R. Budd Dwyer, d. 22 January 1987. Dwyer had called a press conference, seemingly to announce his resignation. He opened his mouth, inserted the gun and pulled the trigger. News cameras caught it all and it went out live

11. "I myself and my wife – in order to escape the disgrace of deposition or capitulation – choose death. It is our wish to be burnt immediately on the spot where I have carried out the greatest part of my daily work in the course of a twelve years' service to my people."

    Adolf Hitler, dictator, d. 30 April 1945

12. "Absolutely no reason except I have a toothache."
Forty-nine-year-old John Thomas Doyle,
d. 17 November 1954, explaining his decision to jump
from Golden Gate Bridge, San Francisco

14 PROSAIC LAST WORDS

1. "Tomorrow, I shall no longer be here."

    Nostradamus

2. "No."

    Alexander Graham Bell, in response
    to his deaf wife's request, "Don't leave me."

3. "Ich sterbe." (I die.)

    Leonhard Euler, Swiss mathematician and physicist

4. "What?"

    Tsar Nicholas II, when informed that he and his
    family were condemned to death by the Bolsheviks

5. "Good morning."

    William Howard Taft, twenty-seventh
    President of the United States

6. "Hold me up, I want to shit."

    Walt Whitman, American poet

7. "Don't let it end like this. Tell them I said something."*

    Mexican revolutionary Francisco "Pancho" Villa

8. "Ich bin Heinrich Himmler." (I am Heinrich Himmler.)

    Nazi SS chief, before biting on a cyanide capsule

---

* Possibly apocryphal, as Villa died in an ambush in a hail of bullets
so it's unlikely he was able to say very much at all.

9. "Dzzhh." (Dzzhh.)
> Soviet leader Joseph Stalin, discovered lying
> on his bedroom floor soaked in stale urine. A terrified
> attendant asked Stalin what happened to him, but all he
> could get was this unintelligible response

10. "Okay, I won't."
> Elvis Presley to fiancée Ginger Alden
> who told him when he was on the way
> to the bathroom, "Don't fall asleep in there."

11. "Hello."
> Graham Chapman, Monty Python comedian,
> to his adopted son who had just arrived at the hospital

12. "Pee pee."
> Freddie Mercury, while dying of AIDS,
> asked to be helped to the bathroom

13. "Oh shit . . ."
> Cozy Powell, rock drummer about to die
> in a car crash while on the phone to his girlfriend

14. "Oh, wow. Oh, wow. Oh, wow."
> Apple co-founder Steve Jobs

CHAPTER ELEVEN
Trial and Retribution

15 CAPITAL ODDITIES

1. In most of Europe throughout the Middle Ages it was considered indecent to hang women because you could see their underwear; they were burned alive instead.

2. Before Britain abolished the death penalty in 1964, the rope used in hanging executions was always made at a factory in Wellington, Somerset. Only the finest Italian silk hemp was used because it didn't stretch; elasticity in a rope is a bad thing because it reduces the deceleration force on the victim's neck, making death more painful. Today, in countries where people are still hanged, the rope is made of Terylene, the least elastic of all the synthetic fibres.

3. The infamous Victorian pornographer Frederick Hankey once attended a public hanging with a friend and took along two girls so they could have sex while they watched. Hankey was so turned on by the experience that he did it again at the execution in Paris of the Frenchman Robert-Francois Damiens, sentenced in 1757 for his botched attempt on the life of King Louis XV.*

4. In December 1479 Bernado di Bandino Boroncelli was hanged for a failed attempt to overthrow Giuliano di

---

* Casanova also attended the horrific execution of Damiens and saw them at it in the crowd, "lifting a woman's skirts" for some "sexual gymnastics".

Piero de' Medici in Florence. Leonardo da Vinci sketched the hanging man and made notes about his clothing: "A tan coloured skull-cap, a doublet of black serge, a black jerkin, lined and the collar covered with a black and red stippled velvet. A blue coat lined with fur of fox's breasts. Black hose."

5. In Britain, beheading as a form of capital punishment was reserved for people of noble birth. For appearances' sake, many victims had their heads stitched back on before they were buried.

6. On 31 January 1606 gunpowder plotter Guy Fawkes cheated his executioners by jumping from the scaffold where he was to be hanged, breaking his neck. He wanted to avoid the lingering death and mutilation that inevitably followed; his lifeless body was nevertheless quartered in the usual way, as befitting a traitor.

7. In 1793 Charlotte Corday met her appointment with "Madame Guillotine" for stabbing to death the French revolutionary leader Jean Paul Marat while he was having a bath. Afterwards, one of the executioner's assistants picked up her decapitated head and slapped it on the cheek, resulting in an expression of "unequivocal indignation" on Corday's face, according to an eyewitness. The slap was an unacceptable breach of guillotine etiquette, so the assistant was sent to prison for three months.

8. On 29 January 1547 Thomas Howard, Duke of Norfolk, was to have been beheaded for treason, but he had a stroke of good luck. The previous day, fifty-five-year-old King Henry VIII died before getting round to signing the death warrant. The condemned noble died in bed, seven years later. Thomas Howard's son Henry was less

fortunate: he was beheaded just a few days before the king expired on the same charge of treason that almost claimed Thomas.

9. In 1827 Levi Kelley was the last man to face a public hanging in Cooperstown, New York, for the murder of his tenant Abraham Spafard. There were so many people packed into the spectators' grandstand that it collapsed under the weight, causing at least two more deaths. The fatal collapse delayed the execution until order was restored. Showing concern for his audience even as the noose was being placed around his neck, Kelley's last words were: "How many are killed and injured?"

10. In Victorian England, the hangman's role was not a salaried job. They were paid a fee per execution: £10 for the hangman and three guineas for the assistant. They could, however, make extra by selling their victims' clothes – a lawful perk of the job. William Calcraft supplemented his income by selling sections of the rope used to hang his victims, charging between five shillings and £1 per inch. During a very lean period in London the hangmen went on strike unless they were paid extra to whip offenders.

11. In January 1846 Elizabeth van Valkenburgh, a mother of four living in New York, was sentenced to be hanged after she admitted spiking the tea of her husband John, a violent drunk, with arsenic. Because of her broken leg and her obesity, van Valkenburgh was carried to the gallows in her rocking chair and the noose was placed around her neck where she sat. She was still rocking away when the trap was sprung.

12. In 1747 Sweden beheaded Scottish-born adventurer Alexander Blackwell for his alleged part in a conspiracy

against their King Frederick I. Blackwell laid his head the wrong way on the chopping block; when the executioner corrected him, Blackwell replied, "I am sorry, this is the first time that I've been beheaded."

13. William "Deacon" Brodie was a respected figure in nineteenth-century Edinburgh. He was also an amateur inventor and is credited with having a hand in designing the device first tested at his own execution – the drop gallows. Until that time, people condemned to be hanged were pushed from a high platform and left to strangle to death. Brodie helped perfect the trapdoor-and-lever system that became the industry standard. Brodie also lived a double life as a highly skilled cat burglar. His cover was blown when an accomplice turned king's evidence. He fled to Amsterdam but was quickly apprehended, returned to Edinburgh for trial, and condemned to death. On the gallows, Brodie asked if he could inspect the apparatus: after pronouncing it satisfactory, he was promptly dropped to his death.

14. In 1949 John George Haigh was hanged at Wandsworth Prison for killing six young women and dissolving them in vats of industrial acid. Anticipating that he would be a major attraction, Haigh bequeathed his clothes to Madame Tussauds Chamber of Horrors so they could use them to dress his wax figure.

15. In America, prisoners waiting to be executed on Death Row are given a medical to ensure they are fit enough to die.

10 DUELS

1127: in Flanders, Herman "the Iron" defeats fellow knight Guy in trial by combat. After being kicked from his horse, Herman pretends he is dead, then reaches up and tears off Guy's testicles.

1565: famous Danish astronomer Tycho Brahe has most of his nose sliced off in a midnight duel over a mathematical argument. Young Tycho goes out and buys a replacement nose made out of gold, silver and wax.

1598: playwright and actor Ben Jonson kills a fellow thespian Gabriel Spenser in a duel. Tried for murder, Jonson pleads guilty but manages to escape the gallows thanks to a legal ploy called "benefit of clergy". He has to prove he can read and write by reciting a chapter from the Bible, forfeits all of his worldly goods and has an "m" for "murderer" branded on his left thumb.

1763: British politician John Wilkes challenges fellow MP Samuel Martin to pistols in Hyde Park after Martin calls him "a stabber in the dark, a cowardly and malignant scoundrel" in the House of Commons. Wilkes is shot in the abdomen but avoids death when the bullet bounces off his coat buttons. It turns out that Martin had been practising in a shooting gallery for six months before making his offensive speech.

1765: William, fifth Baron Byron, known as "the wicked Lord" and great-uncle of the poet Lord Byron, kills his cousin and neighbour William Chaworth during a duel in a dimly lit back room in the Stars and Garters Tavern in London by running a sword through his stomach. Before succumbing to his injury, Chaworth says he regrets not picking his fight somewhere with better lighting.

1791: shortly after his marriage to Rachel Donelson Robards, future US President Andrew Jackson is surprised to learn that she is still married to her first husband – a scandal that elicits a snide comment from one Charles Dickinson. Jackson, bent on defending his wife's name, challenges him to a duel. Dickinson fires first but the impact of his bullet is blunted by Jackson's loose overcoat and only breaks one of his ribs. When Jackson attempts to return the favour, he misfires. Unfortunately for Dickinson, the rules require that he stands his ground while Jackson tries again. He can only stand and watch as his rival reloads then carefully takes aim and shoots him dead. Jackson says later: "I would have stood up long enough to kill him if he had put a bullet in my brain."

1804: American founding father Alexander Hamilton insults political rival and US Vice President Aaron Burr, who challenges him to a duel. When they meet, Hamilton has secretly rigged his pistols with hair triggers, hoping to gain an advantage. Hamilton fires first and misses. Burr then takes careful aim and shoots Hamilton in the groin. Hamilton's last words are: "This is a mortal wound, doctor." Burr wisely flees to Mexico.

1808: two Frenchmen, Monsieur de Grandpre and Monsieur de Pique, choose to fight from balloons after quarrelling over a dancer, Mademoiselle Tirevit, mistress of one and lover of the other. Watched by a huge crowd, the duellists climb into their aircraft near the Tuileries and rise to 2,000 ft. With the balloons about 80 yards apart, de Pique fires his blunderbuss and misses. De Grandpre aims his more effectively: de Pique's balloon collapses and he and his second fall head-first to their deaths on the rooftops below.

1829: British Prime Minister the Duke of Wellington becomes the only elected head of state to fight a duel while in office. The hugely disappointing event takes place in Battersea Park with Lord Winchelsea; Wellington aims at his legs and misses. Winchelsea fires in the air and apologizes.*

1900: Warren Earp, the youngest of the famous clan of gun-fighting brothers, challenges John Boyett to a gunfight in Wilcox, Arizona, but gets drunk and forgets to bring his gun; he is shot in the chest and killed.

---

* In 1809 George Canning (then Foreign Secretary, later Prime Minister) duelled with Lord Castlereagh on Putney Heath. Canning was wounded in the leg; both men resigned from office.

NAME THAT SLAYER:
12 SERIAL KILLER HANDLES

1. The Singing Strangler
   During World War II, US army soldier Edward Joseph
   Leonski killed three women in Melbourne, Australia.
   During his trial he confessed to having a fascination for
   women who were singing and strangled them to "get to
   their voices".

2. Satan in a Skirt
   In 2012 Russian Irina Gaidamachuk murdered seventeen elderly women by bashing their skulls in with a
   hammer. She did it to steal their money to buy vodka.

3. The Chessboard Killer
   In 2007 Russian shop assistant Alexander Pichushkin
   was found guilty of forty-eight murders, which he
   recorded on a chessboard. He said he hoped to kill sixty-
   four people, one for each square.

4. The Lipstick Killer
   An American serial killer who confessed to three
   murders in 1946, William George Heirens acquired his
   nickname from a note he wrote in lipstick at one murder
   scene to the effect that he wanted to be caught before he
   killed again. Heirens recanted his confession and claimed
   he was a victim of police brutality, but remained imprisoned until his death in 2012.

5. The Mad Biter
   In 1974 American serial killer Richard Macek killed at least four women in Wisconsin and two in Illinois. He stabbed his victims then chewed on their body parts.

6. Texas Eyeball Killer
   Charles Frederick Albright was convicted of killing three prostitutes in 1991. A frustrated taxidermist, he skilfully removed his victims' eyes after killing them and took them home with him.

7. The Vampire of Sacramento
   In 1977 Richard Trenton Chase killed six people within a month in Sacramento, California. He was so nick-named because he drank his victims' blood and cannibalized their remains. He said he did this to stop his own blood from turning to powder.

8. Charlie Chop Off
   Unknown American killer of five black children in Manhattan between 1972 and 1974. The nickname came from the genital mutilation inflicted on the male victims. By some accounts, police investigators came up with the moniker; others say it was given to him by neighbourhood children.

9. The Old Lady Killer
   In 2010 Juana Barazza, a Mexican professional wrestler known as "The Silent Lady", was sentenced to 759 years in jail when she was found guilty of murdering sixteen elderly women by strangling or bludgeoning them to death. She said she did it because they reminded her of her mother.

10. The Co-Ed Killer
    Edmund Kemper's profile as a serial killer got off to a

flying start when he murdered his grandparents when he was fifteen years old, but he acquired his nickname after killing and dismembering six female hitchhikers. He was asked: "What do you think when you see a pretty girl walking down the street?" Kemper replied: "One side of me says, 'I'd like to talk to her, date her.' The other side of me says, 'I wonder how her head would look on a stick?'"

11. The Darkroom Murderer
Nothing to do with photography, this one was all about choice of location. In 2012 this German predator allegedly drugged and strangled three men and was suspected in two other murders. One victim was given ecstasy in a dimly lit room, hence the nickname. The other victims were killed in less interesting places.

12. The Gorilla Killer
Earle Edward Nelson killed at least twenty-two people, mostly landladies, after approaching them on the pretext of renting a room. Once he gained their trust he would strangle them and have sex with the corpses, then hide the bodies under a bed. Strangely, no gorillas were harmed during the process: he got his nickname when it emerged in court that he had manic periods during which he took to walking on his hands or lifting heavy chairs with his teeth.

5 INCOMPETENT HANGMEN

1. William Calcraft despatched about 450 offenders during his forty-five-year career as Victorian England's most prolific executioner. He was notorious for miscalculating the drops required to effect a speedy death and would sometimes swing from his victim's legs or climb onto their shoulders in an attempt to break their necks. The Newgate execution of William Bousfield in 1856 was a case in point. The night before his execution, Bousfield, mindful of Calcraft's dismal record, tried to top himself in his cell by hurling himself into a fire. The next morning the condemned man was carried to the scaffold swathed in bandages. Calcraft was more nervous than usual because he had received death threats; he pulled the bolt to release the trapdoor, then ran off leaving the unfortunate Bousfield dangling. The drop was so short that Bousfield was able to haul himself up and lodge his feet on the sides of the trapdoor. An assistant pushed him off, but again Bousfield was able to steady himself. This continued for several minutes until the terrified Calcraft was persuaded to return and finish the job, which he did by clinging to Bousfield's legs until the force of his weight finally succeeded in strangling him. Bousfield struggled for a half a minute before he died. Calcraft was finally forced to retire from office at the age of seventy.

2. John Ellis, a former barber from Rochdale, served as the UK's chief executioner from 1907 until his traumatic encounter with Edith Thompson, hanged for the murder

of her husband Percy in 1923. Unlike some of his predecessors, who went into the profession as a family
business, the grim business of hanging weighed heavily
on Ellis. Although he hanged more than 200 people it
was the ghost of Thompson that came to haunt him the
most. On the way to the scaffold she fainted and had to
be carried by four prison warders, who tied her to a
small wooden chair then placed the noose around her
neck. When the gallows trapdoor opened and Thompson
fell, the jolt from the drop caused her uterus to invert,
spilling a large amount of blood. Ellis was deeply traumatized by the Thompson execution, and he had a
mental breakdown and made the first of several suicide
attempts, but only succeeded in shooting himself in the
jaw.* As suicide was a criminal offence, he was charged
and bound over for twelve months. Eight years later Ellis
was more successful, slashing his throat with a barber's
razor. The Edith Thompson execution had another
legacy; from that day on, all women hanged in Britain
after Thompson were required to wear reinforced canvas
knickers.

3. Arthur English served as Canada's chief executioner
   from 1912 to 1935, going by the pseudonym Arthur
   Ellis, possibly as a tribute to John Ellis (see above). His
   career ended with the botched hanging of an Italian
   woman, Thomasina Sarao, who had murdered her
   husband to collect on his life insurance. By this time,
   hangmen were adopting a more scientific and more
   humane method of calculating the exact level of force
   needed to be applied to the doomed person's vertebrae.
   Unfortunately, Ellis was working to the wrong weight
   for his client. He made a noose for a woman 32 lb lighter
   than the person who mounted the scaffold and the rope

---

* Ironically, he also failed to hang himself.

was more than a foot too long: the extra force ripped Mrs Sarao's head off. It was the last time members of the general public were allowed to buy tickets to watch hangings in Canada.*

4. Bartholomew Binns was England's least successful hangman. His brief four-month career as chief execu- tioner in 1839 was littered with inept hangings, including that of his final customer, eighteen-year-old Michael McLean in Liverpool at Kirkdale Gaol on 10 March 1884. Binns arrived for work drunk, so the prison gover- nor sent for a local man to assist him. Binns refused help and insisted on carrying out the execution alone. After the trapdoor was released, McLean was left choking to death and it took thirteen minutes for his heart to stop. Binns was removed from his job a few days later. Later that year Binns appeared in court when he accused his mother-in-law of stealing his watch. During the trial, it emerged that his daughter had been frightened out of the house by his habit of hanging cats and dogs at home.

5. During an eight-year career James Berry hanged 131 convicted murderers in British and Irish gaols, but is chiefly remembered for the non-execution of John Lee, "The Man They Could Not Hang", on 23 February 1885. Lee was sentenced to death for hacking to death his elderly employee Emma Keyse at Babbacombe in Devon. Although the trapdoor at Exeter Gaol worked every time it was tested, it failed to open three times in the space of seven minutes with Lee on the drop. This was variously attributed to "divine intervention",

---

* His name lives on in the Arthur Ellis Awards, the Crime Writers of Canada's annual awards for best crime and mystery writing. The award statue itself is a little hanging man whose arms and legs move when the statue's string is pulled.

rain-swollen woodwork and wedging by another convict, but the real cause was a faulty hinge on the trapdoor that snagged on the drawbolt while bearing Lee's weight. By all accounts, Lee was the calmest man present: the panicked chaplain refused to have anything more to do with it all and walked away. Meanwhile, the prison warden frantically telegraphed the Home Secretary to ask him what to do. Lee was reprieved and served a twenty-three-year prison sentence instead. After a few more mishaps, including the near decapitation of convict John Conway at Liverpool in 1891, James Berry resigned and became a pig farmer.

DIFFERENT STROKES: 12 CRUEL AND UNUSUAL PUNISHMENTS

1. In ancient Japan, the authorities handed out punishments to people convicted of crimes that were beyond the criminal code called *shikei*, which translates as "private punishment". One such torture was *kusuguri-zeme*: "merciless tickling".

2. In ancient Greece, the verb *rhaphanizo* meant "to thrust a radish up the fundament". It was the standard punishment for adulterers.

3. The ancient Romans had a torture called "the goats tongue". The victim's legs were tied to a tree and the soles of their feet were moistened with salt water. A tethered, thirsty goat would then lick their feet until the flesh was worn away.

4. According to the traditional Roman punishment for parricide,* the condemned person is beaten with blood-coloured sticks, then sewn up in a sack with a dog, a rooster, a viper and a monkey, then thrown into the sea.

5. As any grand inquisitor during the Middle Ages could have told you, waterboarding is not a harsh

---

* The killing of parents or another close relative.

interrogation technique, it is an excruciating and effective form of torture. The use of water to simulate the sensation of drowning, known as the "ordeal by water", was especially convenient because it required only a rag or a funnel and a supply of water; it left no wounds or scars and no bloody mess to clean up and it was a good way to make an accused heretic say whatever the inquisitor wanted to hear. Thanks to the Inquisition's obsession for record keeping, we know that an "ordinary" ordeal called for the application of five litres of water and an "extraordinary" one consisted of ten litres.

6. The sixteenth-century punishment in England for anyone who refused to enter a plea in court was "pressing to death". The victim was stripped, blindfolded, then placed on a rock roughly the size of a tennis ball, after which a large panel of wood was placed on the chest band and gradually loaded with 700–800 lb of rocks and stones, until his or her back broke. Within about fifteen minutes the victim would be dead, although it usually succeeded in eliciting a plea. In 1726 a murderer called Burnworth endured a weight of around 450 lb for nearly two hours before he begged to be released; he pleaded, was found guilty, then was hanged.

7. In sixteenth-century Germany, unmarried mothers suspected of killing their newborn children were arrested, brought to the prison in chains and their breasts examined for milk. A midwife was then dispatched to retrieve the baby's body, which was brought back to the mother, no matter how long it had been dead, to shock her into a confession. Once the mother confessed, she was either drowned or beheaded.

8. In ancient Hindu society, men of the Brahmin caste were not allowed to drink alcohol, or eat meat, onion or

garlic. Anyone who disobeyed was required to commit suicide by repeatedly drinking boiling-hot cow's urine.

9. The Pathans, an ethnic group living mostly in Afghanistan and Pakistan, were famed for the imaginative methods they used to mutilate, then kill any enemies who fell into their hands. A prisoner might be pegged out on the ground and his jaw forcibly opened with a stick so that he couldn't swallow, then women would urinate in his mouth until he drowned. The victim would then have his penis cut off and stuffed in his mouth for good measure.

10. England's cruellest method of execution dates from 1531 when King Henry VIII enacted a law allowing for convicted poisoners to be boiled to death. The last person killed by this method was a servant, Margaret Davy, boiled alive in 1542 for poisoning her boss.

11. The ancient Persian method of execution scaphism* was designed to inflict prolonged torture. The victim was stripped naked and trapped between two narrow rowing boats or hollowed-out tree trunks, joined together one on top of the other, with the head, hands and feet sticking out. The condemned was then force-fed milk and honey until they developed severe diarrhoea. Meanwhile, more honey was rubbed on the exposed parts to attract insects such as wasps. The victim was then left to float on a stagnant pond or exposed to the sun. The faeces accumulated inside the container attracted more insects that would eat and breed in exposed flesh, causing gangrene. The force-feeding was repeated daily to prolong the agony and to avoid a quick

---

* From the Greek word *skaphe*, meaning anything scooped or hollowed out.

death by fatal dehydration or starvation. In 401 BC Mithradates, a soldier condemned for the murder of Cyrus the Younger, was executed by this method and survived the insect torture for a record seventeen days.

12. A common method of capital punishment in southeast Asia was execution by elephant, often employed by royalty to signify the ruler's absolute power and his ability to control wild animals. The elephants were trained to crush, dismember or torture captives in public executions and were capable of killing their victims immediately or torturing them slowly over a prolonged period. Although the practice was suppressed by the European powers when they colonized the region, it was resurrected by the British Army in India to deal with mutinous soldiers.

NEAR DEATH BY CHOCOLATE: 10 FRUSTRATED ASSASSINS

1517: Battista de Vercelli and several others are executed for plotting to kill Pope Leo X, a martyr to his piles, by poisoning his Holiness's rectal bandages.

1835: at a funeral, Richard Lawrence tries to shoot US President Andrew Jackson at close range with two loaded pistols, but both misfire. Jackson retaliates by thrashing his would-be assassin with his cane.

1835: a Corsican, Guiseppe Fiesci, tries to kill King Louis-Philippe of France with an ingenious "infernal machine" comprising twenty gun barrels, to be fired simultaneously from a window overlooking a parade in Paris. The supergun goes off, killing seventeen and wounding many others, including Fiesci, but the king rides off unscathed.

1840: Ennemond Marius Darmès joins the queue to gun down the French King Louis-Philippe, but overstuffs his weapon with powder and when he pulls the trigger the gun blows up in his hands. The wounded Darmès fumes as he is being led to the guillotine: "I had him!"

1840: eighteen-year-old unemployed Edward Oxford cocks his pistol and fires two shots at Queen Victoria as she and Prince Albert make their daily carriage drive on Constitution Hill, London. The first of seven of the queen's subjects with regicidal designs upon Her Majesty, Oxford is found guilty but insane and sentenced to confinement for life in Bethlem hospital.

1898: Italian anarchist Luigi Lucheni vows to kill his King Umberto, but can't find the extra fifty liras he needs to travel to Rome. So he kills the Austrian Empress Elisabeth in Geneva instead.

1912: John F. Shrank shoots Theodore Roosevelt as the US President is leaving a hotel in Milwaukee. The ineffective bullet lodges in Roosevelt's chest after hitting both his steel eyeglass case and a fifty-page copy of a speech he was carrying in his jacket.

1933: Guiseppe Zangara, an Italian immigrant and unemployed bricklayer, attempts to shoot President-elect Franklin D. Roosevelt from a distance of 25 feet while standing on a wobbly chair. His shots miss FDR, but Chicago's Mayor Anton Cermak is mortally wounded in the stomach.

1943: Adolf Hitler plans to assassinate fellow-chocoholic Winston Churchill with a bar of exploding chocolate. The chocolate-coated, thin steel bomb, designed to blow up seconds after a piece is broken off, is packed with enough explosive to kill anyone within several metres and hidden among other luxury snacks in the War Cabinet dining room. However, a British spy in Germany tips off MI5 and so foils the plot.

1944: General Claus von Stauffenberg tries to blow up Hitler with a conventional bomb hidden inside a briefcase. He succeeds in killing four people but only manages to singe the Führer's trousers.

10 LYNCHINGS

1. In August 1870 a young nobleman, Alain de Monéys, rode into the rural French village of Hautefaye and in casual conversation with the locals imparted the latest news from Paris that France's war with Prussia was not going well. The locals, who had been drinking heavily, took the news badly. They accused Monéys of being a spy, then tortured and battered him for two hours, before cooking him alive and then eating him. One of the lynch party, it was said, crunched on his steaming testicles.

2. John Billington arrived in America with the original band of pilgrims at Plymouth Rock on the *Mayflower* in 1620. His journey was fraught with problems on account of Billington's "blasphemous harangues"; at one point the ship's captain bound his feet and hands together to make an example of him. Ten years later, Billington got involved in an argument with neighbouring settler John Newcomen and shot him in the back at close range with a blunderbuss. America's first alleged murderer was summarily hanged by an angry mob of pilgrims in America's first lynching.

3. The nineteenth century was rife with instances of explorers and pioneers who resorted to eating each other for survival. Unusually opportunistic in this respect was the American mountain man Boone Helm, who took human flesh with him just in case he found himself in a survival situation. Helm got his nickname

"the Kentucky Cannibal" for his habit of eating his enemies and travelling companions alike. He once boasted, "Many's the poor devil I've killed, at one time or another ... and the time has been that I've been obliged to feed on some of 'em." Helm and other members of his gang were lynched by a group of vigilantes in front of a crowd of 6,000 on 14 January 1864. Upon seeing one of his accomplices hanged, Helm said: "My turn next. I'll be in Hell with you in a minute."

4. One of the largest multiple lynchings in American history took place on 14 March 1891 in New Orleans. The unsolved murder of a city police superintendent led to a roundup of the "usual suspects" – in this case eleven Italians, recent immigrants from Sicily and southern Italy. A crowd of several thousand people surrounded the prison where they were held, chanting, "hang the dagoes!" A hit squad of about twenty-five well-armed men forced their way in and, finding six Italians huddled together in the prison yard, opened fire from about twenty feet away, hitting them with more than a hundred rifle and shotgun blasts. The rest were hunted down and shot in the cells. Several of the men's corpses were displayed to the mob outside the prison and hung on lampposts for all to see. Witnesses said that the cheering was deafening.

5. The lynching of Henry Smith on 1 February 1893 in Paris, Texas, was one of the first of a southern black by a large crowd of southern whites. Smith was a mentally ill former slave who was the prime suspect in the murder of Myrtle Vance, the three-year-old daughter of a brutal Texas policeman. Although the girl had not been sexually assaulted, a local clergyman fuelled growing local hysteria with lurid tales of child molestation. Smith was captured in Arkansas and brought back by train to Paris

where a mob of about 10,000 whites put him on a carnival float and took him into the countryside. There, he was placed on a scaffold and tortured by members of the girl's family, who stuck hot iron brands into his flesh, starting at his feet and legs and working up to his head. He is said to have torn himself away from the post and fallen off the scaffolding, where he died. The crowd fought over the hot ashes to collect his bones and teeth as souvenirs.

6. In 1904 Luther Holbert, a black sharecropper suspected of killing a white plantation owner, tried to escape from his home in Mississippi with his wife before a lynch mob could dispense its own form of justice. When the mob caught up with them the couple were bound to two trees. The mob's ringleaders forced them to hold out their hands and chopped their fingers off one by one, before cutting off their ears. Nearby, an audience of around 600 whites were meanwhile enjoying a large picnic in an atmosphere described as festive. Luther Holbert was then beaten so severely that one eye was left dangling from its socket. After further torturing, the couple were burned alive.

7. In May 1916 seventeen-year-old Jesse Washington was arrested for raping and beating to death the wife of a white farmer in Robinson, Texas. It took an all-white jury four minutes to find Washington guilty and sentence him to death. Before the penalty could be administered by the state, however, a group of courtroom spectators grabbed Washington, put a chain around his neck and dragged him outside, where another mob had built a bonfire. They poured coal oil over him then hoisted him up over a tree branch, leaving him with the lower half of his body dangling in the fire. After a couple of hours his charred remains were placed in a sack, which was then

placed in front of a blacksmith's shop for viewing. A crowd of around 15,000 people witnessed the lynching; photos of the event were made into souvenir postcards, of which around 50,000 went into circulation.

8. In 1920 the James Robinson Circus was in Duluth, Minnesota, for a performance. Two local teenagers, Irene Tusken, nineteen, and her boyfriend James Sullivan, eighteen, watched the black workers dismantle the big top and load the wagons to get the circus ready to move on. Later that night Sullivan claimed that he and Tusken were assaulted and that Tusken was raped by five or six black circus workers. As rumours circulated that Tusken had died in the assault, the police arrested six men in connection with the alleged rape. A mob of between 5,000 and 10,000 people broke into the prison and, after a mock trial, declared three of the men, Elias Clayton, Elmer Jackson and Isaac McGhie, guilty of the rape. They were taken to 1st Street and 2nd Avenue East, where they were beaten and hanged by the mob from a lamppost. A medical examination subsequently found no evidence of rape or assault on the girl.*

9. In 1955, while visiting his mother's family in Greenwood, Mississippi, Emmett Till, a fourteen-year-old black youth from Chicago, wolf-whistled the white wife of the general store's owner. The following Saturday night, Till was roused from his sleep by a posse of white men seeking to avenge the white woman's "honour". They castrated him and beat him to death before tying him to the propeller of a cotton gin, and dunking him in the Tallahatchie River. At his funeral, Emmett's mother,

---

* The first verse of Bob Dylan's 1965 song "Desolation Row" recalls the Duluth lynchings.

Mamie Till, insisted on an open casket so that the whole world could see the boy's bloated corpse. The story was eventually picked up by the national press and the perpetrators were brought to trial. An all-white jury found all of the men not guilty.

10. In 1959 an African-American, Mack Charles Parker, was being held in the Pearl River County Jail in Poplarville, Mississippi, accused of raping a pregnant white woman. Parker vehemently denied having raped anyone and statements from his supporters after his death suggested that the accusations were fabricated by the alleged victim to conceal an ongoing affair with a local white man. Three days before he was due to stand trial, a mob of hooded, masked men broke him out of his cell, then tortured and shot him to death. Parker's mutilated corpse was found ten days later floating in a river twenty miles away. The killing became known as the "last classic lynching" in America. Despite an extensive investigation by the FBI, no conviction was ever obtained against any of the men who murdered Mack Charles Parker.

BAD HEIR DAYS:
10 FILICIDES

c. 900: the paranoid Northern African ruler Ibrahim II has his son Aghlab beheaded on vague suspicion of treason. All sixteen of his female children, hidden by their mother and secretly reared at her own peril, are also massacred on the spot when Ibrahim discovers that he is their father.

1553: Prince Mustafa, first-born son and heir of Ottoman Emperor Suleiman the Magnificent, is strangled on his dad's orders for allegedly plotting against him. The new heir apparent is Prince Selim, the first of a series of degenerate Sultans under whose sway the Empire goes to ruin.

1568: Don Carlos, the brain-damaged eldest son of King Philip II and heir to the Spanish throne, is arrested and placed in solitary confinement on his father's orders while planning to flee to the Netherlands. He dies in isolation six months later, allegedly poisoned on the orders of King Philip (although he may have starved to death).

1580: Italian tyrant Vespasiono Gonzaga kicks his only son Luigi in the testicles when he fails to doff his cap to him in the street. Within a week Luigi dies of internal rupturing.

1581: the Russian Czar Ivan "the Terrible" beats his pregnant daughter-in-law senseless for wearing immodest clothing, causing a miscarriage. When his eldest son, also called Ivan, tries to defend her, the Czar hits him over the head, causing him to bleed to death.

1718: after a bout of heavy drinking, Russian Czar Peter the Great tortures his unloved son Alexis, whom he describes as "like a gangrened limb", before flogging him to death with a leather-thonged whip. Afterwards, Peter celebrates with a fireworks display.

1762: the Korean King Yeongjo has his mad son and heir Crown Prince Sado locked in a rice chest then buried in the palace garden. He is found dead eight days later. Sado was prone to sudden fits of rage, stalking and raping court ladies and had murdered several servants, eunuchs and miscellaneous commoners.

1941: as Soviet troops overrun Berlin, Magda Goebbels, wife of Nazi Germany's Propaganda Minister Joseph Goebbels, administers fatal doses of morphine and cyanide to her six children. She had been planning their murders for at least a month.

1984: Marvin Gaye is shot three times in the chest by his father, the hard-drinking, cross-dressing Marvin senior, during an argument over a contract.

1987: builder Fred West and his wife Rose kill their seventeen-year-old daughter Heather and bury her in their garden at 25 Cromwell Street, Gloucester. Fred tells his other children that they will "end up under the patio like Heather" if they misbehave.

12 NOVEL CRIMINAL DEFENCES

1478: Simon of Venice is caught having sex with a goat. He claims he was looking for a cure for his impotence.

1660: a Swiss court acquits Pyramus Mermilliod, charged with bestiality. Caught with his pants down behind a cow "with one hand on his genitals and the other in or about the cow's fundament", he says he was urinating on the cow's rear to kill flies.

1980: the founder of the Scarsdale Diet, Dr Herman Tarnower, makes the fatal mistake of dumping his long-term mistress, schoolteacher Jean Harris, for a younger woman. Overwhelmed by jealousy and the pain of rejection, Ms Harris drives to Tarnower's home with a loaded gun and pumps five bullets into him. In court, Harris claims that she had been trying to commit suicide, but Tarnower got in the way. The jury, unconvinced, sentences her to life imprisonment.

1981: after hacking to death his mother-in-law in her garage, Orvell Wyatt Lloyd of Dallas, Texas, tells police that he mistook her for a large raccoon.

1985: London civil servant Thomas Corlett says he strangled his wife Erika because she put a pot of mustard and a newspaper on the wrong side of his plate at dinner. Prosecutor David Jeffreys at Southwark Crown Court observes, "A more trivial beginning to a tragic event would be difficult to imagine."

1986: in Edmond, Oklahoma, postal worker Patrick Sherrill shoots and kills fourteen co-workers, injuring seven others. He said he did it after receiving a poor performance review from his employers.

1987: Canadian Kenneth Parks explains why he drove fourteen miles to his mother-in-law's home near Toronto and beat her to death with a tyre iron, then choked his father-in-law into unconsciousness. He was sleepwalking. Parks is acquitted.*

1993: Julie Amiri, twenty-stone mother of three, claims she can only achieve orgasm by shoplifting. The disorder came to light at Chichester Crown Court when she was arrested after a police car chase following thefts from British Home Stores and Marks and Spencer in Worthing, West Sussex. She convinced doctors that her condition was genuine and, although arrested fifty-three times between 1985 and 1993, she was not convicted once.

1996: Kevin McQuain, an eighteen-year-old student, was caught boiling the skull of the former mayor of Syracuse, New York, in his college dorm room. He said he took it from a local cemetery to help with his art classes.

1998: Frenchman Louis Pilar, charged with shooting his wife, blames a three-week TV strike. He explains: "There was nothing to look at. I was bored."

2003: Erik Kurtis Low is dubbed "the wedgie killer" after fatally shooting Michael Hirschey at a party in Utah. Low says he gunned down his host with a large calibre handgun

---

* In 1999 Scott Falater was unsuccessful when he used a similar defence to explain why he had thrown his wife's body into their swimming pool in Arizona after stabbing her forty-four times.

because he feared for his life after Hirschey pulled up Low's underwear in a move known as a "wedgie". The judge rules: "receiving a wedgie is not a reason to kill somebody".*

2011: a man in Zimbabwe says that the donkey he was caught having sex with was in fact a prostitute whom he had paid $20 for her services at a nightclub; she had mysteriously turned into a donkey overnight.

---

* In 2013 Denver St Clair, fifty-eight, from Oklahoma, died when his stepson allegedly gave him an "atomic wedgie" in which the elastic band of his underwear was pulled over his head and around his neck, asphyxiating him.

12 NOTABLE EXECUTIONS

1. In 1541 Margaret Pole, the sixty-eight-year-old Countess of Salisbury, was beheaded at the Tower of London for treason. The regular executioner was on holiday so a novice stood in for him. Reports conflict on what happened next; according to some, she refused to place her head on the chopping block and put up a struggle. Others say that she ran about screaming while the executioner swung at her. Accounts agree that the novice swung at her with his axe at least ten times, hacking at her shoulders for several minutes before managing to kill her.

2. Thomas Aikenhead, a twenty-year-old student, was the last person to be executed for blasphemy in Britain, hanged in Edinburgh in 1697. His crimes included calling Jesus an impostor and describing his miracles as "pranks".

3. In 1782 a crowd of 20,000 turned out to watch the execution of Scottish spy David Tyrie, the last man to be hanged, drawn and quartered in Britain. Tyrie, who worked as a clerk at a Portsmouth naval office, had been caught in "treacherous correspondence with the French" in time of war. In accordance with the full penalty for High Treason, he was dragged to the gallows facing backwards, forced up a ladder then hanged briefly to cause partial strangulation, after which he was taken down and stretched out on a board, still fully conscious, where the executioner castrated him, slit open his

stomach and pulled out his entrails; the bowels and entrails were burned on a fire prepared near the scaffold, the body was then cut into four portions with a limb attached to each. Bits of Tyrie's corpse were fought and squabbled over by the crowd; some stole his arms, legs and several fingers to keep as trophies.

4. In 1814 a vagrant named John Bibby was sentenced to death at the Old Bailey for stealing sheep from the Duke of Richmond's estate. Bibby ran up the ladder to the scaffold shouting: "I am the Duke of Wellington! I am the Duke of Wellington!" When the trapdoor opened, Bibby bounced back as though he was on a trampoline shouting: "What did I tell you?" After a struggle, he was subdued and finally hanged.

5. Black Jack Ketchum was arguably the most stupid outlaw in the old American West. He and his gang robbed stagecoaches and trains, but lost the element of surprise by regularly attempting hold-ups of the same stagecoaches, at the same location, at the same time: it led to his inevitable arrest and execution. Black Jack's last words on the gallows were "Let her rip!" It was an unfortunate choice of words because, when the trapdoor fell, the noose ripped his head from his body.

6. In 1854 several thousand people gathered in Coloma, California, to watch the hanging of Jeremiah Crane and Mickey Free for the murder of Miss Newnham. Crane's last request was to sing a song he had penned in his cell the night before: "I killed Susan Newnham, as you have heard tell/I killed her because that I loved her so well." Not to be outdone, Free asked the crowd permission to dance a jig. Crane and Free's stage careers were short-lived, although some spectators reported that Free continued to dance as he dangled in mid-air.

7. Spencer Perceval, the only British Prime Minister to be assassinated, was shot dead in 1812 in the House of Commons when John Bellingham, a businessman with a festering grudge against the government, put a bullet through the PM's heart at point-blank range. When news of Perceval's murder got out there were celebrations and street parties and, as Bellingham was being taken to prison, sympathetic crowds surrounded the police carriage to try to help him escape. The assassin was hanged within the week, as onlookers cheered, "God bless you!"

8. In 1789 Catherine Murphy was the last woman to be publicly burned at the stake in England. Convicted of coining false money, she was strangled alive, then burned in front of Newgate Prison. Afterwards, local residents sent a petition to the Lord Mayor demanding an end to this type of public execution at Newgate. It wasn't a protest against the severity of her punishment, it was because some people claimed they became ill from inhaling the smoke from her body. The Treason Act of 1790 abolished burning as a method of execution.

9. Adolf Hitler reinstated capital punishment when he took control of Austria in 1938 and a new guillotine was sent to Vienna by rail, labelled "industrial machinery". One of its first victims was a housewife, Martha Marek, executed for poisoning her husband Emile,* their baby daughter, an elderly relative and a lodger. She was

---

* In happier times, Emile had allowed his wife Martha to chop off his leg in order to collect on $30,000 in accident insurance he had taken out. Martha, however, was not very good at wielding the axe and it took three blows to severe the leg. The insurers didn't buy his story that it was an accident incurred while cutting down a tree and their claim was denied.

thought to be paralysed from the waist down, so was taken from the condemned cell to the gallows in a wheelchair. On the morning of the execution, however, Martha's paralysis mysteriously disappeared; she struggled violently with her guards and was able to land a heavy kick to the testicles of her executioner Johann Reichhart before being subdued and tied down by his assistant.

10. In 1939 convicted murderer Pete Catalina went to the gas chamber in Canon City, Colorado, convicted of shooting a man in an argument over a fifty-cent stack of poker chips. Prison officials, keen to reassure the public that they were despatching their prisoners humanely, persuaded Catalina to meet death wearing a monitor to record his final heartbeats. The official tasked with operating the cardiogram reported that Catalina's heartbeat was strong and even for one minute and ten seconds, then stopped abruptly when he inhaled the poison fumes – proof, according to initial press reports, that it was the "quickest and most humane execution we ever had". The public learned only much later that the gas chamber leaked during the execution causing panicked spectators to flee the room.

11. In 1995 George Del Vecchio was set to be executed via lethal injection, eighteen years after he was convicted of almost decapitating a six-year-old boy and raping the boy's mother during a botched robbery. His lawyers argued that he was too ill to be executed due to a recent mild heart attack; the plea rejected, he was put to death on schedule.

12. In 1997 Pedro Medina, a Cuban refugee, was sent to the electric chair in Florida for the murder of a fifty-two-year-old woman. As he was being electrocuted, Medina's

head burst into flames. It prompted the state attorney to issue a health and safety warning to murderers to stay away from Florida "because we may have a problem with the electric chair".

10 CRAP CRIMINALS

1. In 1971 burglar Rodney Dobson was arrested for the forty-third time when he crashed a getaway car into two other vehicles. The judge suggested that the convicted man should consider an alternative career path. "I think you should give up burglary. You have a withered hand, an artificial leg and only one eye. You are a useless burglar."

2. In 1978 twenty-seven-year-old Ralph Graves entered a doughnut shop in Riverside, California, with a gun and demanded money from the till. As he was making his escape with $60, a customer recognized him when the armed robber lifted up a corner of his pillowcase mask to ascertain the whereabouts of the door. He had forgotten to cut eyeholes.

3. In 1995 an Israeli bank robber in Tel Aviv was foiled by a hard-of-hearing cashier, who could not hear him whispering "this is a hold-up". The robber fled the bank in embarrassment.

4. In 1995 a bank robber in Florida queued in line for twenty minutes for the cashier to bring him a bag of cash. He was arrested as he left the bank.

5. In 1995 a would-be thief in Holland went into a store and handed the owner a note demanding money. He fled when handed a reply saying: "Sod off".

6. In 1997 Christina Mack, a thirty-five-year-old house-wife from Chicago, was arrested on suspicion of the attempted murder of her fifty-year-old partner Chester Parker. Mack had greased the bathroom floor as well as the top of the stairs, intending to send her one-legged boyfriend tumbling to his death. A team of fire-fighters had to give her first aid when she slipped on her greasy kitchen floor, knocking herself unconscious.

7. In 1999 police in Wichita, Kansas, arrested a twenty-two-year-old man at an airport hotel after he tried to pass two counterfeit sixteen-dollar bills.

8. In 2002 a thief at a South African zoo made the fatal mistake of attempting his getaway via the tigers' enclosure. He was mauled to death.

9. In 2002 Patrick Daniel was charged with two counts of murder in Sever County, Utah, when highway patrol officers stopped him in his car and found the frozen, dismembered body of a woman and the body of a man with a noose around his neck. He had a diary in the car with an entry reading: "Torch car. Bury in remote area."

10. In 2007 burglar Mark Smith dosed himself on valium and vodka before plucking up the courage to rob a house in Whitley Bay, Tyne and Wear, and then turned out to be less cat burglar than cat napper when he took an unscheduled forty winks under a bed. When finally woken by police, dozy Smith was on his way to an eighteen-month prison stretch.

CHAPTER TWELVE

Loose Ends

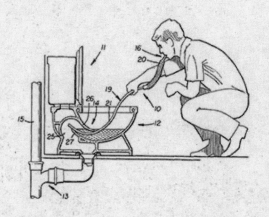

14 LANDMARKS IN CULTURAL SENSITIVITY

1775: Immanuel Kant notes that Africans "are born white apart from their genitals [and] the navel . . . the black colour spreads out from these parts".

1842: British envoy Lieutenant Colonel Charles Stoddart is sent to Bukhara in Central Asia (modern-day Uzbekistan) to negotiate trade with the ruling Emir Nasrullah Khan. Annoyed at being kept waiting for half an hour, when finally introduced Stoddart refuses to bow and tells the Emir to "eat shit". The Emir responds by throwing the Englishman into a thirty-foot-deep, vermin-infested hole named the Bug Pit for a couple of years before chopping his head off.

1869: General Sheridan holds a conference with Indian chiefs at Fort Cobb in Oklahoma. When the Comanche chief Toch-a-way is introduced, the chief says, "Me Toch-a-way, me good Indian." "The only good Indians I ever saw," Sheridan replies, "were dead."*

1884: George Henty, a keen imperialist and author of 122 *Boy's Own* adventures, writes: "The intelligence of an average negro is about equal to that of a European child of ten years old."

---

* Sheridan's remark has gone down in history as the modified "the only good Indian is a dead Indian".

1886: the twenty-sixth US President Theodore Roosevelt notes: "I don't go so far as to think that the only good Indians are the dead Indians, but I believe nine out of every ten are, and I shouldn't inquire too closely into the case of the tenth."

1891: the *Wizard of Oz* author L. Frank Baum calls for "the total extermination of the Indians" [Native Americans] to "protect our safety".

1900: Winston Churchill calls for more British wars in Africa, noting that "the Aryan stock is bound to triumph".

1903: writing for the journal *Medicine*, in an article titled "Genital Peculiarities of the Negro", Dr William Lee Howard notes: "There can never be mutually beneficial relations between the Caucasian and the African" because of their "great sexual differences". He explains that because the genital organs are "enormously developed in Africans, the sexual centres in his [cerebral] cortex are correspondingly enlarged".

1921: when Mahatma Gandhi launches his campaign of peaceful resistance in India, Winston Churchill notes that he "ought to be lain bound hand and foot at the gates of Delhi, and then trampled on by an enormous elephant with the new Viceroy seated on its back". He adds for good measure: "I hate Indians. They are a beastly people with a beastly religion."

1945: Theodore Bilbo, US Senator from Mississippi, observes: "It is a biological fact that a Negro's skull ossifies by the time a Negro reaches maturity and they become unable to take in information."

1947: Arthur Caldwell, Australian Minister for Immigration, notes: "Two Wongs don't make a white."

1983: James G. Watt, US Secretary of the Interior, resigns after assuring critics that his department is well represented by minorities. "I have a black, a woman, two Jews and a cripple. And we have talent."

2001: shortly after the terrorist attacks on 11 September, US Republican Congressmen John Cooksey advises security personnel to be wary of anyone "that's got a diaper on his head, and a fan belt wrapped around the diaper on his head".

2013: Justine Sacco, the communications director for American internet media giant InterActiveCorp (IAC), tweets: "Going to Africa. Hope I don't get AIDS. Just kidding. I'm white!"

12 ELIZABETHAN INSULTS

1. By my trowth, thou dost make the millstone seem as a feather what widst thy lard-bloated footfall. (You are fat.)

2. In sooth, thy dank cavernous tooth-hole consumes all truth and reason. (You have got a big mouth.)

3. Thy vile canker-blossom'd countenance curdles milk and sours beer. (You are ugly.)

4. Thou art an ale-soused apple john. (You are a drunk.)

5. Thou whoreson pale-hearted hedge-pig.

6. Thou saucy fat-kidneyed malt-worm.

7. Thou bawdy hedge-born miscreant.

8. Thou distempered evil-eyed jack-a-nape.

9. Thou queasy paper-faced rudesby. (You are a very bad person.)

10. May thy pigs be set upon by ravens and torne asunder leaving only bespecked bone and curdled fat for which the rats upon to feast.

11. May thy hammer be brittle.

12. May thy cup be as unto a sieve. (Go fuck yourself.)

ELEPHANTS ON ACID AND 10 MORE STUPID EXPERIMENTS

1287: German Emperor Frederick II is interested in the inner workings of the human body. He invites two men to a lavish dinner, then takes one with him on the hunt and has the other man sent to bed. Both men are then disembowelled so Frederick can see if digestion is better aided by exercise or rest; the emperor determines that the man who slept digested his meal better.

1669: Hamburg merchant Hennig Brand, convinced that he can turn human urine into gold, collects between fifty and sixty bucketfuls of his own piss, then allows it to stand and putrefy until, in his own words, it "bred worms", much to the irritation of his neighbours.

1750: Benjamin Franklin electrocutes a chicken, then revives it using mouth-to-mouth resuscitation: the chicken survives, but is blind.

1797: to test the muscle contractions produced by electrical currents, Alexander von Humboldt places a zinc cathode in his mouth and a silver cathode in his anus. He experiences stomach pains, then sees flashing lights, then he soils his trousers.

1803: at the Royal College of Surgeons in London, Giovanni Aldini sticks electric wires into the rectum of a recently executed man, making the corpse "jitter and dance".

1842: Charles Darwin shouts at some earthworms in his drawing room, then plays the piano for them, then the bassoon. He concludes that worms have no sense of hearing.

1862: French neurologist Guillame Duchenne tests his belief that the face is linked to the soul by passing an electric current through the head of an old homeless man, "whose features, without being absolutely ugly, approached ordinary triviality".

1876: despite dissecting more than 400 specimens, Sigmund Freud is unable to find any proof that male eels have testicles.

1953: to investigate the potential of LSD as a truth serum, CIA biochemist Sidney Gottlieb drops tabs of acid into his colleagues' drinks at work, then hangs around to record the effects. Operation Midnight Climax is abandoned when CIA agent Frank Olsen, in the grips of an LSD-induced psychotic episode, leaps to his death from a tenth-floor hotel window.

1954: Soviet scientist Vladimir Demikhov creates the world's first two-headed dog in his lab on the outskirts of Moscow by grafting the head, shoulders and front legs of a puppy onto the neck of a mature German Shepherd. Demikhov parades the dog before the world's press, who watch as both heads simultaneously lap at bowls of milk, then recoil in horror as the milk from the puppy's head dribbles out of the unconnected stump of its oesophageal tube. Demikhov goes on to create a total of twenty two-headed dogs, none of which lives longer than a month.

1962: scientists in Oklahoma inject Tusko, a fourteen-year-old, three-and-half-ton male elephant with 300 mg of LSD

– about 1,500 human doses – in a bid to find out whether it would trigger a temporary form of madness called musth, in which bull elephants become sexually aggressive. After receiving the largest dose of LSD in history, Tusko runs around his pen for a bit, falls over, shits himself and dies.

12 RUDE STREET NAMES

Shiteburn Lane, now Sherborne Lane, London

Pissing Alley, now Cannon Street, London

Gropecunt Lane, now Magpie Lane, Oxford

Rue du Poil au Con (Cunt Hair Street), now Rue du Pelican, Paris

Tickle Cock Bridge, Castleford

Minge Lane, Upton-upon-Severn

Bell End, Worcestershire

Fanny Hands Lane, Lincolnshire

Felch Square, Powys

Cocknmouth Close, West End, Surrey

Butt Hole Road, Conisbrough, South Yorkshire

Funbag Drive, Watford

TOUCHED BY YOUR PRESENTS, DEAR: 12 MEMORABLE GIFTS

1. In AD 800 King Charlemagne gifted Pope Leo III Christ's foreskin; Charlemagne said an angel had given it to him.*

2. Louis IX of France gave Henry III an elephant, the first seen in England since the time of the Romans. While in residence at the Tower of London, the elephant enjoyed a diet of prime cuts of beef, but died in 1257 from drinking too much expensive wine.

3. Pope Leo X had an Indian elephant called Hanno, a gift from King Manuel II of Portugal. It was a star turn in the Vatican and enjoyed pride of place in processions and festivals and was the subject of countless paintings and sculptures. When Hanno died the Pope was devastated and wrote a poem dedicated to his pet pachyderm. Elephants can live up to seventy years, but poor Hanno

---

* The medieval Church had a glut of Holy Foreskins, allegedly removed from Christ eight days after his birth. At one time twenty-one different churches claimed to have one, often at the same time. The seventeenth-century theologian Leo Allatius settled the matter by declaring them all frauds. Allatius asserted that Christ's foreskin had in fact risen to Heaven and was used to create the rings of Saturn.

didn't even make it to seven, having been liberally dosed with a laxative laced with gold.★

4. During a trip to the Congo in 1888, the Irish whiskey heir and budding artist James Jameson bought a ten-year-old girl and gifted her to a local cannibal tribe so that he could sketch her being butchered and eaten. Jameson later rendered his sketches into six watercolours then showed off his works to the chiefs for their approval.†

5. In 1811 the upper-crust eccentric and traveller Lady Hester Stanhope went to see a public execution in Constantinople and afterwards was presented with the severed head on a plate; she was unfazed by the gruesome gift, but said she was sorry it was being passed around "like a pineapple".

6. In 1915 the Shrewsbury millionaire Sir Cecil Chubb bought Stonehenge for his wife on a whim. She wasn't keen, so three years later he gave it to the nation instead.

7. For Christmas in 1936, Salvador Dalí sent Harpo Marx a harp with barbed-wire strings as a present. Harpo replied with a photograph of himself with bandaged fingers.

★ King Manuel's follow-up gift, a rhinoceros, was even less fortunate. Dispatched by ship from Lisbon in 1515 wearing a green velvet collar, it was shipwrecked off the coast of Genoa. The drowned animal was washed up on the shore and its hide was recovered, returned to Lisbon and stuffed. The artist Albrecht Dürer saw a letter describing the stuffed creature and produced his famous print without ever having seen a rhino.

† Jameson never denied paying six handkerchiefs for the girl, but later claimed he only started sketching after they had begun to chop her up; he said he decided to make the best of a bad job and got out his pen.

8. In 1937 Adolf Hitler created a new medal for foreign friends of the Third Reich called The Cross of the German Eagle Order. He created the special award so that no German medal would be "defiled" by a foreigner; it was also a lot cheaper than the gold cigarette cases that the Nazis usually gave to overseas visitors. The first person to receive the medal was fellow Jew-hater Henry Ford.

9. Hitler owned a King George VI coronation mug that played "God Save The Queen" when you picked it up. It was a present from his friend Neville Chamberlain.

10. In 1943 the Australian government gifted Winston Churchill a male platypus, complete with a specially designed "platypussary" containing 50,000 worms. As the ship was nearing Britain, a German submarine attacked and the platypus, called Winston, died of shock. Churchill had it stuffed and mounted on his desk.

11. When the pianist André Tchaikovsky died of colon cancer in 1982 he bequeathed his skull to the Royal Shakespeare Company for use as a stage prop. He has since appeared *post-mortem* in several productions of *Hamlet* as Yorick.

12. In 2007 a woman from Brisbane, Australia, was humped to death by a randy pet camel, given to her by her husband as a sixtieth birthday present. The ten-month-old animal knocked his owner Pam Weaver to the ground before trying to straddle her. It was reported that the camel had a history of erratic behaviour including attempting to shag the family's pet goat. Her husband Noel said he'd thought about buying her an alpaca instead, but it was too expensive.

10 MILITARY EXPERTS

1. "Four or five frigates will do the business without any military force."

   British Prime Minister Lord North, on dealing with the rebellious American colonies, 1774

2. "What, sir, would you make a ship sail against the wind and currents by lighting a bonfire under her deck? I pray you, excuse me, I have not the time to listen to such nonsense."

   Napoleon Bonaparte, when told of Robert Fulton's steamboat, 1800s

3. "Airplanes are interesting toys but of no military value."

   Marechal Ferdinand Foch, Professor of Strategy, Ecole Superieure de Guerre, 1904

4. "You will be home before the leaves have fallen from the trees."

   Kaiser Wilhelm, to the German troops, August 1914

5. "The idea that cavalry will be replaced by these iron coaches is absurd. It is little short of treasonous."

   Aide-de-camp to Field Marshal Haig, at a tank demonstration, 1916

6. "People are becoming too intelligent ever to have another war. I believe the last war was too much an educator for there ever to be another on a large scale."

   Henry Ford, 1928

7. "The Americans are good about making fancy cars and refrigerators, but that doesn't mean they are any good at making aircraft. They are bluffing. They are excellent at bluffing."

Hermann Goering,
Commander-in-Chief of the Luftwaffe, 1942

8. "Defeat of Germany means defeat of Japan, probably without firing a shot or losing a life."

Franklin D. Roosevelt, 1942

9. "That is the biggest fool thing we have ever done [research on] . . . The bomb will never go off, and I speak as an expert in explosives."

US Admiral William D. Leahy,
advising President Truman on atomic weaponry, 1944

10. "A nuclear war could alleviate some of the factors leading to today's ecological disturbances that are due to current high-population concentrations and heavy industrial production."

Official in the US Office of Civil Defense, 1982

10 SPORTING CURIOSITIES

1. In 1848 at the Priory Ground, Lewisham, a team of one-armed cricketers defeated a team of one-legged players by sixteen runs. The greatest contributor to both totals was extras: the One Legged XI conceded thirty, the One Armed XI forty-three, all of them wides.

2. The first person to fail a sport sex test was Polish sprinter Ewa Klobukowska in 1967. The record she had helped set when winning the Olympic gold in the 4 x 100 metres relay in 1964 was struck from the record books and she was banned from performing in female athletic events; none of which prevented her from giving birth to a healthy baby boy a few years later.

3. A 1999 golf tournament in Queensland, Australia, offered penis enlargement to the player with the longest drive and a breast enhancement for the best score by a woman.

4. In 1936 Thomas Hamilton-Brown of South Africa lost his opening-round boxing match at the Berlin Olympics by a split decision, so the disappointed lightweight consoled himself by going on an eating binge. It was only several days later that a scoring error was discovered; one of the judges had accidentally reversed his scores and the South African had actually won the fight and was through to the second round. By this time, Hamilton-Brown had already put on five pounds.

Unable to make the scales for his next bout, he was disqualified for being too heavy for his weight class.

5. At the 1878 FA Cup Final between Wanderers FC and Royal Engineers AFC, the referee really was a bastard. Segar Bastard was one of the best-known referees of the day and went on to become an FA Committee member.

6. During the 1900 Olympic marathon in Paris, the early leader Georges Touquet-Denis took a wrong turn, ran 400 metres in the wrong direction, then stopped at a bar to ask for directions. After a beer, or two, he retired from the race.

7. In 1904 American gymnast George Eyser won six Olympic medals in one day. This haul included gold in the vault, an event that at the time was a jump over a long horse without the aid of a springboard – Eyser was the victor despite having a wooden prosthetic leg.

8. At the 1912 Olympics in Stockholm, Japanese marathon runner Shizo Kanakuri lost consciousness, then strayed off the route in search of a drink. Feeling unwell, he didn't complete the race and went home without telling any of the officials. His official status with the Olympics remained DNF (Did Not Finish) and "missing" until 1967 when the Swedish Olympic Committee invited him back to finish the marathon for the fifty-fifth anniversary of the Stockholm Games. He eventually completed the course in fifty-four years, eight months, six days, thirty-two minutes and 20.3 seconds – the slowest and longest marathon time in history.

9. Gottfried von Cramm, beaten by Fred Perry in the 1936 Wimbledon final, was jailed for six months in 1938 by the Nazis, after he admitted to having a gay relationship

with a young Jewish actor. Von Cramm was denied a visa to play in the US Open the following year because of his "criminal conviction".*

10. Heather Mills, ex-wife of Paul McCartney, was kicked off the GB 2014 Winter Paralympics team for wearing an illegal leg.

---

* Wimbledon also reportedly refused to let him play in the 1939 championships, using the excuse that he was a convicted criminal – a claim refuted by Wimbledon, who said he would have been welcome to play, but he didn't submit an entry.

10 FIRSTS

1. In 84 BC Gaius Marius, seven-times consul and one of Rome's toughest military leaders, became the first person in recorded history to endure surgery without being tied down. Having had the varicose veins removed from one leg, however, he declined to have his other leg treated.

2. In 1884 the American physician William Stewart Halsted, performed the first-ever surgery using cocaine as an anaesthetic. Halsted later became the first-ever cocaine-addicted physician.

3. The first person to wear a top hat in public was English haberdasher John Hetherington in 1797. It caused such a commotion that small children screamed, women fainted and a boy was trampled on by the crowd and broke his arm. Hetherington was found guilty of "appearing on the public highway wearing upon his head a tall structure having a shining lustre and calculated to frighten timid people" and fined £50.

4. The first condoms were moulted cobra skins used by the ancient Egyptians.

5. The first holiday organized by Thomas Cook was an all-inclusive temperance trip to Loughborough.

6. Fiji experienced its first-ever bout of measles in 1875. The king had brought it back from a state visit to Australia and wiped out a quarter of his own people.

7. In 1909 the city of Vancouver in Canada acquired its first ambulance. On the vehicle's maiden trip with the city crew, it ran over an American tourist. He became the first patient transported in the ambulance.

8. The first case of air rage was recorded in 1947 on a flight from Havana to Miami, when a drunken man assaulted another passenger and bit a flight attendant. In another early incident, a first-class passenger shat on the food trolley after being refused another drink.

9. The world's first record-holder for cracking walnuts with one's anus was Jose Luis Astoreka in 1990. The thirty-four-year-old Spaniard cracked an impressive thirty nuts between his buttocks in fifty-seven seconds.

10. The first virtual reality fatality occurred in 2005 when an online gamer from Shanghai, Qiu Chengwei, stabbed to death fellow gamer Zhu Caoyuan. They had argued over an imaginary sword.

15 KEEPSAKES

1. When Henry Grey, the Duke of Suffolk and father of England's uncrowned nine-day queen, Lady Jane Grey, was beheaded in 1554, his widow hid his head in a box under the bed to prevent it from being displayed on a spike on London Bridge.*

2. The Mexican artist Frida Kahlo kept one of her aborted foetuses in a jar by her bedside.

3. In 1586 a German weaver, Leonhard Nadler, was punished for cutting the little toe from an executed man. Nadler said he wanted it as a charm to end his run of bad luck at cards.

4. King Philip II of Spain, husband of Queen Mary Tudor, owned around 7,000 holy relics, including 144 heads, 306 arms and legs and 10 whole bodies. While on his deathbed in 1598 he called for a couple of his favourite body parts to bring him comfort – the arm of St Vincent and the knee of St Sebastian.

5. Kidnapped at the age of seven and sold into slavery, African Angelo Soliman was eventually sold on to the Habsburg royal family in Vienna, Austria. After he surprised his masters with his remarkable intelligence they decided to educate him. Before long he could speak

* Today, the mummified relic is kept in a glass-topped box in the vestry of St Botolph Aldgate in London.

six languages fluently, became a master swordsman, a war hero, a chess specialist, a navigation expert and a tutor to royalty. Known widely as the "princely Moor", he was considered one of the most cultured people of his generation and was a friend to Mozart and Haydn. When he died in 1796 his body was claimed by the Holy Roman Emperor Francis II, who ordered it flayed, stuffed and mounted on a plinth. The emperor wanted it for his private museum of "noble savages".

6. In 1824 Ashanti warriors overran and massacred a British force led by Brigadier-General Sir Charles MacCarthy, who shot himself rather than face capture and torture. After cutting off his head and eating his heart, they then converted his skull into a drinking cup and kept his jawbones for use as drumsticks.

7. The serial killer William Burke sold the corpses of his sixteen victims as dissection material for anatomy lectures, then made one final contribution to science when he was executed in 1829. His body went straight from the gallows to the practised hands of the famous Scottish surgeon Alexander Monro, who performed a public lecture while dissecting the murderer's corpse. Later, several wallets and pocket books made from his skin went on sale. Charles Dickens had a piece of Burke's skin, which he used as a bookmark.

8. The Victorian pornographer Frederick Hankey had a collection of books bound in human skin and said that it was his ambition to see a girl hanged and to have the skin of her backside tanned to bind his copy of *Justine*. In 1863 he asked his friend, the explorer Richard Burton, to bring him back from Africa the skin of a black woman, preferably torn off a live one. Burton said he'd give it a go, but came home empty-handed.

9. The Mimisuka monument in Kyoto, Japan, contains 38,000 severed ears and noses removed from dead Korean soldiers and civilians taken during the war of 1592–98. Traditionally, Japanese warriors would bring back the whole heads of enemies slain on the battlefield as proof of their deeds, but because of the large number killed it was easier to just bring back noses.

10. The romantic poet Lord Byron was irresistible to women. At least a hundred female admirers sent him locks of hair from their heads and pubic regions, including, most famously, Lady Caroline Lamb. Byron would occasionally return the favour, but was more likely to send a tuft trimmed from his Newfoundland dog, Boatswain.

11. After his wife died in 1872, Benjamin Disraeli discovered that she had kept all the hair from the haircuts she'd given him over thirty-three years of marriage.

12. When the Polar explorer Robert Peary returned from the Arctic in 1909 he brought six Inuit back with him so he could show them off on his lecture tour. Four of them died almost immediately of pneumonia. Peary faked their burials then sold their bodies to the American Museum of Natural History. One of the survivors visited the museum and was horrified to find his father's bleached bones in a glass case in the ethnographic department. He begged to have the remains returned to him for a ritual burial, but the museum refused. The skeletons weren't released and reburied in Greenland until 1993.

13. When the artist Robert Lenkiewicz died in 2002, he left behind in a secret drawer, hidden behind some panelling at the bottom of a bookcase, the embalmed corpse of his

friend, a tramp from Plymouth. The painter befriended Edwin McKenzie, after finding him living in a barrel on a rubbish tip and promised him that he would preserve his body after his death as a "human paperweight" rather than handing it over to the authorities for burial. The tramp lay concealed in Lenkiewicz's studio for eighteen years, alongside various other bits and bobs, including the skeleton of a sixteenth-century midwife who was hanged for witchcraft and a parchment desk lampshade that had been brought out of Auschwitz in 1940.

14. In 2006 William Shatner sold a kidney stone he recently passed to an online casino for $25,000. The buyers said they would put it with their other collectables, including a half-eaten toasted cheese sandwich said to bear the image of the Virgin Mary.

15. In 2006 a German woman chopped off her dead husband's penis to pickle it as a souvenir of their marriage. Uta Schneider used a butcher's knife to hack off Heinrich's manhood in a Stuttgart hospital and tried to smuggle it home in a lunchbox but was spotted by a nurse. She told police: "It was his best asset and gave me so much pleasure. I wanted to pickle it for eternity; it's what he would have wanted."

FUTUE TE IPSUM:
10 ROMAN PROFANITIES

1. *Cunnus* (cunt)

2. *Futuo* (fuck)

3. *Mentula* (cock)

4. *Verpa* (erect or circumcised cock)

5. *Landica* (clitoris)

6. *Culus* (arse)

7. *Pedico* (bugger)

8. *Caco* (shit)

9. *Fello* (fellate)

10. *Irrumo* (mouth-rape)

The Romans had around 800 swear words. Ancient Egyptian lawyers of the same period used to seal their documents with a hieroglyph, which translates as: "As for him who shall disregard it, may he be fucked by a donkey." The hieroglyph depicted two large erect penises.

The ancient Greek Socrates was famously potty-mouthed, albeit not in a "fuck this philosophizing" kind of way. His favourite curse was "by the cabbage" – a reference to a variety of cabbage grown in Athens and used as a hangover remedy. The idea behind this was that, if the cabbage could combat the effect of a hangover, it was worth swearing by.

10 ODD ORIGINS

1. The first Barbie dolls were modelled on a German sex doll called Lilli. And they had nipples.

2. The inventor of "Best before" dates, originally for milk, was Al Capone.

3. The first Starbucks logo featured a seventeenth-century Norse woodcut of a mermaid with large bare breasts. In subsequent versions her long hair covered them up.

4. In the 1880s a Scotsman called John Lawson Johnston invented Bovril as a response to the French Emperor Napoleon III's plea for beef to feed his army. Johnston hit on the idea of rendering it down into a concentrated form that could be turned into a drink by adding hot water: it was originally called Johnston's Fluid Beef.

5. The first commercial chewing gum appeared in the shops in 1871. It came after a failed attempt by Thomas Adams to make car tyres from the same ingredients.

6. Zeppo Marx, the youngest of the Marx Brothers, designed the clamping device that held the atom bombs in place before they were dropped on Hiroshima and Nagasaki.

7. Florence Nightingale invented the pie chart.

8. The phrase "Sieg Heil" was thought up by Harvard-educated businessman Ernst Hanfstaengl. He was impressed by the atmosphere generated at Harvard football games and wanted to recreate it at Hitler's rallies.

9. When Adolf Hitler's chauffeur Anton Loibl wasn't driving the Führer to and from work, he was moonlighting as an inventor. One of his brainwaves was a shiny piece of glass mounted on bikes to make them more visible at night – a bicycle reflector. When Heinrich Himmler learned of Loibl's "innovation" he signed a deal to mass-produce them.

10. Sir Charles Isham, a vegetarian spiritualist, introduced the garden gnome to England in 1847. He did it in the hope that it might attract real gnomes to his garden.

12 DAREDEVIL STUNTS

1785: the accident-prone French chemist Jean-François Pilâtre de Rozier and his companion Pierre Romain become the world's first air disaster victims when their hot-air balloon bursts into flame and crashes near Wimereux in the Pas-de-Calais during an attempt to fly across the English Channel. By way of preparation, de Rozier tested the properties of hydrogen by filling his mouth with gas then expelling it over an open flame, thus removing all his facial hair.

1819: Marie-Madeleine-Sophie Armant, wife of North American hot-air balloon pioneer Jean Pierre Blanchard, carries on the family name in ballooning after her husband's death from a heart attack in 1809. She also has the distinction of being the first woman balloonist to die in an aerial accident when her balloon catches fire during a pyrotechnic night flight. She falls out of the basket and strikes a roof before hitting the street.

1841: stunt performer Samuel Scott plans to run from the White Lion Pub in Drury Lane to Waterloo Bridge, jump from a scaffold on the bridge into the river with a noose around his neck, then return to the pub within the hour. A large crowd cheers as he dangles from the bridge and chokes to death, thinking it is part of the routine.

1875: after becoming the first person to swim the English Channel, Matthew Webb attempts a similar feat at Niagara Falls and immediately drowns.

1887: Niagara Falls tightrope walker Stephen Peer performs a tightrope walk over the Falls on a wire cable that's five-eighths of an inch in diameter, successfully completing a double crossing. Three days later Peer is found dead on the bank of the Niagara river directly below his wire cable. It is speculated that he tried an unscheduled night crossing after an evening of drinking.

1920: a barber from Bristol, Charles Stephens, becomes only the third person in history to attempt to go over Niagara Falls in a barrel. Ignoring warnings from his two predecessors that his plan was bound to fail, he secures himself to the inside of the cask with a harness and straps an anvil to his feet for ballast. After the plunge, the only item left in the barrel is Stephens' tattooed right arm.

1961: Commander Malcolm Ross and Lt Commander Victor Prather ascend to 113,740 feet in the Stato-Lab V, setting the all-time balloon altitude record. While being picked up from the Gulf of Mexico after the flight, Prather falls from the helicopter hoist and drowns when his pressure suit fills with water.

1966: skydiver Nick Piantanida aims to break the world record for the highest parachute jump. During his third attempt, he tries to open his facemask by mistake, causing loss of air pressure and irreversible brain damage.

1972: tightrope walker Richard Guzman, performing with the world-famous Flying Wallendas, steadies himself by grabbing a piece of live cable used to hold up the metal rigging. The shock sends him flying to the ground, where he lands on a policeman who is trying to catch him. Despite being tended to almost immediately by an off-duty nurse, he dies from his injuries.

1979: while making the 1979 film *Steel*, stuntman A. J. Bakunas successfully performs a fall from the ninth floor of the construction site. When he learns that Dar Robinson had broken his record high fall for a non-film-related publicity stunt, Bakunas returns to perform the fall from the top of the 300-foot construction site. He falls expertly, but the airbag splits and he is killed.

1988: skydiver Lester McGuire of Durham, North Carolina, is so preoccupied with the video equipment he's set to use during his latest skydive that he forgets to pack a parachute. Lester's wonderful pictures of his freefall continue right up to his final impact with the ground at 150 mph.

2013: Sailendra Nath Roy, a West Bengali Guinness record holder, attempts to cross the Teesta River while hanging from a wire by his hair. The stunt goes wrong when Roy's ponytail gets stuck into the pulley of the 600-foot-long rope. The forty-nine-year-old struggles to free himself for several minutes until succumbing to a massive fatal cardiac arrest.

12 UNSINKABLE FACTS ABOUT RMS *TITANIC*

1. The first victim of the *Titanic* was a shipyard worker, James Dobbins. He died at 12:13 p.m. on 31 May 1911 at the very moment the ship was launched, fatally injured by a collapsing timber support.

2. The 706 third-class passengers on the *Titanic* had two bathtubs to share between them, one for males, and one for females. These passengers were locked behind gated barriers; according to American immigration policy, third class had to be kept apart from everyone else for health reasons.

3. There's no record of anyone making the claim that RMS *Titanic* was "unsinkable". It was only ever promoted as "practically unsinkable".

4. The inventor of the radio, Guglielmo Marconi, was invited on the *Titanic*, but he declined because his son Giulio was ill.

5. Edward John Smith was appointed captain of the *Titanic*, not because of his ability to captain a ship, but for his skills at socializing with first-class passengers. A lifeboat drill was scheduled for the day before the *Titanic* hit the

iceberg, but for reasons unknown Captain Smith cancelled it.★

6. The final song played by the band was almost certainly not "Nearer, My God, to Thee". Survivors said that the last song they heard was "Songe d'Automne"; as none of the band survived, the truth will never be known.

7. In London, the *Daily Mail* reported in its initial 16 April 1912 story: TITANIC SUNK, NO LIVES LOST.

8. Although there were not enough lifeboats to go round, three dogs, two Pomeranian and a Pekingese, made it into them and were rescued. At least nine more dogs drowned.

9. The entire crew of the *Titanic* were fired the instant that the ship sank. The widows of crew members had to rely on charity or get remarried quickly in order to survive.

10. Even in death, class barriers on the *Titanic* were observed. Two days after she sank, the *Mackay-Bennett* sailed from Halifax, Nova Scotia, to retrieve bodies from the Atlantic. The bodies of first-class passengers were returned in coffins, second and third class in canvas bags and crewmen on open stretchers.

11. Although 328 bodies were recovered, 119 were too badly damaged to bring home and were buried at sea.

★ Smith was born and raised in Stoke-on-Trent; however, his statue stands in Beacon Park, Lichfield. It was paid for by public subscription but Stoke's council refused to have anything to do with it and Lichfield was the nearest place to his hometown prepared to accept the disgraced captain's monument.

12. Violet Jessop died in 1971 having survived the sinkings
    of the *Titanic* and *Britannic* (1916) and the near-sinking
    of the *Olympic* (1911).

9 PRE-TWITTER TROLLS

1523: Sir Thomas More says Martin Luther has a "beshitted tongue", adding that Luther's "shitty mouth [is] truly the shit-pool of all shit".

1536: shoemaker William Bowman is arrested for slandering Queen Anne Boleyn, by "saying that her arse is worm-eaten".

1585: Jeremy Vanhill, a labourer from Kent, says of Queen Elizabeth I: "I would to God she were dead so that I might shit on her face." For dissing Gloriana, Vanhill is hanged.

1676: Russian Cossacks write to the Ottoman sultan Mehmed IV, calling him a "goat-fucker" and "the crick in your dick" and suggests he "screw your own mother".

1793: Hébert attends Marie Antoinette's execution, and says, "The greatest of all joys: the head of the female veto removed from her fucking tart's neck."

1861: Abraham Lincoln receives hate mail from Mr A. G. Frick, who invites the President to "suck my prick", "buss my ass" and "call my Bolics [*sic*] your uncle Dick".

1921: John W. Gott becomes the last person jailed for blasphemy in Britain. He is sentenced to nine months' hard labour for comparing Jesus to a circus clown.

1968: US President Lyndon B. Johnson notes about a

subordinate, "He couldn't pour piss out of a boot if the instructions were printed on the heel."

2006: a forty-year-old man from the Netherlands is sentenced to one week's imprisonment when he calls Queen Beatrix "a whore" and tells a police officer that he would like to have anal sex with her because "she would like it".

FRIENDLY FIRE: 10 MILITARY COMMANDERS KILLED BY THEIR OWN SIDE

1643: royalist cannon kills royalist commander the Earl of Kingston when his boat is fired on from the banks of the River Trent.

1672: the French general Jean Martinet, who earned the hatred of Louis XIV's soldiers by beating them into shape with relentless drills, is killed by gunfire from his own troops as he leads a charge at the siege of Duisburg.

1704: after the Battle of Blenheim has been won, an unpopular major in the fifteenth regiment of foot is shot in the head by his own men.

1707: after his ship was lost on rocks off the Scilly Islands Sir Cloudesley Shovell, Admiral of the British fleet, barely manages to struggle ashore, where, according to local legend, an old woman promptly bludgeons him to death. A body washed ashore was regarded as a "derelict" and the woman was assuming legal entitlement to the emerald ring on Shovell's finger.

1718: during the Siege of Fredriksten, King Charles XII of Sweden falls dead with a bullet to the head. It is widely speculated that the shot came from his own troops: his skull complete with bullet hole resides in a Stockholm museum.

1796: at the Battle of Fombio, French general Amadee Laharpe is shot by his men while returning to camp from a reconnaissance mission.

1815: at the battle of Quatre Bas, the commander of 92nd Gordon Highlanders Colonel John Cameron is shot and killed by a soldier whom he had recently flogged.

1862: General Thomas Williams, the tyrannical commander of Union Army troops at the Battle of Baton Rouge, dies from a gunshot wound to the chest. According to one account, he was seized by a group of his own men who held him in front of a cannon before it was fired at the enemy.

1863: Confederate General Thomas J. "Stonewall" Jackson and his staff are returning to camp one evening when they are challenged by a sentry, Major John D. Barry of the 18th North Carolina Infantry Regiment. Jackson's staff give the correct reply but, before they know what has hit them, Barry shouts, "It's a damned Yankee trick! Fire!" Jackson is badly wounded and dies eight days later.

1864: at the Battle of the Wilderness, Union Army Brigadier General Micah Jenkins is shot in the head when his mounted column is mistaken for Federal troops.

10 EUROSCEPTICS

1. "... so why, why should the nation that produced Shakespeare, Dickens, Christopher Wren, Florence Nightingale – and those are just the people on our banknotes for Christ's sakes – kowtow to the continent that produced Hitler, Napoleon, the Mafia and the Smurfs?"

   Alan B'Stard, *The New Statesman*

2. "The last time Britain went into Europe with any degree of success was on 6 June 1944."

   Daily Express, 1980

3. "I loathe abroad, nothing would induce me to live there. And, as for foreigners, they are all the same, and they make me sick."

   Nancy Mitford

4. "'What a dreadful smell!' said the initiated stranger, enveloping his nose in his pocket-handkerchief. 'It is the smell of the continent, sir,' replied the man of experience. And so it was."

   Mrs Frances Trollope recounts an overheard conversation in *Paris and the Parisians in 1835*

5. "We went in [to the EU] to screw the French by splitting them off from the Germans. The French went in to protect their inefficient farmers from commercial competition. The Germans went in to cleanse themselves of genocide and apply for readmission to the human race."

   Jonathan Lynn and Antony Jay, *Yes Minister*

6. "I do not see the EEC as a great love affair. It is more like nine middle-aged couples with failing marriages meeting at a Brussels hotel for a group grope."

Kenneth Tynan

7. "There have been many definitions of hell, but for the English the best definition is that it is the place where the Germans are the police, the Swedish are the comedians, the Italians are the defence force, Frenchmen dig the roads, the Belgians are the pop singers, the Spanish run the railways, the Turks cook the food, the Irish are the waiters, the Greeks run the government, and the common language is Dutch."

David Frost and Antony Jay

8. "This [the EU] is all a German racket designed to take over the whole of Europe. It has to be thwarted."

Nicholas Ridley, MP

9. "We have our own dream and our own task. We are with Europe but not of it. We are linked but not combined. We are interested and associated but not absorbed."

Sir Winston Churchill

10. "Here, then, as a service to future presidents of the European Union, is the Utley Guide to the National Characteristics of the Peoples of Europe:

"Belgians: mad, boring. Frenchmen: arrogant, chauvinistic, garlic-breathed. Germans: humourless, ruthless, efficient, greedy. Spaniards: lazy, hot-tempered, bloodthirsty. Irishmen: drunk, lazy, self-pitying, dishonest. Italians: volatile, sleazy, vain. Swedes: sex-obsessed, robotic, conformist. Greeks: smelly, hirsute, untrustworthy. Austrians: fat, wannabe Germans. Finns: pessimistic, sun-starved, suicidal. Dutchmen: clog-wearing, tulip-fancying dope addicts.

Portuguese, Danes, Luxembourgeoise: too insignifi-
cant to bother about. The Brits: upright, honest,
fair-minded (excluding the Scots, who are mean and
belligerent, and the Welsh, who are blathering wind-
bags) . . . before I am dragged off and lynched, I would
like to make it clear that there are huge numbers of
exceptions to these generalisations."

Tom Utley, *Daily Telegraph*

CURSES! A TIMELINE OF 15 FLIPPING PROFANITIES

527: Byzantine emperor Justinian prescribes death for anyone who swears "by the limbs of God".

900: the Scottish king Donald VI promises to cut out the tongues of anyone who swears.

1068: King Henry I, son of William the Bastard, has a sliding scale of fines for swearing in the royal precinct – forty shillings for a duke, twenty shillings for a lord and a whipping for a page.

1220: King Philip II of France punishes swearers by drowning them in the Seine.

1226: King Louis IX of France decrees that swearers should be branded on the face.

1551: the Scottish Parliament bans "sweiring, execrationnis and blasphematioun of the name of God", punishable by a shilling fine or a spell in either prison or the stocks for those who can't pay.

1558: Queen Elizabeth I calls on parliament to control "lewd and wanton discourse".

1694: England brings in the Profane Swearing Act with a system of fines payable for "suppressing prophane Cursing and Swearing".

1785: in his *Classical Dictionary of the Vulgar Tongue*, Francis Grose includes the verb to huffle, which is "a piece of bestiality too filthy for explanation". The 1788 and 1823 editions decide that discretion is the better part of valour and fail to mention the foul practice at all.★

1825: the first-ever reported case of Tourette's syndrome afflicts the wife of a French aristocrat, the Marquise de Dampierre. She shocks polite French society with her periodic outbursts of "sacre nom de Dieu" (in the name of God) as well as "merde" (shit) and "foutu cochon" (best translated as "fucking pig").

1884: Julian Sharman's *Cursory History of Swearing* contains not one single obscene word, but devotes several pages to the word "bloody", which he describes as a word "exceedingly painful".

1948: in his war novel *The Naked and the Dead*, Norman Mailer substitutes fug and fugging. The actress Tallulah Bankhead quips upon meeting him, "So you're the young man who can't spell fuck."

1971: the US Supreme Court protects a man who wore a jacket into a Los Angeles County Courthouse, wearing a jacket bearing the words "Fuck the Draft". Justice John Marshall Harlan rules, "One man's vulgarity is another's lyric."

★ Grose also refuses to define the verb to bagpipe – "a piece of lascivious practice too indecent for explanation". He goes on to define cunt as "a nasty name for a nasty thing".

1999: a group of offenders are forced to do community service next to a dual carriageway in Rotherham. The next spring the daffodils coming into bloom spell out the words "bollocks" and "shag".

2001: Madonna, selected to present the 2001 Turner Prize on a live British TV show, after being politely asked by the programme's producers to "keep it clean" announces, "I would also like to say . . . Right on, motherfucker! Everyone is a winner!" Three years later, during her Re-Invention tour, Madonna atones by imposing a "cursing fine" on anyone caught swearing. According to the *New York Post*, Madonna was caught during rehearsals screaming at her dancers: "Get it right or get the fuck out!"

10 TECHNOLOGY EXPERTS

1. "What can be more palpably absurd than the prospect held out of locomotives travelling twice as fast as stagecoaches?"

   The Quarterly Review, March 1825

2. "Dear Mr President: The canal system of this country is being threatened by a new form of transportation known as 'railroads' ... As you may well know, Mr President, 'railroad' carriages are pulled at the enormous speed of 15 miles per hour by 'engines' which, in addition to endangering life and limb of passengers, roar and snort their way through the countryside, setting fire to crops, scaring the livestock and frightening women and children. The Almighty certainly never intended that people should travel at such breakneck speed."

   Martin Van Buren, Governor of New York and future President of the United States, 1830

3. "What use would this company make of an electric toy?"

   Western Union President Carl Orton, turning down Alexander Graham Bell's offer to sell him the rights to the telephone for $100,000 in 1877

4. "Good enough for our transatlantic friends ... but unworthy of the attention of practical or scientific men."

   British Parliamentary Committee on Edison's light bulb, 1878

5. "Radio has no future."

> Lord Kelvin, Scottish mathematician and physicist, former president of the Royal Society, 1897

6. "Fooling around with alternating current is just a waste of time. Nobody will use it, ever."

> Thomas Edison, American inventor, 1889

"It is apparent to me that the possibilities of the aeroplane, which two or three years ago were thought to hold the solution to the [flying machine] problem, have been exhausted, and that we must turn elsewhere."

> Thomas Edison, 1895

"The talking motion picture will not supplant the regular silent motion picture. There is such a tremendous investment to pantomime pictures that it would be absurd to disturb it."

> Thomas Edison, 1913

7. "Man will not fly for fifty years."

> Wilbur Wright, American aviation pioneer, to brother Orville, after a disappointing flying experiment in 1901. Their first successful flight was in 1903

8. "The horse is here to stay but the automobile is only a novelty, a fad."

> The president of the Michigan Savings Bank advising Henry Ford's lawyer not to invest in the Ford Motor Co., 1903

9. "I have travelled the length and breadth of this country and talked with the best people, and I can assure you that data processing is a fad that won't last out the year."

> The editor in charge of business books for Prentice Hall, 1957

10. "But what . . . is it good for?"
     IBM executive Robert Lloyd, in 1968 on the micro-
     processor, the heart of the modern computer

16 UNINSPIRING BRITISH ROYALS

1. "The plain truth is, that he was a most intolerable ruffian, a disgrace to human nature, and a blot of blood and grease upon the History of England."

   Charles Dickens on King Henry VIII

2. "Here lies our mutton-loving king, Whose word no man relies on; Who never said a foolish thing, And never did a wise one."

   John Wilmot, Earl of Rochester, on King Charles II

3. "A dull, stupid and profligate King, full of drink and low conversation, without dignity of appearance or manner, without sympathy of any kind with the English people and English ways and without the slightest knowledge of the English language."

   Justin McCarthy, Irish writer, on King George I

4. "Here lies Fred, Who was alive and now is dead: Had it been his father, I had much rather; Had it been his brother, Better than another; Had it been his sister, No one would have missed her; Had it been the whole generation, Better for the nation: But since 'tis only Fred, Who was alive and is dead – There's no more to be said."

   Horace Walpole on Frederick, Prince of Wales, eldest son of King George II

5. "George the Third
    Ought never to have occurred.
    One can only wonder
    At so grotesque a blunder."

    Edmund Clerihew Bentley on King George III

6. "A more contemptible, cowardly, selfish unfeeling dog
    does not exist than this king ... with vices and weak-
    nesses of the lowest and most contemptible order."

    Charles Greville, English diarist,
    on King George IV

7. "King William blew his nose twice and wiped the royal
    perspiration from a face which is probably the largest
    uncivilized spot in England."

    Oliver Wendell Holmes, American writer,
    on King William IV

8. "Nowadays a parlour maid as ignorant as Queen Victoria
    was when she came to the throne would be classed as
    mentally defective."

    George Bernard Shaw on Queen Victoria

9. "A corpulent voluptuary."

    Rudyard Kipling on Edward King VII

10. "His intellect is of no more use than a pistol packed in
    the bottom of a trunk in the robber infested Apennines."

    Prince Albert, Consort of Queen Victoria,
    on his son Edward, Prince of Wales

11. "For seventeen years he did nothing at all but kill animals
    and stick in stamps."

    Harold Nicolson, English diplomat and writer
    on King George V

12. "Did more for republicanism than fifty years of propaganda."

> Labour MP George Hardie on King Edward VIII

13. "You do realise, don't you, that she is an alcoholic? She begins drinking at ten o'clock in the morning, which doesn't make her any easier to deal with.

    "She isn't just two-faced. She is 40-faced."

> The Duke of Windsor on Elizabeth Bowes-Lyon,
> the Queen Mother

14. "All the individuals within the Royal Family, they're so magnificently, unaccountably and unpardonably boring. Has Diana ever uttered a sentence of any vague interest or use to the world?"

> Morrissey on Princess Diana

15. "This is what you get when you found a political system on the family values of Henry VIII. At a point in the not-too-remote future, the stout heart of Queen Elizabeth II will cease to beat. At that precise moment, her firstborn son will become head of state . . . In strict constitutional terms, this ought not to matter much. The English monarchy, as has been said, reigns but does not rule. From the aesthetic point of view it will matter a bit, because the prospect of a morose bat-eared and chinless man, prematurely aged, and with the most abysmal taste in royal consorts, is a distinctly lowering one."

> Christopher Hitchens on Prince Charles

16. "I wouldn't let that family near me with a sharp stick, let alone a sword."

> Keith Richards, on knighthood and Queen Elizabeth II

13 ROYAL ODDITIES

1. Although Queen Elizabeth I never once went to Southwark to see Shakespeare at the Globe Theatre, she did go there to see the bear baiting.

2. Pyrrhus, the King of Epirus, had a divinely blessed big toe on his right foot. He could cure certain ailments by dangling his toe over the afflicted part. When he was cremated, it didn't burn and was kept in a casket in a temple.

3. In ancient Ireland, it was customary to suck the king's nipples as a token of fealty.

4. King George VI enjoyed watching home movies backwards. His favourite was watching swimmers leap from a pool onto a diving board.

5. King John VI of Portugal had a favourite manservant, Francisco de Sousa Lobato. The manservant received a variety of honours, accumulating among others the posts of adviser to the king, secretary of the Casa do Infantado, secretary of the Bureau of Conscience and Orders (Mesa de Consciência e Ordens) and governor of the Santa Cruz fortress, also receiving the title of Baron and later Viscount of Vila Nova da Rainha. According to historians, he regularly masturbated his master.*

---

* A priest named Miguel stumbled upon the scene and therefore was deported to Angola, but not before leaving written testimony.

6. King George V's wife launched the eponymous liner *Queen Mary* on 26 September 1934. The twenty-eight words used by the queen when she launched the ship were the only ones she ever spoke in public.

7. When Pharaoh Ramses IV died in 1149 BC and was mummified, his eyes were replaced with small onions and his anus was plugged with a ball of resin.

8. King George I decreed that all pigeon droppings were Crown property. They were used in the manufacture of gunpowder. The British royal family has kept racing pigeons since 1886 when King Leopold of Belgium gave some to the Prince of Wales, later Edward VII.

9. When Queen Juliana of the Netherlands left the throne in 1980, she proposed a mass pardon for petty criminals. When her Cabinet informed the queen that such a pardon was impossible, she asked whether all prisoners could have a piece of cake instead.

10. The Ostrogoth Theodoric the Great, who ruled Italy from 493 to 526, was almost illiterate and such a slow learner that for the first ten years of his rule he could only sign documents by tracing the word LEGI – "I have read [it]" – through a stencil in a block of wood. The Byzantine emperor Justin was similarly ignorant and traced the letters of the word FIAT – "let it be so".

11. King Ferdinand I, the Bourbon ruler of the Two Sicilies, had little appreciation of the true value of the priceless ancient Roman artefacts being dug up in the excavations at Pompeii and Herculaneum. He swapped eighteen of the priceless Herculaneum papyri, first found in 1785, for eighteen kangaroos for his mistress's theme park.

12. Only three of Prince Philip's four sisters married leading Nazis. Prince Philip's brother-in-law, Prince Christoph of Hesse, was an SS colonel attached to Heinrich Himmler's personal staff and head of the sinister Forschungsamt – a security service under Hermann Goering's command that carried out surveillance on anti-Nazis. He named their eldest son Karl Adolf in Hitler's honour. Philip's uncle Charles Edward, Duke of Saxe-Coburg Gotha, was a fervent Nazi who said that Hitler had done a "wonderful job". In 1936 he turned up for King George V's funeral wearing German military uniform, complete with a stormtrooper's helmet. *

13. Ever since King George I brought the practice over from Hanover, all male royals were circumcised until Diana, the Princess of Wales, refused to continue the tradition when William, the Duke of Cambridge was born in 1982.

---

* Princess Michael of Kent's father, Baron Gunther von Reibnitz, was also a member of the Nazi party and of Hitler's SS, although, according to the official palace explanation, he was only an "honorary" one.

8 PEOPLE WITH DODGY TABLE MANNERS

1. The ancient Greek Philoxenus used to blow his nose over the best morsels at the dining table to put off other diners so he could keep the tastiest bits for himself.

2. The ancient Greeks had a dinner-table game called cottabus, which involved flicking wine from one's cup at a target. It didn't catch on in Rome, but Roman banquets were messy affairs anyway. Their dining rooms were constructed with drains and charcoal flooring to soak up all the vomit and wine that was spat out.

3. At Roman banquets, a human skeleton was sometimes passed around as a memento mori (literally, "remember to die") to remind guests that life was short and should be enjoyed.

4. In 1654 English clergyman Thomas Hall noted that Irishmen have "filthy long hair because they use it to clean their mouth and hands during meals".

5. When the Roman Emperor Hadrian dined he made sure that the food intended for him was much better than that served to his hapless guests. One day he dined on a huge Sicilian lamprey; meanwhile, his guests were served an eel like a water snake, fattened in the Tiber sewers.

6. When Mary Queen of Scots returned to her native Scotland from France she was put out to discover that the men continued to wear their hats while sitting down to eat at her banquets. It was pointed out to the young queen that this was not a sign of disrespect but necessity. Men kept their hats on to prevent their long hair from touching the food and to stop head lice from falling into their plates.

7. In 1833 while dining with Fuegians, Charles Darwin watched as one man vomited up a piece of blubber and passed it to another, "who swallowed it with much ceremony".

8. In 1796 the Scottish explorer Mungo Park was attending an African wedding feast, when an old woman threw a bowl of urine in his face. The piss was a traditional Hottentot blessing "from the bride's own person".

FURTHER READING

Geoffrey Abbott, *The Who's Who of British Beheadings* (2000)

Robert J. Anderson, Juliet A. Brodie, Edvar Onsoyen & Alan T. Critchley, *Proceedings of the Eighteenth International Seaweed Symposium* (2006)

Ronald C. Arkin, *Governing Lethal Behaviour in Autonomous Robots* (2009)

Alice Armes, *English Smocks* (1961)

Peter Atherton, *Understanding Aloe Vera* (2005)

Catalin Avramescu, *An Intellectual History of Cannibalism* (2011)

Reginald Bakeley, *Goblinproofing One's Chicken Coop* (2012)

Charles J. Bareis and James W. Porter, *American Bottom Archaeology* (1993)

David Benatar, *Better Never To Have Been: The Harm of Coming Into Existence* (2006)

Peter L. Benson, *Beyond Leaf Raking* (1993)

Duncan Birmingham, *Pets Who Want to Kill Themselves* (2009)

Roger Blake, *A New Look at Wife-Swapping* (1967)

Robin Borwick, *People With Long Ears* (1965)

Walter Brett, *Pictorial Poultry-Keeping And Gardening And*

Encyclopaedia Of Rabbit, Goat And Bee-Keeping, Pig Keeping And Small Holdings Management (2010)

Franz-Josef Bruggemeier, Mark Cioc & Thomas Zeller, *How Green Were the Nazis?* (2006)

Eleanor Burns, *Still Stripping After 25 Years* (2003)

M. Butterfield & C. J. Church, *Whose Bottom is This?: A Lift-the-flap Book* (2000)

Pat Califia, *Lesbian Sadomasochism Safety Manual* (1990)

Brooks D. Cash, *Curbside Consultation of the Colon* (2008)

Robert Chenciner, Gabib Ismailov, Magomedkhan Magomedkhanov & Alex Binnie, *Tattooed Mountain Women and Spoon Boxes of Dagestan* (2006)

Dorothy L. Cheney and Robert M. Seyfarth, *Baboon Metaphysics* (2008)

Mary Ann Clayton, *Critter Cuisine; A New Twist on Backyard Cooking* (1992)

Alex Comfort, *The Joy of Sex: Pocket Edition* (1997)

Kaz Cooke, *Living With Crazy Buttocks* (2002)

David Crompton, *Afterthoughts of a Worm Hunter* (2009)

Stephen Curry & Takayoshi Andoh, *Mr Andoh's Pennine Diary: Memoirs of a Japanese Chicken Sexer in 1935* (2011)

Douglas Davies & Alastair Shaw, *Reusing Old Graves* (1995)

Roger De Boer, Harvey Francis Pitcher & Alan Wilkinson, *D. Di Mascio's Delicious Ice Cream: D. Di Mascio of Coventry: An Ice Cream Company of Repute, with an Interesting and Varied Fleet of Ice Cream Vans* (2006)

Elaine Dee & Guy Walton, *Versailles: The View From Sweden* (1988)

Wendy Diamond, *How to Understand Women Through Their Cats* (2006)

Saiyuud Diwong, *Cooking with Poo* (2011)

Ronald Duncan & M. Weston-Smith, *Ragnar's Guide to Home and Recreational Use of High Explosives* (1988)

Henrik Eberle and Hans-Joachim, *Was Hitler Ill?* (2012)

Mike Edwards, *Detecting Foreign Bodies in Food* (2004)

Kenji Ekuan, *The Aesthetics of the Japanese Lunchbox* (2000)

Glenn C. Ellenbogen, *Oral Sadism and the Vegetarian Personality* (1986)

David Evans, *Does God Ever Speak Through Cats?* (2006)

James Fitzgerald, *The Best Fences* (1984)

Gerard Forlin, *Butterworth's Corporate Manslaughter Service* (2001)

Stanley F. Fox, *Lizard Social Behaviour* (2003)

Jerry Gagne, *Lofts of North America: Pigeon Lofts* (2012)

Charles George, *What Makes Me Amish?* (2005)

R. S. George, *Atlas of the Fleas (siphonaptera) of Britain and Ireland* (2008)

Peter Gosson, *A Century of Sand Dredging in the Bristol Channel: Volume Two* (2011)

David Grant & Edward Hart, *Shepherds' Crooks & Walking Sticks* (1989)

Jane Hallas & Tina Stephens, *Bullying and Sexual Harassment: A Practical Handbook* (2006)

Jack Hanley, *Let's Make Mary: Being a Gentleman's Guide to Scientific Seduction in Eight Easy Lessons* (1937)

Mykle Hansen, *HELP! A Bear is Eating Me!* (2008)

Elizabeth Hawes, *Fashion is Spinach* (2012)

Tom Hickman, *God's Doodle: The Life and Times of the Penis* (2012)

Gary Leon Hill, *People Who Don't Know They're Dead: How They Attach Themselves to Unsuspecting Bystanders and What to Do About It* (2005)

Amy Hirschman & Kaori Tsuyata, *Crafting with Cat Hair* (2011)

Robert G. Hodgson, *Successful Muskrat Farming* (1927)

Marie Holmes, *Glamour and the Hostess: A Guide to Canadian Table Setting* (1958)

Mark Hordyszynski, *Strip and Knit with Style* (2008)

F. M. Hunter and L. S. Davis, *Adelie Penguins Acquire Nest Material from Extrapair Males After Engaging in Extrapair Copulations* in the journal *Auk* (vol. 115, number 2, pages 526–8) (2011)

Stevens Irwin, *Dictionary of Pipe Organ Stops* (1983)

Richard Jacob & Owen Thomas, *How to Live with a Huge Penis* (2009)

Tara Jansen-Meyer, *What Kind of Bean is This Chihuahua?* (2009)

Alison Jenkins, *Jurassic Towel Origami* (2009)

Titia Joosten, *Flower Drying with a Microwave* (1988)

J. Joyce, *London Transport Bus Garages Since 1948* (1988)

Christine Petrell Kallevig, *All About Pockets* (1993)

Philip Kell & Vanessa Griffiths, *Sexual Health at Your Fingertips* (2003)

Jan Seaman Kelly, *Forensic Examination of Rubber Stamps* (2002)

Guy Kettelhack, *How to Make Love While Conscious* (1993)

Patrick Kingsley, *How to be Danish* (2012)

Jarod Kintz & Dora J. Arod, *Who Moved My Cheese? An Amazing Way to Deal With Change by Deciding to Let Indecision Into Your Life* (2011)

Hiroyuki Kojima & Shin Togami, *The Manga Guide to Calculus* (2009)

Dana Kollmann, *Never Suck A Dead Man's Hand: And Other Life (and Death) Lessons from the Front Lines of Forensics* (2007)

Emmanuel Kowalski, *The Large Sieve and its Applications* (2008)

Rohan Kriwaczek, *An Incomplete History of the Art of Funerary Violin* (2006)

Rev. D. Landsborough, *A Popular History of British Seaweeds* (1857)

David Lawson, *So You Want to Be a Shaman* (1996)

Vicki Leon, *Working IX to V: Orgy Planners, Funeral Clowns and Other Prized Professions of the Ancient World* (2007)

Murray Long, *Breeding Stud Sheep* (2008)

George Macleod, *Goats: Homeopathic Remedies* (2004)

Ethel Marbach, *A Do-it-Yourself Guide to Holy Housewifery* (1964)

Barbara E. Mattic, *A Guide to Bone Toothbrushes of the 19th and Early 20th Centuries* (2009)

Amanda McCall, *Grandma's Dead: Breaking Bad News With Baby Animals* (2008)

William McGrath, *Amish Folk Remedies for Plain and Fancy Ailments* (1986)

Nicolette McGuire, *Royal Knits* (2011)

Chris McManus, *Scrotal Asymmetry in Man and in Ancient Sculpture* (1976)

Carlton Mellick III, *The Haunted Vagina* (2006)

Scott D. Mendelson, *The Great Singapore Penis Panic and the Future of American Mass Hysteria* (2011)

Jan Messent, *Knitted Historical Figures* (1993)

Carolyn Meyer, *The Needlework Book of Bible Stories* (1975)

Kathleen Meyer, *How to Shit in the Woods: An Environmentally Sound Approach to a Lost Art* (1989)

Simon Milledge, *Rhino Horn Stockpile Management: Minimum Standards and Best Practice from East and Southern Africa* (2005)

Julian Montague, *The Stray Shopping Carts of Eastern North America: A Guide to Field Identification* (2006)

Harry Mount, *A Lust for Window Sills: A Lover's Guide to British Buildings from Portcullis to Pebble Dash* (2011)

Jeff Nicholls, *Mole Catching: A Practical Guide* (2008)

Hiroyuki Nishigaki, *How to Good-Bye Depression: If You Constrict anus 100 Times Everyday. Malarkey? or Effective Way?* (2000)

Tatsuju Nomura, *Proceedings of the Second International Workshop on Nude Mice* (1977)

Graciela Nowenstein, *The Generosity of the Dead* (2010)

Ginny Oakley & Stephanie Soskin, *What Not to Wear on a Horse* (2006)

Jonathan Olivares, *A Taxonomy of Office Chairs* (2011)

Frank W. Orme, *Fancy Goldfish Culture* (1992)

Chad Orzel, *How to Teach Physics to Your Dog* (2010)

Alfred & Ellsworth Owen, *Exercises for Gentlemen; 50 Exercises to Do With Your Suit On* (2010)

Philip M. Parker, *The 2009–2014 World Outlook for 60-milligram Containers of Fromage Frais* (2008)

Michel Pastoureau, *The Devil's Cloth: A History of Stripes and Striped Fabric* (2003)

Rick Pelicano, *Bombproof Your Horse* (2004)

Henry Petroski, *The Toothpick: Technology and Culture* (2008)

A. Phear, *Soil Nailing: Best Practice Guidance* (2005)

Howard G. Poteet, *How to Live in Your Van and Love it* (1976)

Aino Praakli, *Estonian Sock Patterns All Around the World* (2011)

Loani Prior, *How Tea Cosies Changed the World* (2012)

Adam Quan, *How to Date a White Woman: A Practical Guide for Asian Men* (2002)

Andrew Rebmann, *Cadaver Dog Handbook: Forensic Training and Tactics for the Recovery of Human Remains* (2000)

David Rees, *How to Sharpen Pencils* (2012)

Mark Remy, *C is for Chafing* (2011)

May Cushman Rice, *Electricity in Gynaecology* (2010)

Doug Richmond, *How to Disappear Completely and Never Be Found* (1996)

Renee Rigdon & Stewart Zabe, *Anticraft: Knitting, Beading and Stitching for the Slightly Sinister* (2007)

Donald Rogers, *Teach Your Wife to Be a Widow* (1957)

John & Roxanne Rossi, *What's Wrong With My Snake? A User-Friendly Home Medical Reference Manual* (1997)

John A. Rush, *The Mushroom in Christian Art* (2011)

Teddy Salad, *A Poseur's Guide to the Potteries & District* (1984)

Jack Scagnetti, *Movie Stars in Bathtubs* (1975)

Ellen Scherl and Maria Dubinsky, *The Changing World of Inflammatory Bowel Disease* (2009)

Calvin W. Schwabe, *Unmentionable Cuisine* (1979)

Jon Scieszka, *Squids Will Be Squids* (2003)

George R. Scott, *The Art of Faking Exhibition Poultry* (2006)

Joel Silverman, *What Color Is Your Dog?* (2010)

C. C. Stanley, *Highlights in the History of Concrete* (1994)

Charles H. Stirton, *Weeds in a Changing World* (1999)

Alisa Surkis, *The Big Book of Lesbian Horse Stories* (2003)

A. Sysoev & A. A. Schileyk, *Land Snails and Slugs of Russia and Adjacent Countries* (2009)

Daina Taimina, *Crocheting Adventures with Hyperbolic Planes* (2009)

Albert Tangerman, *Measurement and biological significance of the volatile sulfur compounds hydrogen sulfide, methanethiol and dimethyl sulfide in various biological matrices* (2009)

Uwe Timm, *The Invention of Curried Sausage* (1997)

Blair Tolman, *Dating for Under a Dollar* (1999)

Robin Torrence and Huw Barton, *Ancient Starch Research* (2006)

Robert Traver, *Trout Madness* (1989)

John W. Trimmer, *How to Avoid Huge Ships* (1992)

A. I. Tselikov, G. S. Nikitin & S. E. Rokotyan, *Unsolved Problems of Modern Theory of Lengthwise Rolling* (1983)

Various, *8th International Friction Stir Welding Symposium Proceedings* (2010)

Various, *High Performance Stiffened Structures* (2000)

Elmore Vincent, *Lumberjack Songs with Yodel Arrangements* (1931)

Mary Lofthus Wales, *How to Make Your Own Shoes* (1992)

Jane M. Waterman, *The Adaptive Fuctions of Masturbation in a Promiscuous African Ground Squirrel* (2010)

Ernest Wilkinson, *Snow Caves for Fun and Survival* (1992)

Derek Willan, *Greek Rural Postmen and Their Cancellation Numbers* (1996)

Gareth Williams, *Development in Dairy Cow Breeding and Management: and New Opportunities to Widen the Uses of Straw* (1998)

Anne Wilson, *The Book of Marmalade: Its Antecedents, Its History and Its Role in the World Today* (1984)

Donald L. Wilson, *Natural Bust Enlargement with Total Power: How to Increase the Other 90% of Your Mind to Increase the Size of Your Breasts* (1985)

R. Lucock Wilson, *Soap Through the Ages* (1955)

John Woodforde, *The Strange Story of False Teeth* (1983)

Genichiro Yagyu, *All About Scabs* (1998)

Lietai Yang, *Techniques for Corrosion Monitoring* (2008)

James Yannes, *Collectible Spoons of the Third Reich* (2009)

Michael R. Young, *Managing a Dental Practice the Genghis Khan Way* (2010)